FRENCH *theatre* SEASON

AUTUMN 1997

A CELEBRATION OF THEATRE FROM FRANCE
Presented in London & Stratford-upon-Avon
30 September – 20 December 1997

THE PROGRAMME OF THE FRENCH THEATRE SEASON

Royal National Theatre
COMÉDIE-FRANÇAISE
Les Fausses Confidences
by MARIVAUX
Directed by JEAN-PIERRE MIQUEL
30 September – 4 October 1997
Performed in French with English surtitles

Presented by the Royal National Theatre on behalf of the French Theatre Season

Orange Tree Theatre
3 plays by MICHEL VINAVER

Overboard
Directed by SAM WALTERS
Translated by GIDEON LESTER
2 October – 1 November 1997

Neighbours
Directed by GEOFFREY BEEVERS
Translated by PAUL ANTAL
4 – 22 November 1997

Dissident, Goes Without Saying
Directed by AURIOL SMITH
6 – 23 November 1997
Translated by PETER MEYER
All three plays performed in English

Presented by the Orange Tree Theatre in association with the French Theatre Season

Sadler's Wells at The Peacock Theatre

STANISLAS NORDEY

Contention

(a curtain faller)

by DIDIER-GEORGES GABILY

preceded by

La Dispute

by MARIVAUX

and other things

Directed by STANISLAS NORDEY

29 – 31 October 1997

Performed in French with English surtitles

Produced by Théâtre Nanterre-Amandiers/Compagnie Nordey

Presented by the French Theatre Season

Sadler's Wells at The Peacock Theatre

ROBERT WILSON

La Maladie de la Mort

by MARGUERITE DURAS

Directed and designed by ROBERT WILSON

5 – 8 November 1997

Performed in French with English surtitles

Co-produced by Théâtre Vidy-Lausanne E.T.E./MC 93 Bobigny/Festival d'Automne à Paris/Ruhrfestspiele Recklinghausen-Europäisches Festival. Co-presented by Wiener Festwochen/Holland Festival

Presented by the French Theatre Season in association with Cultural Industry

Royal Court Theatre Downstairs

ROYAL COURT/THEATRE DE COMPLICITE

The Chairs

by EUGÈNE IONESCO

Translated by MARTIN CRIMP

Directed by SIMON McBURNEY

From 19 November 1997

Performed in English

Presented by the Royal Court Theatre and Theatre de Complicite in association with the French Theatre Season

Royal Court Theatre Upstairs

NEW VOICES FROM FRANCE

World premiere of

One More Wasted Year

(Encore Une Année Pour Rien)

by CHRISTOPHE PELLET

Translated by MARTIN CRIMP

Directed by MARY PEATE

18 – 22 November 1997

and in repertory from 8 – 20 December 1997

Rehearsed readings

Agnès

by CATHERINE ANNE

Le Renard du Nord

by NOËLLE RENAUDE

Mickey la Torche

by NATACHA DE PONTCHARRA

Une Envie de Tuer sur le Bout de la Langue

by XAVIER DURRINGER

19 – 22 November 1997

All plays in NEW VOICES FROM FRANCE performed in English

Presented by the Royal Court New European Writers Season and the French Theatre Season

The Other Place, Stratford-upon-Avon
ROYAL SHAKESPEARE COMPANY
Roberto Zucco
by BERNARD-MARIE KOLTÈS
English version by MARTIN CRIMP
Directed by JAMES MACDONALD
In repertoire 26 November 1997 – 11 February 1998

Performed in English

Presented by the Royal Shakespeare Company as part of the French Theatre Season

The Other Place, Stratford-upon-Avon
ROYAL SHAKESPEARE COMPANY
Beckett Shorts
a season of 6 short plays by SAMUEL BECKETT
Directed by KATIE MITCHELL
22 October – 13 November 1997

Performed in English

Co-produced by the Royal Shakespeare Company/Hahn Produktion, Reithalle Munich/The Belfast Festival/Mercat de los Flors, Barcelona/ Archa Theatre, Prague/Arte Carnuntum, Vienna. Presented in association with Offshore International Projects

Presented by the Royal Shakespeare Company as part of the French Theatre Season

Riverside Studios
PETER BROOK
Oh Les Beaux Jours
by SAMUEL BECKETT
Directed by PETER BROOK
27 November – 6 December 1997

Performed in French

Co-produced by Centre International de Créations Théâtrales – Paris and Théâtre Vidy-Lausanne E.T.E.

Presented by the Royal National Theatre on behalf of the French Theatre Season

Institut français
STAGE ON SCREEN
A season of films and videos, with guest appearances by directors and actors, including films by acclaimed directors ARIANE MNOUCHKINE and PETER BROOK; documentaries on French theatre luminaries such as KOLTÈS, PATRICE CHÉREAU, and SAMUEL BECKETT; and the British premiere of **Amoureuses**, the directorial debut of MICHEL PICCOLI, on the occasion of his appearance in **La Maladie de la Mort**.
29 September – 17 December 1997

Presented by the Institut français in association with the French Theatre Season

EDUCATION, TALKS AND DISCUSSIONS
A large number of education projects including:

Le Ballon Rouge – Performed in French and English by the European Theatre Company on a nationwide tour from 29 September to 5 December 1997

Le Mariage de Figaro – Performed in French by Théâtre Sans Frontières on tour across Britain from 15 September to 12 November 1997

A programme of workshops for GCSE and A level students, and for secondary school teachers and university lecturers

A ticket scheme designed to enable pupils to attend performances at a reduced rate

A range of talks, discussions and seminars exploring aspects of French theatre as revealed by the Season's programme

FRENCH THEATRE SEASON SUPPORTERS

The French Theatre Season gratefully acknowledges the generous
support of the following public funding agencies:

THE ASSOCIATION FRANÇAISE D'ACTION ARTISTIQUE

THE FRENCH MINISTRY OF FOREIGN AFFAIRS
(Direction Générale des Relations Culturelles Scientifiques et Techniques)

THE FRENCH MINISTRY OF CULTURE AND COMMUNICATIONS
(Direction des Théâtres et Spectacles, Département des Affaires Internationales)

THE CITY OF PARIS
(Direction des Affaires Culturelles)

THE FRENCH EMBASSY IN LONDON

THE SOCIÉTÉ DES AUTEURS ET COMPOSITEURS DRAMATIQUES
(Action Culturelle, Entr'Actes, Beaumarchais)

THE VISITING ARTS OFFICE OF GREAT BRITAIN AND NORTHERN IRELAND

The French Theatre Season would also like to thank the following sponsors and supporters
for their generous contribution:

Founding Contributors
BAGATELLE
Capital Home Loans Limited
De Dietrich
GEC ALSTHOM
GENERAL UTILITIES PLC
Norman Insurance, a Member of Les Mutuelles
du Mans Assurances Group
Publicis
ROBSON RHODES
THOMSON multimedia Sales UK Limited
TPL Logistics Management

Overall Season Sponsors & Supporters
Associated Newspapers Limited
B.A.T Industries p.l.c.
CCF
CRÉDIT AGRICOLE INDOSUEZ
EVIAN Natural Mineral Water
THE GENERAL ELECTRIC COMPANY P.L.C.
GENERAL UTILITIES PLC
Ibis UK Ltd, part of the ACCOR World-wide
Group of Hotels
LVMH - Moët Hennessy . Louis Vuitton
Paribas
The Peninsular & Oriental Steam Navigation
Company
Publicis
RAIL EUROPE UK LIMITED
The Rayne Foundation
Rothmans UK Holdings Limited
N M Rothschild & Sons Limited
Rothschild & Cie Banque
Monsieur Albert Roux
The Royal National Theatre Foundation
Monsieur et Madame Wafic Rida Saïd

Performance Sponsors
Oh Les Beaux Jours by Beckett
(directed by Peter Brook)
CITROËN

Les Fausses Confidences by Marivaux
(Comédie-Française)
The British Petroleum Company p.l.c.
COMITÉ COLBERT
GEC ALSTHOM
Kingfisher plc
Manches & Co. Solicitors
RAIL EUROPE UK LIMITED
Monsieur et Madame Wafic Rida Saïd
SAUR UK Limited

La Maladie de la Mort by Marguerite Duras
(directed by Robert Wilson)
GLOBAL ASSET MANAGEMENT

Corporate Members
Bank of Ireland
BULGARI
CARTIER Ltd
CHANEL
Commercial Union plc
Robert Fleming Holdings Limited
L'ORÉAL
MARKS & SPENCER
Matra BAe Dynamics
Renault UK
Société Générale
Tarmac plc

Educational Projects' Supporters & Sponsors
The Central Bureau for Educational
Visits & Exchanges
The Vivien Duffield Foundation
Ecovert South Limited
Elf Exploration UK plc
The Paul Hamlyn Foundation
The Lever Charitable Trust
Matra BAe Dynamics
The Reuter Foundation
The Sir John Swire Charitable Trust
TOTAL

The French Theatre Season Ltd is a registered charity

FRENCH *theatre* SEASON

AUTUMN 1997

MISE EN SCÈNE
FRENCH
THEATRE NOW

DAVID BRADBY AND
ANNIE SPARKS

Published with the support of the
French Theatre Season – a celebration of theatre from
France presented in London and Stratford-upon-Avon
30 September–20 December 1997

METHUEN DRAMA

Published by Methuen 1997

2 4 6 8 10 9 7 5 3 1

Text copyright © David Bradby and Annie Sparks 1997
Illustrations copyright © Claude Gaffner 1997

David Bradby and Annie Sparks have asserted their rights under the
Copyright, Designs and Patents Act, 1988 to be identified as the authors of this work.

First published in the United Kingdom in 1997 by Methuen,
Random House, 20 Vauxhall Bridge Road, London SW1V 2SA
with the support of the French Theatre Season

Random House Australia (Pty) Limited
20 Alfred Street, Milsons Point, Sydney,
New South Wales 2061, Australia

Random House New Zealand Limited
18 Poland Road, Glenfield
Auckland 10, New Zealand

Random House South Africa (Pty) Limited
Endulini, 5A Jubilee Road, Parktown 2193, South Africa

Random House UK Limited Reg. No. 954009

A CIP catalogue record for this book
is available from the British Library

ISBN 0 413 71230 3

Typeset in Bembo by MATS, Southend-on-Sea, Essex
Printed and bound in Great Britain by Mackays of Chatham Plc

CONTENTS

INFORMATION SECTION

ILLUSTRATIONS

The photographs included in this book are the personal choice of Claude Gaffner, his own record of the visual and theatrical qualities which have emerged since he began to photograph French theatre in the early 1980s. His first commissions were from Jean-Louis Barrault and Antoine Vitez. Since then he has photographed thousands of productions, and his work has been published and exhibited all over the world. For this book he was invited to contribute a 'photo-essay', a portfolio of images which would give readers a sense of the visual richness of French Theatre Now.

All the photos are © Claude Gaffner with the sole exception of *Les Atrides* © Bernand.

Table of Illustrations

Laug, with Pierre Arditi as Vladimir, Marcel Maréchal as Estragon, Robert Hirsch as Pozzo, Jean-Michel Dupuis as Lucky.

3. *Dom Juan* by Moliére at the Comédie-Française, 1993. Direction: Jacques Lassalle, design: Rudy Sabounghy, with Andrzej Seweryn as Dom Juan and Rolan Bertin as Sganarelle.

4. *Le Martyre de saint Sébastien* by Robert Wilson, after Gabriel D'Annunzio with music by Claude Debussy at MC93, Bobigny, 1988. Direction and design: Robert Wilson, with Sylvie Guillem.

5. *Le Vieil Hiver* by Roger Planchon at the Théâtre National Populaire, Villeurbanne, 1991. Direction: Roger Planchon, design: Ezio Frigerio.

6. *Le Mahabharata* by Peter Brook and Jean-Claude Carrière in the Boulbon quarry, Avignon Festival, 1985. Direction: Peter Brook, design: Chloé Obolensky, with Andrzej Seweryn.

7. *Les Atrides: Iphigénie à Aulis* by Euripides at the Cartoucherie de Vincennes, 1990. Direction: Ariane Mnouchkine, design: Guy-Claude François.

8. *Savannah Bay* by Marguerite Duras at the Théâtre du Rond-Point, 1982. Direction: Marguerite Duras, with Madeleine Renaud and Martine Chevalier.

9. *Les Bonnes* by Jean Genet by the Comédie-Française at the Théâtre du Vieux-Colombier, 1995. Direction: Philippe Adrien, design: Goury, with Catherine Hiegel and Dominique Constanza.

10. *Les Voisins* by Michel Vinaver at Théâtre Ouvert, 1986. Direction: Alain Françon, design: Yannis Kokkos, with Anouk Grinberg as Alice.

11. *Le Mariage de Figaro* by Beaumarchais at the Théâtre National de Chaillot, 1987. Direction: Jean-Pierre Vincent, design: Jean-Paul Chambas.

12. *L'Ile des esclaves* by Marivaux at the Théâtre de l'Athénée, 1994. Direction: Jean-Luc Lagarce, design: Laurent Peduzzi.

13. *Terra Incognita* by Georges Lavaudant at Les Taillades, Avignon festival, 1992. Direction: Georges Lavaudant, design: Jean-Pierre Vergier.

14. *Le Libertin* by Eric Emmanuel Schmitt at the Théâtre

Montparnasse, 1997. Direction: Bernard Murat, design: Nicholas Sire, with Bernard Giraudeau and Claire Keim.

15. *Le Jeu de l'amour et du hasard* by Marivaux at the Théâtre de la Commune, Aubervilliers, 1987. Direction: Alfredo Arias, design: Claudie Gastine.

16. *Dans la solitude des champs de coton* by Bernard-Marie Koltès at the Manufacture des Oeillets, Ivry, 1995. Direction: Patrice Chéreau, design: Richard Peduzzi, with Patrice Chéreau as the Dealer.

ACKNOWLEDGEMENTS

We should like to express our gratitude to Michael Earley, publisher of Methuen Drama, whose tireless energy and vision have helped to bring this project to fruition. Our thanks go to the many people in France who have been generous with their time and expertise, especially Lucien and Micheline Attoun, Annette Barthélémy, Sabine Bossan and Annie Christôme, Mireille Davidovici and Yann Richard, Michel Fournier, Claude Gaffner, and the writers, directors and administrators who agreed to be interviewed: Bernard Faivre d'Arcier, Lucien and Micheline Attoun, Michel Azama, Philippe Minyana, Eric Emmanuel Schmitt and Roger Planchon, with thanks also to Gilles Costaz and Michel Bataillon for permission to use Costaz's interview with Planchon. The support and encouragement of Luc Bouniol-Laffont, Cultural Attaché at the French Embassy, has been invaluable throughout. Our thanks also to the staff and resources of the French Theatre Season (London, 1997) who provided special funding for the colour plates used to illustrate this volume. But the views expressed in this volume are ours alone.

David Bradby
Annie Sparks
1997

PREFACE

Spectateurs is the word conventionally used for a group of people attending a theatre performance in France. It emphasises their sense of sight and the pleasures of watching a *spectacle* or a *mise en scène* (literally: something set on the stage). In English-speaking cultures the word is audience, suggesting that people gather to *hear* more than to *see* a play. The very different connotations of these two commonplace words indicate something of the gulf separating the French theatre tradition from that of Britain and North America. This gulf is a complex one, however, and cannot be reduced purely to the differences between seeing and hearing. A great many other factors, both cultural and historical, have their part to play, as this book will show. It is the only book of its kind, intended for anyone who knows a little of the English-language theatre tradition and wants to know more about the state of French theatre now.

In the course of this century the most influential movement to have its roots in France has been the Theatre of the Absurd. This flourished in the 1950s and 1960s, and brought international fame to playwrights such as Beckett, Ionesco, Adamov, Genet and many others. Their plays challenged every preconception and inherited 'rule' of the stage, renewing our sense of what was possible, both in dramatic form and in theatrical presentation. Like all great dramas, their impact made itself felt on both eye and ear, but at first it was the visual originality of, for example, a corpse which grows to fill the whole stage, which disturbed and stimulated theatre-goers. They found themselves confronted with performances which rejected the familiar drama of rational debate or conversation in favour of raw images making a direct assault on the sensibilities of their *spectateurs*. To people who puzzled over the meaning in his plays, Beckett replied that it was the *shape* of the ideas which mattered to him.

So original were the plays of the Absurd, and so great was their impact, that, for many people, they still *are* contemporary French theatre, to the point where they have eclipsed everything that has followed in the past three decades. But the story of what has happened since the Absurd is an absorbing one, beginning with the revolutionary upheavals of 1968. Just as the French Revolution paved the way for the dictatorship of Napoleon, so the events of 1968 opened the way to a decade of all-powerful directors in French theatre. If our guide to French theatre now had been written in 1977 instead of 1997, it would have given a very different impression. The 1970s saw the high point of sophisticated and costly directors' theatre, characterised by lavishly spectacular stagings which drew on Surrealism, on painting, architecture, sculpture, installation art, film, opera and dance, as much as on dramatic traditions of play-making.

The biggest change to have taken place in the last two decades concerns the role of the playwright in the French theatre. This is the phenomenon we aim to survey here. Absurdist shock tactics had demolished the traditional dramatic conventions so conclusively that playwriting seemed to have reached a dead end during the 1970s. At the same time the creative achievements of productions devised by companies like the Théâtre du Soleil, together with the baroque brilliance of much directors' theatre, combined to make it seem as if the playwright was an extinct species. The major development of the 1980s and 1990s is the story of the playwright's return to life, sometimes in surprising new incarnations, sometimes reassembling traditional elements in different configurations.

Mise en scène follows one quite particular story throughout. It concentrates on showing how theatre directors acquired such power and control over institutions in the first place, and how the playwrights have slowly recaptured some purchase on the creative processes of live theatre in France. In order to explain this progression, we have had to condense a great deal and omit a great deal more. To redress the balance we have included a separate information section, listing as many as possible of those who are active in the 1990s, shaping French theatre as it approaches the next century and a further series of turning points. These listings also include theatres, organisations and institutions, festivals and training schools, reviews and publications. All contribute to the range and diversity of contemporary French theatre. We have attempted to mix analysis and factual data in such a way as to create something approaching a Michelin guide to theatre in France.

London and Paris
May 1997

PART I

MISE EN SCÈNE
AND THE PLAYWRIGHT

CHAPTER 1

THE FRENCH THEATRICAL TRADITION

French theatre-goers take the three unities of Aristotelian tradition for granted. Just as football fans expect a game of two halves, so theatre-goers in France expect the three unities of time, place and action to be respected. Not that they reject all experimental plays which break these rules: on the contrary, when such plays are valued it is often for the self-conscious way they reject those very rules. The neo-classical respect for Aristotle, which took root in *le grand siècle* – the age of Cardinal Richelieu and Louis XIV, the age of Jean Racine, of Pierre Corneille and of Molière – has proved remarkably durable over the last three centuries. To understand why is to understand something of the deep divide between theatre in France and the theatre of the English-speaking world.

In the 1630s, when the Puritans were preparing to close down the theatres all over England, Richelieu was establishing the Académie Française, founded with the mission to shape the literary and dramatic taste of the French nation. When a critical quarrel developed, in 1637, over whether or not Corneille's *Le Cid* respected the three unities, the Académie was called upon to arbitrate in the dispute. Louis XIV (who reigned from 1661 to 1715) was the first centralising monarch to understand the value of theatre in his drive to establish cultural hegemony. He exercised personal control over court entertainments, often taking part himself (as a dancer) and providing personal protection to men of the theatre, notably Molière. In 1680 he established the Comédie-Française, intending the company to have the same authority in the world of the theatre as the Académie had acquired in the world of letters.

Although its statutes have undergone alteration since Louis

XIV's time, the Comédie-Française still survives and is proud to call itself the oldest theatre company in Europe. Its director must be nominated by the President of France, but its organisational structure retains something of the old 'share' system, giving to each member of the permanent company an equal say in deciding matters of policy and choice of repertoire. Because of its orgins, in a fusion of the major companies of the time (the one which had been Molière's, until his death in 1673, and the company of the Hôtel de Bourgogne) it is also the sole guardian of performance traditions which link today's theatre to that of Molière, Racine and Corneille. Certain comic routines, especially in performances of Molière, were handed down from player to player and are the basis of the company's claim to perpetuate performance traditions that have survived for three hundred years, although actors today aim for more originality.

When Louis XIV created the Comédie-Française, he gave it the monopoly over all French-language performances in the capital. Any other performers were forbidden to use spoken text, so they had to use mime or song, or perform in another language, like the Italian Company. This partly accounts for the rapid growth of interest in opera, both comic and serious, in the course of the late seventeenth and eighteenth centuries: words that were sung escaped the monopoly restrictions placed on spoken text. Under Louis XV the right to perform in French was extended to the Italian Company, which enabled them to perform the plays of Pierre Marivaux, among other authors; Marivaux wrote many of his plays especially for the Italian actors, using characters drawn from the *commedia dell'arte*. But the Comédie-Française remained the only theatre for a playwright with serious ambitions. It was here that Voltaire's numerous tragedies were staged, and here that Beaumarchais's *Marriage of Figaro* was performed in 1784, after repeated refusals from the censor over the previous three years. Not until 1791, under the French Revolution, was the privileged position of the Comédie-Française finally overturned. Even then, the general freedom for any citizen to open a theatre was short-lived, since Napoleon was as keen as the Bourbon kings before him to maintain control over public performances in French and it was he who reintroduced a licensing system only slightly more liberal than that which had been in force before the Revolution.

This system of monopoly was not unique to France. Similar restrictions existed in London and in other European cities. Unique to France is the way that successive Republican governments have been eager to exercise the same proprietorial control over theatre as the king had done in the seventeenth and eighteenth centuries. In consequence of this, theatre has enjoyed the same respect and prestige in France as the arts of music or painting. In the course of the nineteenth century in Paris, as everywhere else, monopoly legislation was gradually relaxed, bringing theatre management into line with any other commercial operation. But the continued existence and protected status of the Comédie-Française ensured at least a show of respect for the classical tradition. As theatre became effectively the first modern mass medium, critics and commentators deplored the growing materialism and superficiality of the theatre industry. There were also powerful advocates for the reform of theatre, unafraid to adopt a tone of high moral seriousness, and for such men the authority of the classical tradition was a useful weapon. Even Emile Zola, when promoting Naturalist theatre in the course of the 1880s, was able to claim inspiration from the classics. No real equivalent of this reliance on the classical traditon exists in Britain, where Royal control of theatre went little further than censoring it. The activities of the Lord Chamberlain, responsible for granting (or refusing) licences to any play produced in public, were seen as an irritating necessity rather than an opportunity for promoting English culture. In the debate which led to the abolition of the Lord Chamberlain's censorship powers (in 1968) nobody thought to defend his office as guardian of the nation's dramatic tradition.[1]

---

[1] In France, censorship has largely withered in the course of this century: in 1906 the central office of theatre censorship ceased to exist, without having been officially abolished, as the result of a budget in which the office was not voted any funds. In 1945, as part of legislation designed to reinstate democratic rule after the years of German occupation, government censorship of theatre was explicitly abolished, but municipalities were given the right to forbid performances which might be prejudicial to peaceful government in their locality.

The living memory of the classical tradition, a tradition in which theatre plays a central role in the cultural life of the nation, has inspired a succession of twentieth-century stage reformers. The first and most influential was Jacques Copeau (1879–1949). Copeau's campaign had begun not as an actor or director (which he later became), but as a critic and commentator. In a series of articles published during the early years of the century he aligned aesthetic reform with moral and ethical purity, arguing that only by rediscovering the 'bare stage' of the Elizabethans, or of the *grand siècle* in France, could the theatre rediscover a sense of purpose and cultural necessity.[2] When he set up his theatre company, combined with a training school at the Left-bank Vieux-Colombier theatre, his aim was to recreate something of the collaborative company traditions that he believed had made for the greatness of Molière's or Shakespeare's theatre. His appeal to the renewal of traditions based on close collaboration between players and playwright was bound to find echoes in France, with its strong sense of an unbroken line handed down from actor to actor within the framework of companies who often specialised in performing the work of particular playwrights. It was also to prove one of the most influential ideas in the development of French theatre throughout the twentieth century.

After the brief star-burst of the Romantic verse dramas of Victor Hugo in the 1830s, the nineteenth century had seen the emergence of few major dramatists; playwrights with the highest ambitions, such as Alfred de Musset, author of *Lorenzaccio*, never expected their plays could be staged because of their disregard for the unities. France played an important part in the development of Naturalism, through the work of Zola and the founding of André Antoine's Théâtre Libre in 1887, but no French playwright emerged to compare with Ibsen, Strindberg or Chekhov. The Symbolist theatre similarly thrived under Aurélien Lugné-Poe, but the Belgian Maurice Maeterlinck was the only francophone playwright he discovered, with the

---

[2] Copeau's writings on theatre are being published by Gallimard under the heading *Registres, 1974* (in progress). A selection was published in English translation by Rudlin, J. and Paul, N. H., as *Copeau: Texts on Theatre*, Routledge, 1990.

exception of Alfred Jarry, whose *Ubu Roi* startled devotees of the Symbolist art briefly in 1896, provoking William Butler Yeats, who was in the audience, to comment: 'after us the savage god.' Jarry's play only had two performances and was not successfully revived for another sixty years, when Jean Vilar produced it, although it is now frequently revived as a pre-modern classic. In the second half of the nineteenth century the profitable 'boulevard' theatre nurtured the genre known as 'French Farce', whose major exponents were Eugène Labiche, Georges Courteline and Georges Feydeau. 'Grand Guignol' horror plays also developed in this period, just before the rise of the cinema, when large fortunes could still be made from managing a theatre. Not until after the First World War was there a major renewal of French dramatic art. This was the time when a group of powerful actor–directors, drawing inspiration from Copeau and known as 'Le Cartel', succeeded in restoring the theatre to the place it had held in the *grand siècle*. In the words of Charles Dullin, one of the 'Cartel' directors, they were 'forced to teach the authors what they no longer know, namely the rules of the theatre game'.[3]

Dullin's term, 'the rules of the theatre game', carries a clear reference to the Italian dramatist Luigi Pirandello and underlines the link between the new Modernist movement in art and the frank theatricality of the 'Cartel' style. It was no coincidence that Pirandello's meditation on theatre and its relation to human identity, *Six Characters in Search of an Author*, had its greatest success in Paris during this period, in a production by the company of Georges Pitoeff – later a member of the 'Cartel'. The chief playwrights to emerge from this rediscovery of theatricality were Jean Cocteau, Jean Giraudoux and Jean Anouilh, authors whose work was sometimes criticised for being witty but shallow. Nevertheless, they paved the way for the challenging and quintessentially theatrical qualities of the great post-war playwrights such as Jean Genet, Eugène Ionesco and Samuel Beckett who were to change the whole way we think about theatre.

---

[3] Dullin, C., cit. Gouhier, H., in *L'Essence du théâtre*, Paris: Plon, 1943, pp. 228–9.

A more radical reformer of the same period was Antonin Artaud (1896–1948). His ambition was to develop performances in which everything on stage was expressed in language specific to theatre, 'written directly in the stage space', and emphasising movement, gesture, music, rhythm and colour as much as the spoken word. His ideas were not seriously taken up until after the war, but in the 1950s and 1960s they also contributed (like the work of the Absurdist playwrights) to a re-evaluation of theatrical art, its power and its specific methods of constructing meaning. His collection of essays, *Le Théâtre et son double,*[4] gradually grew in influence during the post-war period and became a much-quoted text around 1968, when all the inherited beliefs and practices of French theatre were being thrown into doubt. Although he was the most revolutionary of modern directors, Artaud was also one of the most obsessed with tradition – not the traditions of Western classical text-based theatre, but those of Eastern theatre and of mystical thinkers from all parts of the globe. He saw no difficulty in juxtaposing ideas drawn from the Kabbala, from alchemy, from Mexican peyote rituals and from Balinese dance dramas; in this he can be seen as the father of late-twentieth-century 'intercultural' theatre.

From the Liberation to 1968

The experience of defeat and occupation during the Second World War paved the way for the two distinctive developments in post-war French theatre: the theatre of the Absurd and the decentralisation movement. The blow to national pride manifested itself in two distinct phases: the first was during the occupation of France, when the response to German propaganda in daily life was only to strengthen people's sense of attachment to French traditions. The theatres of Paris were never so full as under the Occupation, when the plays performed were either classics or recent plays inoffensive enough to

[4] Paris: Gallimard (idées 114), 1964. (First published in 1938.) *The Theatre and its Double*, in English translation by Claude Schumacher, in *Artaud on Theatre*, Methuen, 1989.

be passed by the *Propagandastaffel*, although a few oppositional plays did slip through the net, such as *Antigone* by Jean Anouilh and *Les Mouches* by Jean-Paul Sartre, produced by Charles Dullin. After the Liberation in 1945, the enthusiasm of theatregoers did not diminish, but the post-war plays began to reflect the shattered sense of all trusted values having been swept away by the terrible events of the Hitler years. First came the Existentialist dramas of Jean-Paul Sartre and Albert Camus, both of whose early plays placed contemporary problems in Classical settings, thus laying claim to the unbroken tradition stretching back through Giraudoux and Cocteau to Racine and Corneille.

These post-liberation plays embodied an Existentialist philosophy which emphasised the arbitrary quality of all existence. The absence of a Creator, the dramatists argued, meant that there are no values given in advance. Insofar as human beings wish to ascribe value to certain ideas or actions, these values must be understood as freely chosen, not pre-ordained by a Creator, and only to be justified by a personal commitment which might frequently appear absurd. This modern philosophy, born of bitter wartime experience, stressed the need for individuals to take their destiny into their own hands. They had to accept the limitations of their situation (since no outside force could be counted on to change it) and exercise their freedom of choice within the constraints of that situation. This philosophy lent itself well to dramatic expression and both Sartre and Camus attracted large audiences. But although their ideas were novel, the dramatic structure of their plays was extremely conventional and it was left to the dramatists of the Absurd to modernise French drama and make an authentically new beginning.

With hindsight, it is clear that the existential anguish evident in Absurdist plays such as Samuel Beckett's *Waiting for Godot* or Eugène Ionesco's *The Killer* were expressions of the same intellectual mood, made up, in equal parts, of despair, cynicism and the desire for radically new beginnings. But at the time when the first plays of The Absurd were produced, both audiences and critics found them baffling. This was because they rejected the traditional conventions of dramatic construction, especially plot and character. As Martin Esslin observed, 'The theatre of the Absurd has renounced arguing *about* the absurdity of the human condition; it merely *presents* it in being – that is, in terms of concrete stage images.'[5] The dominant stage image of the 1950s, that still haunts us today, became that of Vladimir and Estragon bleakly waiting for a Godot who never comes. Vladimir and Estragon lack the usual defining features of stage characters: they have no past, since they can remember almost nothing, and no future, since they are convinced they must stay and wait for Godot. So they exist in a perpetual present, in which the only thing that keeps them (and the play) going is a series of habitual routines, some comic, others not. Many critics have pointed out their affininty with clowns, since they exist only in a condition of pure play. But they are not content, like circus clowns, to offer their nonsense as entertainment. Instead, they are stuck, like Pirandello's six characters, with nothing but the fragments their author has written and have to try to make sense of their existence in that context alone. The same self-conscious theatricality is present in both Pirandello and Beckett, but Beckett takes the development one stage further, since Pirandello's play maintains the distinction between the two worlds of art and reality, whereas Beckett's erases it.

The other writers grouped together by Esslin as Theatre of the Absurd (Ionesco, Genet, Arthur Adamov, Fernando Arrabal) developed similar images of the world as a site of sense-less, circular play-acting, from which there was no escape and whose antics are made to appear, at one and the same time, both farcical and tragic. Apart from their intense theatricality, these plays had so little in common with the traditional rules and conventions of drama that audiences did not at first know what to make of them. In fact, it is doubtful whether they would ever have been staged at all, had it not been for the existence of a number of small 'art' theatres in the Latin Quarter of Paris. Their stages were so small that they seemed crowded with more than two or three actors on them and their seating capacity was

[5] Esslin, M., *The Theatre of the Absurd*, Harmondsworth: Penguin, 1980, p. 25 (revised edititon). Esslin was the first to coin the term Theatre of the Absurd.

often limited to less than fifty. But because they had very low running costs they could afford to take chances and it was in these theatres that plays by Adamov, Ionesco, Beckett, Arrabal, Jean Tardieu, Jean Vauthier, Jacques Audiberti and many others were first performed. Most of these tiny stages disappeared in the course of the sixties or were turned into cinemas. Just one still survives: La Huchette, where Ionesco's double bill of *The Bald Prima Donna* and *The Lesson* has had an uninterrupted run since its first revival in the late 1950s.[6]

The French theatre tradition, as this brief summary has shown, combines respect for the classical heritage, both in acting and in dramatic literature, with a vigorous experimental or reforming strain. Shared by both these apparently opposed tendencies is a strong awareness of the specific quality in which all dramatic art is rooted, namely theatricality. Because of this attraction to artifice, realism has never enjoyed the same privileged position in France as it does on the English-speaking stage. This did not change in the post-war period, since the two major influences, the Absurd and Brecht, have both stressed the self-conscious theatricality of dramatic performance. An additional factor was that France failed to experience the steady development of television drama which, in Britain, tended to reinforce the realistic trend. Instead, the French cinema industry has flourished in the post-war years, becoming known for 'art' movies which look back to the theatricality of Jean Renoir and which make extensive use of self-consciously filmic devices of the New Wave.

Theatricality is sometimes associated with superficiality, but this is not always the case: it can accompany intensely serious investigations of the human condition, as the works of Shakespeare demonstrate. This is well understood in France, where theatre is seldom seen as 'mere' entertainment. To any Frenchman even remotely interested in cultural matters, theatre appears to be a necessary part of urban existence. The twentieth-century pioneers and reformers of the French stage, from

[6] For a history of these pocket theatres see Cohn, R., *From Desire to Godot: Pocket Theater of Post-war Paris*, Berkeley and Los Angeles: University of California Press, 1987.

Jacques Copeau to Jean Vilar, have all been able to appeal to the deep-seated Republican belief that to bring a number of citizens together for a performance based on some matter of common concern was an activity of unquestionable value to society at large. This connects with a second and equally deep-seated belief, namely that the members of any society are made more humane by being exposed to works of art at their most demanding. Thus Copeau, in the early years of the century, could appeal to the need for 'a heightened sense of, and love for, one's own humanity',[7] and Vilar, in 1944, could write that his theatre was intended 'for all those for whom theatre is not mere entertainment, but also a painful pleasure for mind and heart'.[8]

The name of Jean Vilar evokes a complex set of associations clustering around Republican ideals of Liberty, Fraternity and Equality, and rooted specifically in the hopes for a new, more democratic society which followed the liberation of France in 1945. He is remembered above all as the founder of the Avignon Theatre Festival in 1947 – see pp. 127–36 – and for his concern that Avignon should be a place of reconciliation where young people from all over Europe could come together, in a holiday atmosphere, overcome recent hatreds and discover a shared heritage in the great works of the European repertoire. Alongside works by Shakespeare and Corneille, he also produced Kleist and Brecht at a time when any work from Germany was still viewed with suspicion in France. Although a great innovator in his own right, Vilar had a strong sense of the theatrical tradition he inherited: his first published book was entitled *De la tradition théâtrale*.[9]

Vilar's view of the 'Theatrical Tradition' was that the great works of the classic repertoire constituted a birthright of all people, no matter what their class or condition in life. Provided that these works were performed honestly, without excessive decoration, the words of their authors possessed the power to

---

[7] Cit. Whitton, D., in *Stage Directors in Modern France*, Manchester: University Press, 1987, p.59.
[8] Cit. Wehle, P., in *Le Théâtre Populaire selon Jean Vilar*, Avignon: Barthélémy, 1981, p.115.
[9] Paris: L'Arche, 1955.

awaken the public to an understanding of the world and of society that they could not gain anywhere else. His avowed aim in choosing his repertoire – especially the plays of Molière, Corneille, Shakespeare – was to provide a means for ordinary people to gain access to education and to culture. It was an article of faith for him that this would make wars less likely and tyranny less possible. But for this to happen, theatre needed to be seen as a public service, as necessary to the well-being of a community as gas, water or electricity. Vilar's other belief was in the festive nature of all great theatre – that the above aims were best realised in an atmosphere of common celebration and that the function of theatre was to bring together a whole people in rediscovery and reaffirmation of deeply held beliefs.

As the successful director of the new Avignon Festival, Vilar was given the job, in 1951, of breathing life into the Théâtre National Populaire. This institution, dating back to 1920, had never been given the money or the prestige to do anything more than offer reduced-price performances of productions from the Comédie-Française and other leading Parisian companies. Moreover, its location in one of the smartest districts of Paris, on the right bank opposite the Eiffel tower, was not exactly ideal for appealing to a popular audience. But it had one great advantage: size. With a stage eighteen metres wide and an auditorium that could hold over 3000, it offered the chance to recreate the mass excitement of the Avignon Festival performances in the courtyard of the Papal palace. The key to the success of such an enterprise was in organising the audience. Vilar built up an extremely large 'association of the friends of the TNP', and arranged for free buses to bring parties from factories and businesses. He also made sure that there would be no hidden costs, such as the obligatory tip for the usherette, that good, cheap food could be bought before the show and that it would start on time (at this time Parisian theatres almost always started around forty-five minutes after the advertised time).

Vilar was a man of the Left. He was unafraid of voicing his opposition to de Gaulle when he inaugurated the Fifth Republic in 1958. But he considered that the primary role of theatre was not to involve itself in political struggle over individual issues. Rather, its strength was in providing a space for debate and reflection, where the great issues confronting any society in any age could be aired. His choice of repertoire laid a heavy emphasis on the classics, and his choice of modern plays tended to be those which stressed the individual's responsibility for the shape and direction of society (e.g. Brecht's *The Resistible Rise of Arturo Ui;* Robert Bolt's *A Man for All Seasons*). Roland Barthes explained this by distinguishing between Vilar's conception of theatre, which he described as a theatre of civic awareness or conscience (*'conscience civique'*), and Brecht's more explicitly political theatre: 'Vilar's civic awareness/conscience is of course not so radical as Brecht's *Verfremdung.* Vilar does not recreate the social gestus of an epoch; but he does sketch in its moral gestus: the historical conflict between order and disorder, legitimacy and usurpation.'[10]

His idea of the civic and moral dimension of his mission was inseparable from the material conditions in which the theatre operated. His experiences at Avignon had convinced him that theatre with a broad popular appeal had to get away from traditional theatre buildings whose dress circles and galleries reproduced the class divisions of society. Even the separation between actors and audience was something to be minimised, in his view: 'The theatre with footlights, proscenium arch, boxes and balconies must disappear if it is not already dead. It does not reunite its spectators, it divides them.'

But for Vilar the essence of theatre was in the experience of common humanity: 'Our aim is to bring to all people that pleasure which has been wrongfully denied them since the time of the cathedrals and mysteries. Our aim is to bring together in dramatic communion the little shopkeeper from Suresenes and the high court judge, the worker from Puteaux and the stockbroker, the postman and the professor.'[11] His success in achieving this egalitarianism is hard to measure, but from 1951 to 1963, while French public life slithered in the moral and

---

[10] Cit. Leclerc, G., in *Le T.N.P. de Jean Vilar*, Paris: Union Générale d'Editions, 1971, p. 213.

[11] Vilar, J., *Le Théâtre, service public*, Paris: Gallimard, 1975, pp. 146–7.

political ambiguities of the Algerian war and the demise of the Fourth Republic, Vilar's TNP acquired a moral authority of a rare kind. When he resigned as director of the TNP in 1963, he continued to direct the Avignon Festival. The disruption of the Festival in 1968 signalled the end of an era when communion was the watchword and the beginning of a period of more openly divisive political theatre. When the radical American company The Living Theatre branded his way of running the Festival as 'reactionary' and encouraged audiences to 'rebel' by not paying for their tickets, Vilar felt (correctly) that his whole vision of the theatre of communion was being rejected (see chapter on Avignon, pp. 127–36).

Before this happened, however, Vilar's vision of theatre which could unite and educate a mass public was an inspiration to a wide movement for decentralisation of the theatre. Those inspired by Vilar also looked back to Copeau and his work in the 1920s and 1930s. Just as Copeau had withdrawn from Paris to the countryside in the early 1920s, so his disciples had taken up the challenge, a generation later, of bringing performances to towns and regions deprived of permanent theatre. Copeau's last published book was entitled *Le Théâtre populaire* (1941), a plea for performers and playwrights to leave behind the hothouse atmosphere of Paris and to seek instead an unsophisticated, pop-ular audience who would value being given the opportunity to discover the great masterpieces of the European tradition. This plan of action was adopted by Jean Dasté at St Etienne, by Michel Saint-Denis at Strasbourg and by many others in the course of the 1950s. Their enterprise was rewarded by a favourable climate at the Ministry of Education, where a far-sighted civil servant, Jeanne Laurent, set up a scheme for subsidising regional theatres. These were known as CDNs – Centres Dramatiques Nationaux (National Dramatic Centres) – and although only five were established (in Colmar, Saint-Etienne, Rennes, Toulouse and Aix-en-Provence) before Jeanne Laurent was moved to another post, they showed that a combination of local and national subsidy could effectively sup-port permanent producing theatre companies in the French regions.

The early pioneers of the decentralisation movement aimed, like Vilar, to justify their existence by appealing to a wide constituency. All of them shared Vilar's concern to build up loyal audiences who would feel 'ownership' of the theatre company's activities. In many cases they were supported by the organisations for workers' education which had grown out of the cultural wing of the Resistance movement. All of them published newsletters or house journals and the awareness of their innovations began to spread throughout France so that by the time the Fifth Republic was inaugurated (in 1958) many towns were eager to welcome a new CDN.

In 1959, de Gaulle established the first Ministry of Culture and placed the eminent author André Malraux in charge of it. Under the Minister were placed 'directors' of the various artistic disciplines. The directorate for theatre was established under Emile Biasini in a beautiful mansion situated at 53 rue Saint-Dominique in the seventh *arrondissement*. It is still there today and the continuity of this organisation has done a great deal to ensure the favourable conditions for the expansion of theatre provision in France over the last four decades. Funds were made available and Biasini moved rapidly to establish new National Dramatic Centres along similar lines to those already in place. In 1960 alone four were established (at Tourcoing, Grenoble, Reims and Angers). Two years later the status of CDN was awarded to the Théâtre de la Cité, directed by Roger Planchon at Villeurbanne, a working-class suburb of Lyon, whose communist mayor was a strong believer in the civic benefits to be derived from spending municipal funds on theatre.

Malraux's major preoccupation was the setting in place of Maisons de la Culture – culture palaces which he imagined having something of the grandeur and appeal of the great Gothic cathedrals which sprang up all over France in the late Middle Ages. The plan was for these to be multi-disciplinary organisations, with provision for theatre, music, fine arts and libraries. All were planned with a large stage and auditorium at their centre, since their governing principle was, in Malraux's words, 'the end of Paris's privileged status and the development in the provinces of centres of artistic creativity'; he went so far as to say that he hoped they would eliminate the hideous word 'provinces' from the vocabulary of French cultural life. So the intention was for them to be centres of creative activity, providing the base for a producing company (and, in many cases, an orchestra, dance and opera company as well). But their structure was cumbersome and not as attractive to theatre directors as the CDNs, where they had a freer hand. Moreover, they were expensive to build and even more expensive to run. In the long term, the gradual proliferation of CDNs was to be rather more important for the extension and decentralisation of theatre than were the Maisons de la Culture.

Among the practitioners who shaped the direction of work in the CDNs there was a remarkable measure of unanimity concerning the purpose of their activities. Their aim was to promote theatre as a means of developing a critical analysis of the social structures upon which capitalism depends. The decade from 1958 to 1968 was when Brecht's work and influence had the greatest impact in France and his plays were produced in almost every one of the CDNs. In this respect their orientation was more politically motivated than that of Vilar, but still retained ties with the broad humanist view of any cultural enterprise. A continuity existed between the work of the more radical, such as Roger Planchon's company at Lyon, and those who were politically neutral, such as the company of Jean-Louis Barrault and Madeleine Renaud, which occupied the Odéon throughout the 1960s and whose repertoire successfully combined classic authors with 'difficult' modern texts by playwrights from Paul Claudel to Samuel Beckett.

1968 and Its Aftermath

The strikes and student revolts which spread across France in 1968 had a profound effect on every aspect of theatre development and on how the tradition was viewed. It changed the relationship of individuals to their institutions, it changed the expectations of audiences, of actors, directors and writers. Above all, it changed the relationship between those who worked in theatre and those who provided its funding. In

Malraux's ten-year period as Minister of Culture there had been broad agreement between ministry and workers about aims and objectives. The broad aim was to increase the amount of high-quality theatre available throughout the French-speaking world (overseas territories like Martinique were not neglected) and the objectives were to establish as many new theatres as there were people with the energy, talent and vision to make them work. Anyone who could demonstrate a local need, and could convince the director of theatres about the quality of his or her work, was sure to receive funding. The amount available for subsidy grew substantially throughout the 1960s, resulting in a sense of buoyancy and optimism.

To many people who had achieved recognition and state funding in the 1960s the events of 1968 were experienced as a betrayal, a sudden rude awakening from a deceptive dream of harmony. The ideology fuelling the decentralisation movement had always been broadly Left-wing, focusing as it did on the education and empowerment of the working class and those who had hitherto felt excluded from the domain of culture. It was thus natural, when the wave of strikes spread across France in May 1968, for the theatres to express their solidarity with the workers and to open their establishments for meetings or debates. In panic at the speed with which control seemed to be slipping away, the government sacked any director of a theatre who had allowed (or had merely been unable to prevent) a state theatre being used for political meetings. A number of leading directors of provincial theatres met this fate, notably the widely respected Gabriel Monnet, then head of one of the first Maisons de la Culture, at Bourges, and the internationally famous director of the Odéon in Paris: Jean-Louis Barrault.

As a response to the crisis Roger Planchon invited all theatre workers to convene at his theatre in Villeurbanne for detailed discussions about the nature of the crisis and the responses that could be made to it. From this conference there emerged a large measure of disillusionment about the achievements of the decentralisation movement and the expansionist cultural policies of Malraux. Reviewing the previous decade, speaker after speaker admitted that although theatre provision had undeniably increased, the proportion of working-class members of the audience was still tiny. In the course of these discussions there was a growing feeling that the decentralisation movement had fallen into a trap. While imagining that they were creating conditions for a re-examination of society and its workings (as Vilar had always claimed), had they in fact provided the Gaullist government with a convenient alibi, allowing it to claim that it promoted capitalism with a human face, since it made theatre available to the masses?

The extraordinary explosion of utopian slogans and ideas that were characteristic of the events of May 1968 doubtless had its effect. Slogans such as *L'Imagination au pouvoir* (Put Imagination in power) or *Soyez réalistes, demandez l'impossible* (Be realistic, request the impossible) created an atmosphere in which modest cultural gains seemed like failures and nothing short of a complete cultural revolution would have gained approval. In such circumstances it was easy to accuse Malraux of doing no more than supplying '*un supplément d'âme*' (a little extra sprinkling of soul) to make the capitalist state more acceptable. The fundamental aim of Malraux's policy had been to maximise the opportunities for artistic expression and to spread them more evenly across French territory. To theatre people in the wake of May 1968, it seemed that such activities merely amounted to rehearsing the cultural patrimony, and that they always benefited the bourgeoisie rather than the working class. Even the presentation of socially critical plays by Brecht and his followers could never guarantee the raising of revolutionary consciousness in the audience. Two things were necessary, it was argued, and these were set out in a document known as *La Déclaration de Villeurbanne* (The Villeurbanne Declaration). The first was to go out in search of all those people who still thought theatre was not for them; they were baptised 'the non-public'. The second concerned the performances which were to be taken to this newly identified constituency. Rather than the old formula of the classics with a few modern plays by Brechtian writers, the demand was for a more pro-active conception of culture. In future, the only worthwhile touchstone of cultural value was to be its usefulness to the dispossessed of society:

Any cultural activity now seems to us to be entirely in vain
if it does not have the avowed aim of *politicisation*: that is,
to ceaselessly invent, in view of the 'non-public', opportunities for them to raise their political awareness, to make
a free choice of themselves, to transcend the feelings of
impotence and absurdity constantly aroused in them by a
social system in which human beings are almost never
enabled to invent *together* their own humanity.[12]

The Declaration went on to define a concept of culture 'which
can modify existing relations between men, in other words,
something which can genuinely be termed cultural action'. In
the years following 1968, fuelled by such thinking, there was an
enormous increase in *'animateurs culturels'*, activists who combined some of the skills of Theatre in Education with those of
Community Theatre activists. Their aim was expressed as *donner
la parole* (to give a voice) to those who have none and usually
involved working outside the normal cultural establishments,
going out into factories or community centres and facilitating
performances whose purpose was to provide participants with
opportunities for new political awareness.

For theatre people who did not wish to go so far as to trans-
form themselves into *animateurs culturels*, the same arguments
provided a powerful incentive for work according to the
method known as *'la création collective'*. This term conveys a cultural form growing out of the experience of May 1968 and has
no direct equivalent in English (the closest English term is
'devised theatre'). Its roots are both theatrical and ideological.
The theatrical pedigree links up with Copeau and the Comédie-
Française tradition of a company of actors who share
responsibility for all their creative work. But *la création collective*
which swept through French theatres in the wake of 1968 went
far beyond this in its Jacobin egalitarianism. A recurrent leit-
motif of the social criticism which surfaced in 1968 was the
rigidity of the social hierarchies governing French society. The
division of labour and the compartmentalisation of skilled

---

[12] Cit. in Abirached, R. (ed.), *La Décentralisaton théâtrale 3: 1968, le tournant*, Arles: Actes
Sud, 1994, p.197 – the full text of the Declaration is on pp.195–200.

employment, to which only those with official diplomas were admitted, were both denounced as weapons used by the boss class to keep the people 'in their place'. Opposing this, *la création collective* proclaimed that everyone in a theatre company should have an equal say in devising every aspect of the performance and company management.

A Model Collective – The Théâtre du Soleil

Although many companies took up the challenge of devising their own material, one company stood out from the very beginning and continues to this day as an acknowledged leader in French theatre: Le Théâtre du Soleil directed by Ariane Mnouchkine. Mnouchkine's earliest intervention in French theatre dates back to 1959, when, together with Martine Franck, she set up a student company at the Sorbonne. She persuaded both Sartre and Planchon to be the presidents of this new group and organised a lecture by Sartre as the first public event. In the course of the 1960s Mnouchkine worked, like many other young directors, towards realising her own vision of theatre for the people, drawing on the inspiration of Vilar and touring with her company of semi-professional enthusiasts, encouraged by the thought that Molière's company had also spent many years on the road before becoming established in Paris. In 1963 the Théâtre du Soleil was created, run as a co-operative, its collaborative structure further reinforced when, after 1968, it was decided that every member should take an equal salary. The group's repertoire was similar to that of many other young companies at the time, but their determination to take the theatre beyond its normal limits led to performances in a disused circus in Montmartre of *The Kitchen* (by Arnold Wesker) and of *A Midsummer Night's Dream* (by Shakespeare). The events of 1968 led the company to question the purpose and effectiveness of its policy. The urgency of the situation seemed to demand that they devise their own commentary on contemporary France, rather than using plays by established playwrights.

Their first steps in this direction were tentative and highly theatrical: the production was entitled *Les Clowns* and consisted of a series of improvisations in which each member of the company presented a particular clown, mask or routine which they had researched, and through which they could comment on contemporary events. Most significant was their rejection of a traditional stage and evocation of a fairground setting: a small box set was constructed, with a ramp that thrust out into the audience. Inside the box, reflective panels covered with tiny light-bulbs evoked the dazzling but slightly tawdry glamour of a fairground booth. The ramp extending into the audience enabled the clowns to step outside this artificial environment to a point where they were in direct contact with the audience on either side, or to make their entrances and exits through the audience. This production was taken to the Avignon Festival, where they insisted on performing for audiences in the un-fashionable working-class districts of the town. They had intended to bring it back to the Montmartre Circus building, but were refused permission by the owner and so took it to the Elysée Montmartre, a former boxing hall in which Barrault had staged his *Rabelais,* after being dismissed from his directorship of the Odéon in the wake of the 1968 events.

The frank theatricality of *Les Clowns* had enabled the company to experiment with different performance styles, but had limited their ability to comment on political realities. In their next production, entitled simply *1789*, this problem was overcome. A retelling of the early years of the French Revolution, *1789* came to be seen as a key production and one that served as a model for *la création collective*. It was performed in a disused ammunition store, the Cartoucherie at Vincennes, whose enormous open hangars have been home to the company ever since. Just as Vilar had insisted on spatial innovation going hand in hand with a new approach to theatre, so an innovative performance space became a fundamental element in the creative process of the Théâtre du Soleil. Audiences milled about in a large open area, surrounded by five small stages, and this was the most striking novelty for theatre-goers in 1971: they were placed in an entirely unexpected relationship to the action. Most important was the atmosphere established before the play began and, here again, the arrangement of the space was crucial. The first of the huge hangars of the Cartoucherie was set up as an area in which the audience could be welcomed, buy the text (which also functioned as a programme), eat a rye-bread sandwich, drink some *vin ordinaire* and absorb the carefully created mood in which the revolutionary virtues of liberty, equality, fraternity were celebrated. It was the actors themselves who took the tickets and served the food, some of them in costume. Through these practical details the audience imbibed the ideology of the group in which all tasks were shared around by rota and all members were paid the same. Occasionally spectators could spot Mnouchkine herself sweeping the floor or showing people to their seats, something she continues to do to this day. Through the time they spent in this 'entrance hall' the audience were made to feel at home and welcome as a group, before being swept into the second hangar, where the five stages were set up.

All of this established the right atmosphere for what followed: a company of fairground performers setting out to tell the story of the French Revolution in their own way, using games, puppet shows, conjuring tricks, dumb-show, trials of strength and other street-theatre techniques in order to put their message across. The play was the responsibility of the whole group and was constructed entirely by means of improvisations. These were based on historical and political research shared out among different members of the company. The results of the research would be pooled and different groups of actors would work on improvisations designed to embody the events or characters researched. These would then be shown to the assembled company and Mnouchkine would give a judgement: whether the scene was to be abandoned, or reworked, or retained for further development and possible incorporation in the final show.

What emerged from this process was a performance in which not only the salient historical facts, but also the very difficulty of reconstructing history at all, became the subject of the performance. Each of the scenes depicted an event that was well known to its audience from their study of the French Revolution in school, but each was presented from a different point of view and frequently the points of view contradicted one another. Out of this process emerged a densely layered picture, demonstrating, as much as anything else, that there are a great many ways of telling the history of the French Revolution, and that our version of the events cannot avoid being coloured by our own social and political viewpoint. This was particularly important, since the ambition of the company was to make the show into a kind of commentary on the disappointment of May 1968. Just as the Gaullists had been returned to power in the autumn of 1968, they showed how the bourgeoisie had managed to 'confiscate' the gains made by the people in the early stages of the French Revolution.

The atmosphere in the promenade space during the performances was one of high emotion. The actors encouraged the audience to experience all the extremes, from elation to despair and from rational debate to irrational necromancy. More remarkable still was the fact that the sense of having been through something exceptional together did not end with the performance, but continued afterwards. On most evenings a considerable portion of the audience felt unwilling to leave the building, but stayed, locked in heated discussion. Very soon they were joined by the cast and the debates would continue until the early hours of the morning. The play assumed a therapeutic role for many people, who had welcomed the events of May 1968 with enthusiasm and who were plunged into despair (like Mnouchkine and her company) by the subsequent reassertion of right-wing forces in France. The post-performance discussions gave them an opportunity to talk through their disappointment with like-minded people. The atmosphere was not unlike that of a gathering of true believers in a country where religion had been outlawed.

This production represented an extraordinary achievement in French theatre, one that could be compared with the opening season of the Moscow Arts Theatre in 1898–9 or the early productions of Absurdist theatre in Paris in the early 1950s. All were occasions when audiences had the experience of being confronted with a representation of the world that both astonished them and convinced them by its rich, multi-layered quality, so that it seemed like a completely new theatre form. The secret of the appeal of *1789* was that Mnouchkine had succeeded in generating a compositional method in which the creative power of every member of her company was liberated to the maximum extent. This was an achievement consciously sought after, as she explained: 'Remember that the director has already achieved the greatest degree of power he's ever had in history. And that our general aim is to move beyond that situation, by creating a form of theatre where it will be possible for everyone to collaborate without there being producers, technicians and so on, in the old sense.'[13] In *1789* the political and the aesthetic aims of the creative work were in perfect harmony, both at the level of the company's own process and at that of their understanding of history.

This was demonstrated even more clearly by the success of their following production, *1793,* in which the social and historical focus was narrowed, but the research methods, the performance style and the demonstration of how history is constructed through a clash of different political choices and visions, all built on the experiences of *1789.* Nearly 400,000 spectators visited these two shows in the early 1970s and the influence of *1789* has continued well beyond that, through the film record that is still available. The method of *création collective* exerted a powerful fascination on theatre companies, both in France and beyond. For a while, *création collective* became almost a new orthodoxy in France, to such an extent that it seemed as though the individual playwright and the authored play were doomed to extinction.

The method of collective devising had its drawbacks, however. Although it could provide a complex and completely convincing means of rediscovering a precise historical moment, it was fraught with difficulties when applied to the modern world, or to fictional material where there was no historical data to research. The third and last play in the Soleil's cycle of the early 1970s, *L'Age d'or*, was never completed. Subtitled *première*

---

[13] '*L'Age d'or.* The long journey from 1793 to 1975', *Theatre Quarterly*, Vol.V, No.18, 1975, p.12.

ébauche (first draft), it marked the end rather than the beginning of a stage in the company's artistic life. Mnouchkine and members of the company encountered unexpected difficulties in trying to give a picture of the contemporary world that would have the clarity and the political force of *1789* and *1793*. In the long term, Mnouchkine appears to have concluded that the vision of a single playwright was, after all, necessary, since in the plays of the 1980s and 1990s that dealt with contemporary political reality she always began from written texts. But at the time she was much more preoccupied with the group dynamic within the company, and with the sheer difficulty of finding a coherent vision and voice for dealing with contemporary reality.

Her solution, like Vilar's and Copeau's before her, was to delve back into the traditions of popular performance, notably the *commedia dell'arte*. The story of the death of one apparently unimportant immigrant worker was to be contextualised in the social and political climate of the France of Giscard d'Estaing (1974–81) by means of masks and representative comic figures. Aesthetically and theatrically, the show was a triumph. The audiences who moved around the Cartoucherie space, stretched themselves on the gently undulating slopes covered with coconut matting and bathed in the warm glow of the thousands of tiny orange bulbs in the ceiling, experienced once more the sense of festive warmth that the two previous performances had engendered. They also warmed to the astonishing versatility of actors who, using absolutely nothing in the way of props or scenery, could conjure up a rich range of differing settings, situations and conflicts. But politically the show failed, since it lost the complexities of the analysis in *1789* and *1793,* and adopted a crude perspective, in which the poor were good-hearted but powerless and the rich heartless and unassailable. Because of this the play fell into one of the familiar traps of popular theatre: giving such convincing images of the exploitation of the poor that it suggested that nothing short of a miracle could ever change the situation.

At the same time the internal dynamics of the company were developing towards crisis. This was because the working method that had been developed since *Les Clowns*, despite its brilliant results, had one serious drawback: it depended on making the actors feel that they were constantly competing with one another for Mnouchkine's approval. Despite her idealistic statement, quoted above, about limiting the power of the director, the company's day-to-day working method placed her in a position of domination even more effectively than the traditional way of rehearsing a play, where the actors have to submit to the director's interpretation of the play. Here, there was no play, just a series of improvisations, but in the process of presenting these improvisations, deciding which should be kept and which abandoned, the sole arbiter was Mnouchkine herself. This meant that, in order to retain a sense of contributing to the development of the work in hand, every actor was constantly in competition with every other actor: all, naturally, wanted *their* improvisation to be retained. During the performances of *L'Age d'or*, Mnouchkine abandoned the company for the first time in several years, in order to write the script of her film about Molière. In her absence the company's unity of spirit disintegrated: in Philippe Caubère's words, 'She had kept us like children for too long.'[14]

Caubère's subsequent career as a solo performer illustrates the sometimes fatal attraction that Mnouchkine exercises over young actors. Having taken leading roles in the three *créations collectives* discussed above, Caubère went on to play Molière in Mnouchkine's film and to direct a highly theatrical production of Molière's *Dom Juan*. After this, he left the company. But he found that it was not so easy to leave behind the dominant influence of Mnouchkine. He began to elaborate a one-man show in which he could express his own journey from boyhood in Provence to the discovery of Mnouchkine's vision of theatre at the Cartoucherie. This was devised following the improvisational method learned from Mnouchkine, but was performed by Caubère alone. The first performances, entitled *La Danse du diable,* were a triumph at the 1981 Avignon Festival. He continued to devise further one-man shows throughout the 1980s:

[14] Caubère, P., 'Les Réchappés du Soleil', *Acteurs*, No.70, May 1985, p.150.

Ariane ou l'Age d'or, Les Jours de colère ou Ariane II and others.
These were tributes to Mnouchkine's inspirational directing
methods but also caustic send-ups of her tendency to make
everything revolve around herself. By 1994, when he performed
the complete cycle of what he called his *Roman d'un acteur*, his
show had grown to fill a dozen episodes, each of some three
hours' playing time. To watch these performances is to appreciate the exceptional, protean quality of an actor who can bring a
whole theatre company to life in front of our eyes, on a bare
stage, by dint of his virtuosity alone; but one cannot help also
being struck by the paradox that a decade of collaborative work
at the Théâtre du Soleil seems to have left him incapable of performing with anyone but himself.

Création Collective – **Other Companies**

The high profile achieved by the Soleil should not obscure the
fact that the methods of *la création collective* were adopted by
many other theatre companies in the 1970s, with varying
degrees of coherence. A dominant theme in much of this work
was the relationship between power and the flow of images in
contemporary society. The radical philosophers, writers and
visual artists' movement known as the Situationists had seized
on the public demonstrations and meetings of May 1968 as an
opportunity to develop their denunciation of the use of the way
modern states exploit the power of images to reinforce control
over their citizens. Guy Debord's book *The Society of the Spectacle*
(1967) developed the theory that, in a culture dominated by
television, all experience is set at one remove from reality,
processed through a series of predigested images or scenarios,
which can only be consumed in a passive state. The
Situationists' ideas had a powerful appeal to people working in
a theatre already influenced by Brecht, and who were looking
for more radical theories to demystify and account for the use of
images by those in power. The Théâtre du Soleil's *1789* included
many striking examples of such use of images: for instance, a
tableau vivant of the king as Good Shepherd, surrounded by his
adoring flock. This image was used to set the king's own view

of his paternalist bounty in opposition to the neglect and poverty in which the French people really languished in the 1780s.

A more contemporary commentary was provided by Le Grand Magic Circus, a collective grouped under the leadership of the flamboyant Jérôme Savary. Savary's training was in music and design, and these aspects of performance feature prominently in all his work. In the years leading up to 1968 he had directed plays by Arrabal, culminating in a production of his play *Le Labyrinthe*, as a result of which the Grand Magic Circus was formed. Savary's ambition was to generate a performance in which the text was genuinely subordinated to the visual, musical, festive dimension. The group's first show (1970) was entitled *Zartan*; it adopted a comic-strip format and showed an anti-Tarzan going on a picaresque journey across the world, demolishing all the cliché images of power current at the time. This was followed by *Robinson Crusoé* (1972) which attacked myths of colonial supremacy. *De Moise à Mao* (1973) went further, attacking all the icons of Western cultural supremacy, including Molière and the French classical tradition. Show followed show with great rapidity and inventiveness throughout the 1970s, but by the end of the decade all the sacred cows had been demolished and the Grand Magic Circus ran out of steam. In the 1980s Savary turned his considerable talents to directing light opera and comedies such as *Le Bourgeois Gentilhomme* (1981) and *Cyrano de Bergerac* (1983). In the last ten years he has extended his repertoire to include musicals such as *Cabaret*.

Another director who worked with Arrabal was Jorge Lavelli. Having come to prominence with a number of highly theatrical and aesthetically dazzling productions in the 1960s, he agreed to join with Arrabal and a company of TNP actors for an experiment in *création collective* in 1972. The title of the play was *Bella Ciao, la guerre de mille ans* and the aim was to devise it entirely as a team effort. As David Whitton reports, 'initially the team included everyone involved in the production – Lavelli and Arrabal, the designer Michael Raffaelli and a composer, André Chameaux, technicians, a score of actors and a Marxist pop group, Komintern, consisting of some fifteen musicians.

This unwieldy team soon split into two groups, those like Arrabal and Lavelli whose concerns were artistic, and others who were motivated by political aims.'[15] Strong political control was exerted by the cultural committee of the local communist party and the production which resulted was rich in images but lacking in argument. It used theatrical devices such as a bullfight or a rugby match to suggest the struggle between right- and left-wing forces in society, but fell into the trap of many similar shows, where the creation of images was subjected to a grid of politically correct clichés, resulting in an overall effect of banality.

Lavelli learned from this experience and never again became embroiled in an overt political programme. He became the focus for a group of Latin-American writers and directors, the best known of whom was Copi: alongside his well-loved work as a cartoonist, Copi also wrote mordant plays of Surrealist inspiration. Another was the Cuban Edouardo Manet, whose grotesque play *Les Nonnes* was a huge success in 1969 and who has written regularly for the stage ever since. The Argentinian director Victor Garcia was part of this group until his death in 1982 and so also is his compatriot Alfredo Arias. To a greater or lesser extent, the productions of this group were always characterised by an expressionist, often elaborately decorative style, having identifiable roots in Latin-American Catholicism. They did not ignore social issues – the poor and the dispossessed were frequently the subject of their plays – but they tended to be presented through the distorted or sumptuous images of a baroque nightmare, rather than in realistic or Brechtian mode. A recent example of this style was Alfredo Arias's 1993 production of Copi's *Cachafaz* (Uruguayan slang for 'big-mouth') presented at the Théâtre de la Colline under Lavelli's leadership. In the same season Arias also directed an entirely new show at the Folies Bergères, in which he abandoned the simple unveiling of breasts and buttocks, replacing it with more complex images of seduction. Lavelli himself, after introducing the work of the Polish playwright Witold Gombrowicz to the French public, alongside

---

[15] Whitton, D., *Stage Directors in Modern France*, Manchester: University Press, p. 204.

that of Arrabal and Copi, devoted much of his energies to opera. But in 1987 he was appointed the first director of the new Théâtre National de la Colline (see below pp. 153–4).

A second dominant theme of *créations collectives* in the post-1968 years was the questioning of the structures through which power is exercised in the bourgeois state. In their search for new material to match the urgency of the revolutionary ideas thrown up in 1968, many companies naturally turned to documentary methods. An outstanding example was the Théâtre de l'Aquarium, under the leadership of Jacques Nichet. He expressed very clearly the transition, as he saw it, between theatre before and after 1968: 'we abandoned story, plot and psychology . . . our theatre was transformed by the use of documentary material; we no longer used the stage as a place to celebrate eternal cultural values, but as an instrument for elucidating social issues, and as a form of group expression.'[16] In 1972 the Aquarium put on a production entitled *Marchands de ville* exposing corruption in government policies on housing and property development, which was entirely based on research conducted by the members of the company. The banks were personified by actors dressed in outlandish capitalist costume, including several top hats each, and the set consisted of blocks of housing not more than three feet tall which they manhandled about and used as bargaining counters. In contrast to this, the tenants of the buildings in question were presented as believable characters who used direct address to involve the audience in their housing problems.

The documentary method for exposing the real centres of power in bourgeois society was taken to an extreme in *Un Conseil de classe très ordinaire* (1981), which was based on a clandestine tape recording made of the end-of-year meeting in a lycée, where the progress of each pupil is discussed by the teaching staff. This recording revealed the extent to which each pupil's fate was decided by the whims and peculiarities of the teachers concerned. In deciding how to flesh out what was only

---

[16] Nichet, J., 'La Mise en pièces du document', *Théâtre Public*, No.38, 1981, p. 15.

an audio recording and give it a visual dimension, the company at first thought they should try to 'explain' everything that was said, by recreating a plausible psychological motivation for each of the speakers. But they rejected this solution and concluded that the words (since they had, in reality, been spoken at a real staff meeting) would preserve a greater impact if allowed to appear strange and difficult to fathom. In this way they adopted a rather Brechtian aim 'to render strange what is familiar, so that one can laugh it it'.[17] This was achieved by the movements, positions and incidental activities of the various participants, which were used to express their relationships with institutional power. The production showed how institutions typically create their own little worlds with self-perpetuating ceremonies and their own idioms. As Nichet put it, 'these teachers are caught in the trap of their language, which is not theirs, but the language of the institution speaking through them.'[18]

Although grounded in documentary methods and commenting on the social set-up, the productions of the Aquarium were characterised by a poetic emphasis in the selection of word or image and a lack of interventionist political stance. More directly involved in the political process was Armand Gatti, who responded to the upheavals of 1968 by deciding that theatre within theatre buildings was no longer able to reach working-class audiences and that the only solution was to take his company to the workers and involve them in the creative process. This was a bold decision, since he had been one of the most frequently performed playwrights in the years leading up to 1968, having written a dozen plays between 1958 and 1968. The experience which convinced Gatti to turn his back on the established theatre was the banning of his *La Passion du Général Franco* when it was already in rehearsal at the TNP late in 1968. At the same time he had been reflecting on the role of the spectator in theatre and concluded that conventional theatre performance could not avoid casting the spectator in a passive role: 'I'm for a spectacle without spectators,' he wrote, 'where each person

---

[17] Ibid., p.29.
[18] Ibid., p.26.

participates in the creation, where each learns from the other. I don't want the voyeur.'[19]

In the course of the 1970s Gatti and a number of collaborators arranged to spend time in factories or cultural centres working on projects which involved the people of that community and which culminated in a variety of different outcomes. In Schaalbeek, in Belgium, he occupied a disused factory and developed a project on the Spanish anarchist leader Durruti; in Montbéliard he set up a project among the workers in the Peugeot factory which culminated in a series of television films; in St-Nazaire he devised a project about Russian dissidents which enraged local communist party officials but engaged local people in the production of a journal, the creation of a number of small plays, video projects, kite-dramas and a vast sculpture of a wild duck, to symbolise the person who flies against the wind of the dominant ideology. A similar project in Derry engaged unemployed youths in creative work which resulted in a variety of different outcomes, including a video film entitled *Our names were the names of trees* which was shown on British television.

In these projects, Gatti's function is similar to that of the *animateur*, but also goes beyond it, since he imposes an image like the wild duck flying against the wind, which he then uses to draw all the people involved in the project into his creative field. He is best seen as a contemporary folk artist, working with film, video and all the modern means of communication. The most important part of his projects is to provide access to these to people who would not normally think of using them. He is a poet whose aim is to stimulate others to acts of poetry. He is fascinated by the images people use to describe themselves: for example, his 1968 play, *Les Treize Soleils de la rue Saint-Blaise,* took its title from a participant who answered his question 'what would you like to be?' by replying: 'a sun.' Since 1968 his search for this kind of intense image has been as much through stimulating the creativity of others as through his own work.

---

[19] Cit. Champagne, L., in 'Armand Gatti: toward spectacle without spectators', *Theater,* Vol.13, No.1, 1981, p.29.

Of all the *animateurs* who changed direction after 1968, Gatti has been the most consistent in developing work outside theatre structures and involving members of the 'non-public'. He has come to define his intervention as 'plural writing', since it involves liberating expressive language in other people, giving back to them the powers of articulacy which, he believes, late capitalist society does everything to stifle. His work in the 1980s and 1990s has all been done with people whom he describes as '*les exclus*', i.e. social outcasts, those who are marginalised or disempowered. There are similarities between his approach and that of Augusto Boal (who made a base in Paris when forced into political exile from his native Brazil). But where Boal seeks to apply creative performance methods to concrete political situations, Gatti denies that his work has immediate political applications. He seeks rather to generate the poetic image that can set up a creative distance between the constraints of an oppressive situation so as to liberate the imaginations of those caught up in it.

A good example of his recent work was the performance developed in the prison of Fleury-Mérogis near Paris in 1989.[20] In this bicentenary year of the French Revolution, there were official celebrations all over France. Gatti decided to explore the meaning of the Republican ideals of *Liberté, Fraternité* and *Egalité* for a group of prisoners. His method was to supply the prisoners with quantities of documentary material about the French Revolution, but at the same time to encourage them to tell their own stories. He contrasts his work with conventional political art whose aim he describes as '*la prise du pouvoir*' (to take power). His aim is, rather, '*la prise de la parole*' (to take the power of speech). He defines the people he chooses to work with as social outcasts 'under sentence of death': 'They are sentenced to be what they are by the language that locks them in: the language of bad council housing, the language of the media. Our theatre is not a theatre of psychology – the fatal disease of our time. Nor is it a historical theatre, or a political theatre, or a character

[20] See Knowles, D., 'Armand Gatti's Theatre of Social Experiment 1989–91', *New Theatre Quarterly*, No.30, May 1992, pp.123–39.

theatre. It is a language theatre brandished, against a background of squalor, by the people language has rejected.'[21] Through his work in prisons, on council estates, in factories or the urban wastelands which surround the prosperous centres of contemporary French cities, Gatti seeks to develop a vigorous language that will give back dignity to the dispossessed. In this way he links up with his own origins as the son of an Italian immigrant in Marseille, who worked as a refuse collector, and whom Gatti commemorated in his 1962 play *La Vie imaginaire de l'éboueur Auguste G.* In the same spirit he has written and directed epic plays on the concentration camp experience: *Le Chant d'amour des alphabets d'Auschwitz* (1989), reworked and staged in Marseille as *Adam quoi?* (1993).

Another group to have remained faithful, in its own way, to the spirit of *la création collective* is the Théâtre du Campagnol, which moved into a brand-new theatre, built to their specifications, as the 'Centre Dramatique National de Corbeil-Essonnes' in 1993.[22] This company was formed by Jean-Claude Penchenat in 1975, after he had been part of Ariane Mnouchkine's Théâtre du Soleil for the previous ten years. Its most notable success was *Le Bal* (1981), a group-devised performance without words, using only dance and music, and set in a popular dance hall. This becomes the setting for a series of confrontations of different kinds through which the history of twentieth-century France is evoked. It was filmed by Ettore Scola and remains, like Mnouchkine's film of *1789*, an example of the extraordinary conviction and energy brought to their roles by actors when they are given responsibility for the whole creative process. It also demonstrates how humour and powerful emotions can be brought to socially conscious theatre without diminishing its political bite. The Campagnol believes in the importance of establishing close relations with the public in its locality and many of its *créations collectives* use stories or memories recounted by local people as their starting point. Penchenat sees no reason

[21] Gatti, A., 'Seventeen Ideograms and the Search for the Wandering Word', *New Theatre Quarterly*, No.38, May 1994, p.114.
[22] But see below, p. 148.

why such work should not go hand in hand with a more traditional repertoire, and has regularly alternated collectively devised shows with productions of plays by dramatists, both classic and contemporary.

Chapter 2

THE DIRECTOR AS
CREATIVE ARTIST

Antoine Vitez

From the widespread practice of *la création collective* in the 1970s there followed an unforeseen result: the tendency of directors and companies to turn to textual material which was not originally written for theatrical performance. Just as the defenders of *création collective* had insisted on the right of every member of the company (not just the specialised playwright) to share in the creative process, so a further challenge was mounted against the idea that only certain kinds of writing could be accepted as dramatic. An influential pioneer in this respect, and a key figure for the development of French theatre in the 1970s and 1980s, was Antoine Vitez. He was a man of many talents: translator, director, teacher, critic, actor. He worked with Vilar on the journal of the 'Friends of the TNP', *Bref*, and was active in the decentralisation movement, before becoming known as a director and acting teacher at the end of the 1960s. He taught at the Jacques Lecoq school from 1966 to 1970 and in 1968 was appointed to a teaching post at the Conservatoire, where, for the next thirteen years, he developed his own methods of actor training. These have been open to public scrutiny for the past ten years thanks to a series of video tapes entitled *Leçons de théâtre* which are still commercially available.

In 1972 he established a company at Ivry, Le Théâtre des Quartiers d'Ivry, where he directed a company of young actors, many of whom he had recently trained, in an eclectic repertoire which included plays by modern authors (e.g. *Iphigénie Hôtel* by Michel Vinaver, 1977) and the great classics. His most successful classical staging was in 1978, when he presented four Molière plays in repertoire, using a bare stage and employing only those few props or items of furniture which were mentioned in the inventory kept by Molière's stage manager (the plays were: *L'Ecole des femmes; Le Tartuffe; Dom Juan; Le Misanthrope*). His style, both in teaching and in directing, was to draw out the virtuoso qualities of his actors, giving them free rein to develop gestures, movements or vocal intonations having little to do with mimetic reproduction of real life, but seeking to emphasise poetry, rhythm or movement for its own sake. In 1975 he directed this company in a performance entitled *Catherine*, based on a novel (*Les Cloches de Bâle*) by Louis Aragon, the well-known communist poet, for whom Vitez had worked as secretary in the early 1960s.

Catherine was not an adaptation in the normal sense, but rather a reading of Aragon's novel, in which a group of actors passed the book around and read out passages in turn. By treating the text in this way, Vitez aimed to put on display for his audience not simply the plot and ideas contained in the novel, but its particular narrative texture as well. While passing the novel around, the actors demonstrated their own continuing reality as people reading a book (not characters in role) by eating their way through a complete dinner that was served up for them on the stage. To people who objected that Vitez should have made a more traditional adaptation of the story he responded that what interested him about stage performance was to find material that offered a kind of resistance and did not allow itself to be easily absorbed into the theatrical machine. He insisted, in a much quoted phrase, that '*il faut faire théâtre de tout*' – theatre can be made from anything . . . novels, poems, press cuttings, the Gospel'.[1]

From 1981 to 1988 he was director of the Théâtre National de Chaillot, the theatre that had housed Vilar's Théâtre National Populaire two decades earlier. While in control of the Chaillot theatre, he continued to present a mix of classic and modern plays similar to the repertoire he had directed at Ivry. He included the great works of the European repertoire, such as *Faust* and *Hamlet*, while also reviving neglected works by

[1] Cit. in Temkine, R., *Mettre en scène au présent*, Lausanne: La Cité, 1977, p.197.

Le Soulier de satin by Paul Claudel

En attendant Godot by Samuel Beckett

Dom Juan by Molière

Le Martyre de saint Sébastien by Robert Wilson

Le Vieil Hiver by Roger Planchon

Le Mahabharata by Peter Brook and Jean-Claude Carrière

Les Atrides by Théâtre du Soleil

Savannah Bay by Marguerite Duras

Robert Garnier and Victor Hugo. When accused of turning the former popular theatre into an élite institution, he famously delared that his aim was '*un théâtre élitaire pour tous*' (an élitist theatre for all). At Chaillot he also continued to use the methods he had applied to Aragon's novel. He took a similar approach to the staging of Pierre Guyotat's *Tombeau pour cinq cent mille soldats*, a notoriously subversive stream-of-consciousness novel whose dense verbal texture attempts to embody all the sordid horror and fascination of the Algerian war. In this, just as in his productions of more conventional texts, he created the sense of overlapping time-scales, of clashes and contradictions, interrupting smooth narrative flow with moments when the audience had to take stock, or recognise the strangeness of something previously taken for granted. As a director, he shared the intellectual, restlessly questioning style of Brecht, so it was fitting that his last production before his untimely death in 1990 was Brecht's *Life of Galileo* at the Comédie-Française, where Vitez had been appointed director in 1988.

By their sparkling intelligence, their qualities of seduction and surprise, Vitez's productions exercised considerable fascination over his colleagues. In particular his insistence that no form of writing was a priori unsuitable for theatrical presentation had a powerful influence. Numerous directors turned their attention towards ever more unlikely sources for theatre performances and, in the course of the 1970s and 1980s, one might have been forgiven for thinking that there was an official competition for who could make a successful theatre performance from the most unlikely text. If there had been such a competition, the prize would have gone to Jean-François Peyret, who collaborated with Jean Jourdheuil on a number of productions, culminating in 1990 with a staging of the scientific discourse of Lucretius, *De Natura Rerum*.

The career followed by Antoine Vitez in the course of his last two decades can serve to exemplify the principal paradox of the theatre post-1968. Anne Ubersfeld, in her recent book on Vitez, makes the following comment: 'May 1968 left no man of the theatre intact – let alone a man concerned with political matters. He constantly asked himself the key question: for whom do I work? To whom is my art directed? He continued to ask it until the end of his life when, as head of the Comédie-Française, he wondered how to democratise and renew that theatre's audience.'[2] The paradox is that so many directors shared Vitez's genuine desire to democratise the theatre, and yet the years since 1968 have seen an ever greater concentration of power in the hands of theatre directors at the expense of every other participant in the theatrical enterprise: writers, actors, designers, technicians and audiences.

From the point of view of dramatists, the decade of the 1970s was a very lean period. The success of devised performances led to sharp decline in the number of new plays reaching the stage. At the same time there was a crisis in theatre publishing, so that even fewer plays were getting into print. The combination of these things led some to declare that the playwright was dead. Although there were honourable exceptions, including Vitez himself, few directors made it their business to search out new playwriting talent when they could achieve spectacular effects with group-devised shows and their own reworkings of classic texts.

The causes for the growing power of directors were both institutional and artistic. The institutional causes had their roots in the expansion of the Ministry of Culture in the years leading up to 1968. The programme of new arts buildings inaugurated under Malraux, and inspired by the vision of the Maisons de la Culture, resulted in a large number of new theatres being opened in the early 1970s. This was something of an embarrassment to the government, which was trying to keep the Gaullist spirit alive after de Gaulle. On the one hand, it was under pressure from Pompidou, newly elected President, to continue with de Gaulle's *politique de grandeur* in cultural matters. On the other hand, it had no intention of allowing the new culture palaces to become hotbeds of revolt. The best solution appeared to be to direct subsidy towards lavish productions of the classics. It is clear that the directors who benefited from this largesse in the

---

[2] Ubersfeld, A., *Antoine Vitez, metteur en scène et poète*, Paris: Editions des Quatre Vents, 1994, p.18.

course of the 1970s were uncomfortably aware of how they were playing into the hands of right-wing forces. But they were caught in a trap of their own devising. They had issued a strongly worded declaration in favour of increasing subsidy to *les créateurs*; they could hardly turn down what little subsidy they were still being offered (it continued to decline in the course of the decade). The greatest ambiguity, which gradually became apparent, was over the term *créateur* and the question of who it meant.

Roger Planchon

In the heroic decade of the 1960s Planchon had coined the phrase '*écriture scénique*' – scenic writing, to be seen on an equal footing with the author's written words – to express the creative responsibility of the director. It was a notion whose origin he traced to Brecht's work with the Berliner Ensemble: 'The lesson of Brecht is to have declared that a performance contains both dramatic writing and scenic writing; but the scenic writing . . . has an *equal responsibility* with the dramatic writing. In fact, any movement on stage, the choice of a colour, a set, a costume, etc., involves a total responsibility.'[3]

Rather than tracing the origin of this idea to Brecht, Planchon might just as well have gone back to Edward Gordon Craig's prophetic vision, in the early years of the century, of the theatre director as the complete creative artist of the future, bringing together and mastering all the different expressive idioms of the stage.[4] By ignoring the Symbolist origins of this idea and locating it instead in the practice of Brecht, Planchon steered the concept away from the aesthetics of art for art's sake and towards a more socially committed stance. This lent a left-wing alibi to the director's claim to be treated as a creative artist, a claim which was nevertheless bound to bolster the power of the director, and therefore militate against more democratic control of the creative process. An additional factor was the emergence of the New Wave cinema in France in the

[3] Cit. in Adamov, A., *Ici et maintenant*, Paris: Gallimard, 1964, p.214.
[4] Craig, E. G., *On the Art of the Theatre*, London: Heinemann, 1911.

1950s and 1960s. This grouped together a number of directors – Jean-Luc Godard, François Truffaut, Alain Resnais, Louis Malle, Roger Vadim – who were seen as '*auteurs*' (authors) in their own right. Planchon, who had been a film fanatic since his boyhood, saw his role as comparable to that of the New Wave directors.

Planchon's standing was high among theatre professionals. Not only were his productions widely admired, but he had provided the forum for the debates taking place in May 1968. Even the government recognised his high standing by offering him the post of director of the Chaillot Théâtre National Populaire; when he refused to move to Paris, the title TNP was conferred on his theatre in Villeurbanne. In view of this it was not surprising that his concept of scenic writing was taken up with enthusiasm by other directors and his insistence that the director be treated as a creative artist, on the same footing as the playwright, found wide approval.

In the early years of the new TNP, Planchon enhanced his authority by a series of dazzling productions which were not limited to the revivals of classic authors, but included work by contemporary playwrights. Ionesco's last play, *Voyages chez les morts (Journeys Among the Dead,* Calder, 1985), for example, was given its first production by Planchon at Villeurbanne in 1983. The production was far from being a simple presentation of Ionesco's play, however. Instead, Planchon argued that it was more interesting to use the play as part of a larger project to put on stage the whole life and times of its author. In line with this idea, he retitled his production *Ionesco*, added material from other writings by the author and built up a picture of what it was like to be a Romanian in exile during the cold war. The production was monumental, incorporating sets which moved in a menacing way and crowd scenes not written by the author. It represented a triumph for Planchon's concept of 'scenic writing', where the work of the director contributes to the meaning on an equal footing with that of the playwright, but many critics complained that it altered the thrust of Ionesco's play. It transformed the play, originally conceived by its author as a personal journey into a private dream world, into a vast chronicle of the damage inflicted on Western Humanist philosophies by the struggles of the cold war period.

This production drew on methods developed by Planchon some years earlier in a production entitled *A. A. Théâtres d'Adamov* (1975), which collaged scenes from a number of Adamov's early plays in order to build up a picture of his life and times, exploring the link between his private neuroses and the political challenges he faced. Planchon's own plays *Le Cochon noir* (1973) and *Gilles de Rais* (1976) displayed a similar ambition to paint the portrait of a whole epoch through the depiction of individual characters whose personal anguish could be seen as representative of the larger ideological conflicts through which they lived. Planchon made no clear distinction between this new work and his reinterpretations of classic plays by Molière, Shakespeare or Racine. In all of these he was pursuing what was, for him, a consistent project: to discover new ways of staging the individual's relationships with history. In this respect his work was fuelled by similar concerns to that of Ariane Mnouchkine. He was endeavouring to develop a performance language sufficiently complex to express truths of both a personal and a political nature. He took as his model Shakespeare, whom he admired because: 'In Shakespeare the social analysis never crushes the individual psychology of the characters while at the same time the characters do not mask the general view of the society that is being described.'[5] 'Scenic writing' was thus seen as carrying a weighty artistic responsiblity and was far from the self-indulgent 'decorativism' for which many directors were criticised at this time.

In the 1980s and 1990s, Planchon's leadership faded somewhat and his position of authority was challenged by a new generation of directors who built on his idea of 'scenic writing' without always sharing his Shakespearian vision of the artist's responsibilities. Planchon became obsessed with making films and expended a great deal of his energies in negotiations with different producers and film companies in pursuit of his projects.

[5] Cit. Bataillon, M., in 'Expoplanchon' (exhibition catalogue), Vénissieux: Centre Culturel, 1982.

He succeeded in making two films: *George Dandin* (a film version of Molière's play) in 1987 and *Louis, enfant roi*, which came out in 1992. In 1991 he returned to his Shakespearian vision of earlier years with the staging of two linked plays of his own, set in the sixteenth-century wars of religion: *Le Vieil Hiver* and *Fragile forêt*. The dramatic action traces people's changing relationship with the ideologies, Catholic or Protestant, that they are enlisted to fight for. In their reflection on the difficulties entailed in accepting any belief whole-heartedly, these plays are addressed to our contemporary anxieties in the period following the cold war. Their characterisation is subtle and they offer wonderful opportunities for actors; just occasionally the narrative drive becomes bogged down, like the progress of the conflict it depicts, in the dreadful monotony of armed conflict the world over.

Although his powers as a director remain undiminished, Planchon appears to have lost some of the passion and urgency which made his earlier directing work so exciting. He continues to write and to mount his own plays, for example *Le Radeau de la Méduse*, seen at Villeurbanne in 1996 and at the Théâtre de la Colline in 1997. As a playwright he retains his belief in the value of the Brechtian historical epic, which can make his style of writing appear old-fashioned to trend-spotting critics. He has also received a bad press for using the considerable resources of the TNP exclusively to produce his own work. This judgement is unduly harsh, since his plays are unique in the French theatre today: Planchon is one of the very few contemporary authors willing to take on historical subjects that are epic in scale and that dare to emulate the scope of the Shakespearian history play.[6] Moreover, as a director he has not entirely neglected the modern repertoire, mounting new works by Vinaver, Ionesco and Dubillard, as well as an outstanding production of Pinter's *No Man's Land* (1979), which led to many subsequent productions of Pinter's work in France.

---

[6] For an assessment of his work as a playwright, see Daoust, Y., *Roger Planchon*, Cambridge: University Press, 1981, and Bradby, D., *Modern French Drama 1940–1990*, Cambridge: University Press, 1991 (chapter 6).

Planchon's initial successes, in the 1950s and 1960s, were partly due to the fact that he maintained a relatively stable company, which functioned as an ensemble. Planchon would invite well-known film actors to join for particular productions, but the continuity of the company was ensured by the loyal presence of versatile actors, such as Jean Bouise and Isabelle Sadoyan, who had been with Planchon since the beginning. By the end of the 1970s Planchon's company finally disintegrated and he abandoned the principle of maintaining a permanent ensemble in order to pursue his own work, both writing and filming. This change of direction perhaps accounts for the fact that, though widely admired, he never acquired the same status or generated the same affection in the theatre profession as Mnouchkine or Vitez (see above, p. 37–40) or Peter Brook, who is the other major figure most responsible for ensuring that the theatre director is seen as a creative artist in his own right in France.

Peter Brook

Peter Brook moved into the Northern Parisian variety theatre called Les Bouffes du Nord in 1974 and it has remained his permanent base ever since. His opening production was *Timon of Athens* in a French version by Jean-Claude Carrière and his subsequent repertoire included other plays by Shakespeare, work by Chekhov and Jarry, some opera (*Carmen* in 1981 and *Impressions de Pélléas* in 1992), but no new plays. Instead, his major contribution has been a series of devised productions based on textual material drawn from all over the world. They include *The Ik* (1975), based on the anthropologist Colin Turnbull's observation of an East African tribe, *The Conference of the Birds* (1979), based on a twelfth-century Sufi poem, *The Mahabharata* (1985), based on the great Indian epic cycle, *The Man Who* (1993), based on Oliver Sacks's record of psychiatric observations, *The Man Who Mistook his Wife for a Hat*, and *Qui est là?* in 1996, which was a theatrical essay on *Hamlet*, drawing together reflections on theatre and performance in general, as well as a meditation on Shakespeare's play.

In devising productions based on such disparate material,

Brook has drawn on the creative energies of an international group of actors, all of whom came to work with him because they were interested in the idea of the Centre for International Theatre Research which he set up in Paris in 1970 (now known as CICT – Centre International de Création Théâtrale). Initially the aims of the Centre were to investigate the basic conditions through which theatre could speak to an audience, any audience, not just a collection of habitual theatre-goers. In pursuit of suitable conditions, Brook took a group of actors on a journey through the poorest regions of Africa, presenting improvised performances and trying to establish what, if anything, could be said to communicate across cultural and linguistic boundaries. Some of the actors who accompanied him on this journey still work with him today, and the experience has shaped his work ever since. Brook summed it up by saying: 'In terms of my own life and my own search, the work with the group has shown me that it is possible to make a theatre experience in a purer, simpler, more essential way.'[7] The fact that actors of the calibre of Yoshi Oida, Maurice Bénichou, Bruce Myers, Sotigui Kouyaté or Ryszard Cieslak have returned many times to work with Brook explains the essential strength of his work: he is able to create conditions in which actors feel challenged to go beyond their usual limits, and liberated to create work which cuts across traditional cultural and national boundaries. The adaptations listed above were mostly scripted by Jean-Claude Carrière, but their elaboration also relied on creative improvisational work by the group of actors. In this way, Brook's Bouffes theatre has come to be seen as a centre of attraction for actors from all over the world and the CICT, rather like the Théâtre du Soleil, draws much of its strength from the rich ferment of international energies.

This work has had an extraordinary influence on the evolution of theatre practice in France and, such is his authority, Brook has never had any difficulty in securing the subsidies he needs. Like Planchon's, Brook's vision of the director's work goes far beyond that of Vilar, who saw himself as the servant of

---

[7] *New York Times*, 4 May 1980.

the play text. For Brook, the director's job is to create conditions in which all the deadly routines inherited from theatrical tradition can be challenged and broken open so as to make a space for the unexpected seeds of new life to emerge. Theatre, for him, is an empty space in which magical transformations can arise from the simple encounter of an audience hungry for imaginative stimulus, and actors who are ready to leave behind everything they think they know and begin again from the simple act of making believe. This belief finds expression in his refusal to renovate the extraordinarily vibrant interior of the old Bouffes du Nord theatre, leaving the walls in their flaking, decrepit state and performing at floor level without the benefit of a technologically equipped stage. The fact that his working methods displace the writer from the central role in the process of creating theatre has led to him being seen as a prime example of how the director is himself a creator. Brook might dispute this: he has always insisted that his role is only as facilitator. This is backed up by the fact that, unlike Planchon and Vitez, he never performs in his own productions. Nevertheless, his world-wide standing and his pre-eminent status at the heart of the Parisian theatre world has helped to reinforce the climate of French theatre, in which the director is considered to be a (if not *the*) central creative force.

In the work of Mnouchkine, Vitez, Planchon, Brook, the vision of the director as the complete creative theatre artist, set out by Edward Gordon Craig at the beginning of this century, has finally come of age. Some of the most thrilling theatre of the past few decades has come about because of their creative daring. Of course they are not an isolated phenomenon; their work and status is underpinned by similar work of dozens of other directors, many of whom are well-known names, at least as well known, if not better, than those of actors or playwrights (see list of directors below, pp. 254–79). Many of the younger generation of successful directors are themselves playwrights (such as Jacques Lassalle, head of the Comédie-Française 1990–3) or actors (such as Daniel Mesguich, now head of the National Theatre of Lille). Even when they are not, their status has been built on the claim that to direct productions requires much more than simply telling actors where to move. It has become received wisdom that directing involves a complicated negotiation between bodies of inherited material and groups of people with varying stakes in the cultural enterprise. Mesguich, for example, has argued that to stage *Hamlet* one has to stage both the text *and* the history of its different productions and its development into a cultural icon. Accordingly, his production (in 1977) included two different stages on which contrasting versions could be performed simultaneously. A recent production by Mesguich entitled *Boulevard du Boulevard* (1992) was a compilation of different plays by Georges Feydeau, Georges Courteline and others, which built up a complex commentary on the farcicality of French Farce (and followed in the footsteps of a similar production by Planchon in 1976 entitled *Folies Bourgeoises*).

The Director and the Classics

The reinterpretation of classic plays, ranging from Shakespeare and Molière to French Farce, has become the accepted way for young directors to make their mark. Brecht had shown how a reworking of *The Beggar's Opera* or *Coriolanus* could be used to shed light on contemporary realities. His productions were much discussed in the 1960s and his idea of using historical material for contemporary relevance was reinforced by the success, in 1962, of Jan Kott's *Shakespeare our Contemporary*. This was the book which inspired Peter Brook's famous *King Lear*, performed in a style deliberately reminiscent of Beckett, and it had a comparable impact on directors in France. For some French directors Kott's arguments seemed to reinforce their committed ideal of making the classics of the Western repertoire comprehensible to all. If the work of the pioneers in the 1950s and 1960s had not had more impact, maybe it was because they had failed to make their productions of the classic repertoire comment explicitly on the modern world? Relevance became a fetish and for a while it was impossible to consider a classic play on its own merits without asking how its production shed light on the contemporary situation.

After the disappointments of 1968, some directors rejected

this line of thinking and began to lay claim to a different status: that of restorer. The argument used here was the same as that used by enthusiasts of early music or partisans of the cleaning of old masters. It was that the masterpieces of the past had become obscured or distorted by the passage of time. This being so, it was not only possible but necessary to scrape away the accumulated deposits of history, so as to rediscover the impact of the work on its original audiences or spectators. Justifying his production of *Le Tartuffe*, for example, Planchon stressed the novelty of a play that dealt with both domestic politics and religion on the same footing. He called it the first bourgeois comedy of adultery, with the added twist that it was not another woman who tempted Orgon, but a confidence trickster (Tartuffe) playing the part of the puritanical man of God. Planchon's production of *Tartuffe* visited London's National Theatre in 1976, together with Patrice Chéreau's staging of *La Dispute* by Marivaux. Chéreau's production emphasised the modernity of this discussion piece, which plays with the ideas of the eighteenth-century Enlightenment about the extent to which human behaviour is influenced by environment. The outstanding example of this approach applied to a classic work was Chéreau's production of Wagner's *Ring* cycle at Bayreuth, in which he used the designs of Richard Peduzzi and the performance of his singers to suggest links between the stories of heroic Norse legend and the industrialisation of Germany in Wagner's time. Apart from Planchon and Mnouchkine, almost every one of the directors who have become the stars of French theatre in the past twenty-five years have devoted as much time to producing opera as they have to straight plays. This is not only because the budgets for opera are normally between three and five times greater than those of plays, but also because opera offers such rich opportunities for this kind of 'restoration'.

This approach to classic texts was, paradoxically, reinforced by the impact of the avant-garde performance artist Robert Wilson. Wilson was invited to the Nancy Festival, a major importer of state-of-the-art new work into France at this time, to give the first performances of a new work. This was *Deafman Glance*, which premièred at the Nancy Festival in 1971 as *Le*

Regard du Sourd. The impact was extraordinary. The stir it caused was increased by an 'open letter' written by Louis Aragon and addressed to the father of Surrealism, André Breton (although he had died fifteen years earlier), in which he said: 'I never saw anything more beautiful in the world since I was born. Never has a play come anywhere near this one, because it is at once life awake and the life of closed eyes, the confusion between everyday life and the life of each night; reality mingles with dream . . .'[8]

In the view of the critic Bernard Dort, 'a large number of productions in France towards the end of the 1970s owed their inspiration to Wilson's "theatre of images": Chéreau's work appeared justified by it, Planchon was seduced by it, Georges Lavaudant's work was nourished by it.' In productions by these directors, and many others, Planchon's definition of 'scenic writing' was taken one stage further: Wilson had demonstrated that 'scenic writing could exist independently of text'.[9] The experience of Wilson's work had a galvanising effect on directors seeking to define the specificity of their art: it gave them permission to cut loose from dramatic text altogether and to broaden the range of their field of research for materials from which theatre could be made (see, too, the discussion of Vitez above, p. 38). Apart from the obvious boost this gave to the vogue for *la création collective*, it also encouraged directors to adapt novels or other forms of writing for dramatic performance. By the end of the 1970s, one out of every five Parisian stage productions was an adaptation, for which the director usually took the credit as both adapter and director.[10] The number of adaptations continued to grow in the course of the following decades and they remain a major element in the repertoire of the French theatre today.

This cultural and artistic predominance of the director has been facilitated by the institutional and financial structures of the

[8] Aragon, L. in *Les Lettres Françaises*, June, 1971.

[9] Dort, B., 'L'Age de la représentation' in Jomaron, J. (ed.), *Le Théâtre en France,* Vol.2, Paris: Armand Colin, 1989, p.530.

[10] Miller, Judith G., 'From novel to theatre', *Theatre Journal*, Vol.33, No.4, 1981, p.431.

theatre in France. The CDNs all share the same legal status, requiring them to provide a public service in return for which they are granted subsidies. The subsidies come with certain conditions attached (see below, p. 151) and the person responsible for dealing with the Ministry, receiving the subsidy and guaranteeing the conditons is the director. His legal status is that of boss in his own business, but he is subject to certain government constraints and not entitled to make a profit on his own account. After the upheavals of 1968, the directors of the CDNs were worried by the summary sackings of those in charge of Maisons de la Culture, and so banded together as a 'Syndicat des directeurs d'entreprise d'action culturelle' (SYNDEAC – Union of directors of enterprises devoted to cultural action). This union established a powerful voice in the evolution of the profession over the following decades and is still a major power to be reckoned with.

One of the bones of contention, from the very beginning of the Malraux years, had been the status of the Maisons de la Culture. These were set up on a similar model to most English repertory theatres, that is to say they had a board of directors made up of local worthies, to whom the artistic director of the Maison was subject. The directors of CDNs were clear that they intended to remain masters in their own house and not to allow the imposition of any board. By means of the collective power they were able to wield through the SYNDEAC, they defended their independence so successfully that the administrative structure of the CDN became the norm and it was gradually accepted that the Maisons de la Culture should be adapted in order to fit in with it. In 1988 the Maisons were brought under the aegis of the Theatre section of the Ministry of Culture and their directors were able to join SYNDEAC. The SYNDEAC today has more than 200 members, directors of the major theatres drawn from all parts of France. Through this organisation, they are able to make their views known and their voices heard, while the case of the playwrights receives less attention.

This has led to a situation in which directors are often accused by authors of having megalomaniac tendencies. Michel Vinaver, for example, has argued that, despite their authority and the increasing subsidies devoted to theatre (which grew in real terms every year throughout the 1980s), the directors represented by SYNDEAC have lost their sense of direction. He pointed out that the first generation of directors who worked to decentralise the theatre in the post-war years were driven by a sense of mission. They believed that theatre was tantamount to a human right. Hence the basic tenet that theatre activity should not be required to pay for itself, but should be construed as a public service.[11] This sense of mission, he pointed out, crumbled under the force of the post-1968 disillusionment. Nevertheless, he maintained, there is a fundamental irony in that, despite this evaporation of missionary certainties, the organisational and financial structures it put in place have continued to be expanded and consolidated. This process has produced a lavishly funded apparatus, run by powerful theatre directors, who no longer feel obliged to justify their position by reference to the old utopian dreams of buiding up a mass popular audience.

So what is it, asks Vinaver, that motivates today's directors? His reply is that they are driven by 'the logic of difference': 'The logic whereby a director is compelled, as it were, to show himself as being extraordinary, in order to justify the extraordinary amount of money he requires and in order to obtain even more, which will allow him to mount things even more different and even more extraordinary, and so on *ad infinitum*.'[12] In this situation, he argues, the successful claim of the directors to be creative artists in their own right has turned into a sterile trap: they are caught in an upward spiral of their own making, where every new production has to appear even more startlingly original than its predecessor and the idea of developing a coherent repertoire over a number of years has entirely disappeared.

The critical picture built up by Vinaver is not all black, but is, as he says, one of 'chiaroscuro'. This is well exemplified in the career of Georges Lavaudant, who was co-director of the TNP in Villeurbanne (with Planchon) from 1986 till 1996, when he

[11] Vinaver, M., 'Decentralization as Chiaroscuro', *New Theatre Quarterly*, No.25, February 1991, pp.64–76.
[12] Ibid., p.72.

succeeded Lluis Pasqual as director of the Odéon-Théâtre de l'Europe. As a young director in the 1960s, Lavaudant had felt that the theatre as it was then practised was boringly old-fashioned. Coming to theatre at a time when the ideas of thinkers such as Derrida and Foucault were being developed, Lavaudant determined to try to generate his own performance material which would match the intellectual daring of avant-garde thinkers, cineastes or novelists. He has staged several collages of texts by writers who have challenged accepted literary norms, from Proust, Kafka and Borges to Gombrowicz, Pasolini and William Burroughs, as well as putting on the 'monsters' of the repertoire, such as *King Lear, Lorenzaccio* and *The Mountain Giants* (by Pirandello). His reputation earned him the honour of being invited to stage Genet's *Le Balcon* for the first time at the Comédie-Française in 1985. He has also produced plays of his own, such as *Terra Incognita* (Avignon Festival, 1992), and has developed a close working relationship with Jean-Christophe Bailly, whose monumental, poetic texts he has directed, from *Les Céphéides* in 1983 to *Pandora* in 1992. His productions are distinguished by great visual brilliance and are costly to mount (thus justifying Vinaver's critical comments) and the raw material from which he works is more often devised by him than written by a living playwright. Nevertheless, he has also made a notable contribution to developing the aesthetic range of theatre and has nurtured at least one new writing talent in Jean-Christophe Bailly.

An exceptional feature of Lavaudant's career is that he has mostly worked with a small, stable group of actors. One of the most telling of Vinaver's criticisms was that the career structure established for directors, where they are expected to move up the promotional ladder every few years, militates against the continuing existence of stable companies. Directors such as Mnouchkine or Planchon or Brook, who remain in one theatre and work with the same actors over a long period of time, have become very much the exception. Most directors move around every few years, and this game of musical chairs has become part of the spiral effect, with little relevance to the needs of theatre, but acquiring its own peculiar fascination, in much the same way that cabinet reshuffles of government ministers are always newsworthy.

Sarraute, Duras, Beckett

Thus the 'creative' activities of some directors appear to be motivated by the desire to establish originality at any price and have often led to productions which displace the dramatist in favour of adaptations of material never intended for theatre performance. But responsibility for this state of affairs cannot be laid solely at the door of the directors, because it is also true to say that some of the impulse towards blurring the lines between dramatic and non-dramatic writing has come from the authors themselves. This trend has been exemplified in the work of a small number of authors who carry immense authority, though their output may be relatively sparse and their plays may have failed to achieve commercial success. These authors – Beckett, Duras, Sarraute – are novelists as much as playwrights. Their dramatic work, which is sometimes indistinguishable from prose narrative, questions the limits of theatre and problematises two of drama's most familiar structural supports: time and identity. Both Beckett and Duras had written major full-length plays in the period before 1968. In the 1970s and 1980s Beckett's work became progressively shorter and rarer, while Duras extended her preference for film over theatre (her first film script had been for Alain Resnais's *Hiroshima mon amour* in 1959). Her 1972 *India Song* was subtitled '*Texte, Théâtre, Film*'. It is made up of images and voices, dissociated most of the time, so that the characters become depersonalised, or hazy, and one is never sure where one character ends and another begins.

The writer who first defined the principle behind this approach was Nathalie Sarraute who, as early as 1939, borrowed the term 'tropisms' from the vocabulary of the biological sciences to convey the impulses, emotional, physical or psychological, which precede linguistic expression, and which give rise to both our words and our actions. Her short stories, gathered together under the title *Tropismes*, show people reacting to stimuli from outside, or to the proximity of other people, with instinctive movements, which are presented in an almost scientific tone. The stories do not generally contain much action in the conventional sense, but beneath their calm exterior intense activity is taking place which may be extremely violent. They are 'veritable dramatic actions concealed beneath the most ordinary conversations and the most everyday gestures. They constantly bubble up to the surface of appearances which serve both to mask and to reveal them.'[13]

It was not until the mid-1960s that Sarraute began to write plays, encouraged by a commission from Radio Stuttgart, but the dramatic potential of her work had been present from the beginning, because theatre, especially the European theatre since Chekhov, is such a powerful medium for exploring the conflict between speech and the underlying impulses which precede it. Her prose fictions dispensed with anything resembling plot and when she began to explore the world of tropisms through drama, she had to abandon any realistic notion of time, presenting minute movements of the psyche stretched out over an enormously expanded present moment. In this way her plays are similar to those of Beckett, who set all his plays in an expanded present tense, where time has almost ceased to have any meaning. Most important of all, she focuses on all those things which are not normally spoken of or admitted to, so that her plays appear very odd, almost shapeless, as a flayed body might after being stripped of its skin. Hers is a theatre entirely constructed of sub-text. She refuses to give her characters contexts or outer characteristics. Often they do not even have names, being designated simply as 'Him', 'Her', or 'Man 1', 'Man 2', 'Woman 1', 'Woman 2'.

Duras's characters have names, but they share something of the anonymity of Sarraute's 'Him' or 'Her'; they seldom look at one another and talk obsessively of memories which appear more and more unreliable with the unfolding of the dramas. As in Beckett's late plays a silent character is frequently accompanied by voices 'off' which may or may not be his or her own. All these writers question the common assumptions underpinning our sense of

---

[13] Sarraute, N., Preface to *L'Ere du soupçon*, Paris: Gallimard, 1956, p.9.

identity by asserting the unreliability of memory. In Duras's plays, especially, the past can never be taken for granted. In the dialogues of her plays characters invent the past or change it and challenge it, leaving out things we expect them to say and describing keenly felt moments which may or may not have happened. In her late plays the voices are almost exclusively feminine and Duras's work has been read by feminist critics, in the light of Julia Kristeva's theories, as mounting a challenge to the structures of patriarchal society. Her plays explicitly reject the classical model of a conflict brought to resolution. In *Savannah Bay*, for example, the only two characters on stage are a mother and her granddaughter. As they talk, exchange memories, go over the same subjects, the audience begins to glimpse the realities of three generations of women, each seen from the perspective of the other two. Rather than enacting a conflict, they reconstruct the life of the dead mother/daughter and explore the shape that each has given to the lives of the other two.

As in Nathalie Sarraute's plays, their words often seem mysterious or unmotivated, there is no linear action and very little dramatic conflict of the traditional kind: since the boundaries between the characters are so fluid, there is very little space for antagonism and the Oedipal model of masculine power-struggle is entirely absent. The setting for key memories is constantly evoked, for example the rock, the sea and the salt marshes where Madeleine's daughter is first seduced and then commits suicide in *Savannah Bay*. This remembered place acquires a solidity denied to the characters themselves: it remains the same, while they change, merge into one another, even speak about themselves in the third person. They appear uncertain of whether they are really responsible for the words which they speak, or if perhaps they belong to someone else. In 1983 *Savannah Bay* was given a memorable production by Duras herself, with Madeleine Renaud and Bulle Ogier, at the Théâtre du Rond-Point. Attending a performance gave one the same kind of pleasure as a Beckett play, akin to that of poetry: there was very little movement on stage and most of the dramatic effects were achieved by the use of voices, but an atmosphere of intense concentration was established in which the smallest move or change of rhythm could touch the emotions.

Duras's plays, like Sarraute's, were mostly staged either by Jean-Louis Barrault or by Claude Régy. But in the 1970s and 1980s Simone Benmussa, who had worked for Barrault for many years, began to put on their work, also bringing that of Hélène Cixous to the stage for the first time with an influential production of *Portrait de Dora* (1976). Benmussa's special gift was to find a spatial poetry to correspond to the verbal impulses, hesitations, ellipses of the texts. She followed her production of *Portrait de Dora* with an adaptation of a story by George Moore: *The Singular Life of Albert Nobbs* (1977). Adaptations of other stories by Henry James followed and, in 1984, of Natalie Sarraute's autobiographical *Enfance*. Her most recent triumph was another adaptation from Henry James's story *The Real Thing* at the Comédie des Champs-Elysées.

The struggle to remember and, in the process, make sense of one's past is also an enduring theme in Beckett's work. His characters attempt, in desperation, to produce a coherent narrative of their life, so as to establish their subjective existence, but these attempts are frustrated by alternative versions, which may come as challenges from others, or swim up from the depths of their own consciousness. Towards the end of his life Beckett wrote more and more about ghostly characters, as Anna McMullan has pointed out: 'Beckett's plays of the late 1970s and 1980s, reveal an increasing preoccupation with . . . the notion of "between zones". In *Footfalls, Rockaby* and *Ohio Impromptu*, Beckett again explores experiences of absence and loss and how to represent those experiences.'[14]

While Beckett's early plays have become modern classics and are frequently revived (the 1996–7 season included a star-studded *En Attendant Godot* at the Rond-Point and a production by Brook at the Bouffes du Nord of *Oh les beaux jours*), the late plays have not received such frequent stagings in France. All except *Catastrophe* were first written in English and have been taken up with greater enthusiasm in Germany, England and North America than in France. This was partly due to a rift between Beckett and

---

[14] McMullan, A., *Theatre on trial: Samuel Beckett's later drama*, Routledge, 1993, p.90.

Barrault, who had championed his work in earlier decades. A season of late Beckett plays was directed by Pierre Chabert at the Rond-Point in 1983, including *Catastrophe, Berceuse (Rockaby), L'Impromptu d'Ohio (Ohio Impromptu)*. But Barrault was upset that Beckett did not want Madeleine Renaud to perform *Rockaby*; she had been a memorable Winnie in the first French production of *Oh les beaux jours (Happy Days)* in 1963, but Beckett had been uneasy with her performance in *Pas moi (Not I)* in 1975. This was the last time Beckett was to collaborate with Renaud and Barrault.

In his last two decades, Beckett became more and more involved in directing his own plays, and one of his happiest memories was directing Delphine Seyrig in *Pas (Footfalls)* in 1978.[15] Given the 'in-between' status of these plays – part narrative, part play – it is natural that authors such as Duras and Beckett should take responsibility for directing them, controlling not just the words, but the rhythm, tone, speed in which they are said, as well as the visual images which accompany them. James Knowlson's biography demonstrates how profoundly pictorial Beckett's productions were, containing many references to paintings he admired. He also reports how, time and again, actors would comment on the musicality as well as the precise imagery that he imposed. Billie Whitelaw (Beckett's favourite British actress) said that when Beckett directed her in *Footfalls*, she felt 'like a moving, musical, Edvard Munch painting', and Rosemary Pountney reported that 'conducting is a more appropriate word for what he was doing as a director . . . as the actors spoke their lines, his left hand was beating out the rhythms like Karajan'. Bud Thorpe, playing Clov in Beckett's 1980 production of *Endgame*, described it as 'all rhythm and music . . . He said to us, "Now I am going to fill my silences with sounds." And he added: "For every silence there will be sounds, be they the shuffling of feet, steps, dropping of things, and so on."' Eva Katarina Schulz, who played Winnie in Beckett's Berlin production of *Happy Days* (1971), said: 'His aim was to achieve a musicality of gesture as striking as that of voice.'[16]

[15] See Knowlson, J., *Damned to Fame: The Life of Samuel Beckett*, London: Bloomsbury, 1996, p.657.
[16] Quotations all reported by Knowlson in op. cit., pp.584, 624, 668.

CHAPTER 3

THEATRE OF THE EVERYDAY
AND AFTER

Both Beckett and Duras took on productions of their own work to counter the excessively 'creative' tendencies of certain directors. But through directing they were able to achieve much more than this negative aim would suggest, exploring for themselves the boundaries between speech and movement, inner and outer dialogue, narration and action. Their example has been extremely influential on recent theatre practice. It is now commonplace for writers to direct their own works and many of the texts written for the theatre in the last ten years demonstrate clearly the influence of a minimalist approach to dramatic action in which much of the play is concerned with voices that echo in the head and the identity of the speakers is ambiguous. Playwrights such as Michel Azama and Philippe Minyana, both of whom began their theatre careers as performers, undoubtedly owe a great deal to the haunting, disembodied voices of Sarraute, Duras and Beckett. But the playwrights of the 1990s also draw on a more recent tradition, one that calls for some explanation: the Theatre of the Everyday (*théâtre du quotidien*).

Although less distinguished in its achievements than the work of Beckett, the Theatre of the Everyday has had an important shaping influence on French theatre. Its distinctive contribution is to have extended Beckett's aesthetic of failure and discontinuity so as to explore not only private dramas, but also the effect of society at large on those private existences. Almost all of the authors associated with the Theatre of the Everyday have also worked as actors or directors (sometimes both) and the movement is closely connected to the concern for 'scenic writing' inherited via Planchon from Brecht. In these plays there is no room for fine writing or for witty epigrams. The plays are

often difficult to read on the page, only coming to life in performance. Nevertheless the playwrights of the Everyday shared
Beckett's central preoccupation with language. The difference
was that they emphasised its socially constructed nature.

The first theatre entirely devoted to this work was founded
by Jean-Paul Wenzel in 1975; he directed his own plays and
those of Michel Deutsch, and both playwrights have continued
to be a major force in the French repertoire to the present day.
Others whose work had similar aims and ambitions were
René Kalisky, Xavier Pommeret, Georges Michel, Bernard
Chartreux, and many of these were influenced by similar work
in German, especially that of Kroetz, Achternbusch, Fassbinder,
Handke and Bernhardt. Translated into French, the work of
these authors has also had frequent staging in recent years.

The plays of the Everyday may be compelling in performance
but are often difficult to read because, similar to those of the
Absurd, they are devoid of plot, character or conflict, in the
traditional sense of these terms. Plot is replaced by attention to
the latent possibilities for action contained within each situation
explored in the play, many of which are evoked without being
realised. Characterisation is replaced by depiction of how the
plays' dramatis personae internalise their own social alienation.
The articulation of conflict is replaced by characters who no
longer master their own language. These playwrights follow
Beckett's lead in presenting men and women who do not control the words they speak. Instead, it is as if the words 'speak
them': they are shaped by a language to which they give utter-
ance, but which they neither initiate nor control. These plays
represent human situations in which different language systems
confront one another and do battle for supremacy; the casualties
left behind on the battlefield are the broken bodies of the people
or communities who were the site of the struggle. They go
beyond the display of absurd, stereotyped language that we find
in Ionesco, to show how the reification of language is not just
arbitrary but is generated by social institutions.

Violence is a constant factor and, especially in the work of
Deutsch, has become more evident in recent years. This
violence is all the more disturbing since the most common

setting for these dramas is the home or the intimate space of private life, into which external structures are seen to penetrate, influencing and shaping the lives of characters even when they think they are at their most private. One of Deutsch's earliest plays, *Dimanche*, produced by Dominique Muller at Strasbourg in 1976, centres on Ginette, her mother and father, and her friends who take part in the local majorette troop, a new phenomenon imported from America at that time. Ginette finds herself under a compulsion to practise at all hours of the day and night. She even records instructions for her own exercise routine on to tape and plays them back to herself so as to subject herself to the language of physical commands. She can think of nothing else, losing touch with her own reality in her desire to win the competition and become the perfect majorette. The alien, mechanical image of the long-legged American high-kicker imposes itself upon her, mentally and physically, to the point where she can only live for her training, submerges every personal feeling in pursuit of this image and finally dies of exhaustion. Outside her private world, her community is also in crisis (the union is fighting to prevent the factory which gives employment to her family from being closed down) and this emphasises her powerlessness to shape the events which destroy her.

A similar alteration in the subjective realities of two women is shown in *Convoi* (1980) set in south-west France during the German occupation. Anne, a sixty-year-old peasant woman takes in an eighteen-year-old refugee. She names her Marie, disguising her real name of Hannah Friedman, and treats her as if she were a young relative who had lost her memory. For a while 'Marie' almost becomes Anne's daughter, but she cannot rid herself of the memory of the concentration camps she has experienced nor of the column of refugees on the road being strafed by planes. In long passages of poetic monologue she returns obsessively to the violence that has been done to her and to the other women refugees with her. She keeps trying to establish a separate space for herself, but in the small country village there is no escape from relations and neighbours. With the German take-over of the 'Free Zone' she is denounced by

Anne's own sister and the militia come to arrest both women. Jean-Pierre Vincent, who directed the play at Strasbourg in 1980, commented that the theme of the play was 'exile, physical exile or interior exile, a way of reacting to misfortune'.[1]

Misfortune is a common experience for the characters of these plays. Like those of Franz-Xaver Kroetz, the German dramatist who exerted a strong influence on these French playwrights, they are usually drawn from the bottom rungs of the social scale, peasants or urban workers. When he first began to write Deutsch felt a compulsion to dramatise the lives of people who made up the newly identified 'non-public'. His first thought was that he would have to observe, record, copy their ways of speaking. 'That did not last long. I realised that the only thing one could record was *silence* and the rhythm of that silence; the speech of these people escaped me.'[2] But, unlike Kroetz, he did not concentrate on the representation of inarticulacy, feeling that this resulted in a kind of Naturalism whose effect on an audience was bound to be reactionary – suggesting that these people were subhuman and incapable of change. Instead, his characters became the centre of competing discourses, struggling for supremacy: the slogans of advertising, the small talk of neighbours, the daily discussions around meals and shopping, the glamorised dialogue of Hollywood. His plays have an emotional impact on audiences, but it is largely the product of irony: we observe characters struggling for independent life but at the same time we see that, because they are so deeply alienated, they seize on just that language or behaviour which is the very instrument of their destruction.

Deutsch's recent plays have continued to explore the territory of the everyday. In *El Sisisi* (1986; 'El Sisisi' is the name of a celebrated bar in Barcelona) the dialogue is almost entirely devoid of structure or dramatic development, consisting purely of the exchanges between a group of people who drink in the same bar in the course of one uneventful evening. Here the danger of 'reactionary Naturalism' seems closer than in many of

---

[1] Cit. in Deutsch, M., *Convoi*, Paris: Stock, 1980, p.109.
[2] Cit. in Sarrazac, J-P., 'L'Ecriture au présent', *Travail Théâtral*, Nos.24–5, 1976, p.97.

his plays. But although the dialogue is as true to life as any Naturalist could want, the play refuses the shaping devices common to Naturalist drama, pointing audiences towards conclusions to be drawn from the presentation of daily life. Instead, Deutsch simply offers life in the raw.

His work points the way towards younger dramatists, such as Xavier Durringer, especially since Deutsch has also displayed a growing preoccupation with violence. *Partage* (1981) dealt with two of the Manson girls in prison reliving their murder of Sharon Tate. *Tamerlan* (1987) shows two men in suits, in an ordinary kitchen, rehearsing the tale of Tamburlaine the Great, his conquests and destruction of peoples. Deutsch also manifests his interest in more abstract intellectual or historical questions in plays such as *Thermidor*, a series of debates between Robespierre, Saint-Just and other characters from the French Revolution about the ethics and tactics of revolutionary action. His most recent work consists of brief, fragmentary scenes, set in instantly recognisable everyday situations (e.g. a street, a room) where people confront one another but fail to communicate or to control their own language. Frequently, they appear to be over-determined by a literary model or mythical archetype. In *John Lear*, for example, a journalist named Cordelia interviews John Lear, a famous actor who appears equally at home in Hollywood and in Europe, but who ends up delivering a terrifying monologue which recalls the madness and violence of Shakespeare's King Lear in the storm scene.

Jean-Paul Wenzel, who directed Deutsch's early plays, has also developed a career as a playwright. One of his first plays, *Loin d'Hagondange*, was a bleak chronicle of a retired couple whose lives have been sucked dry by stupefying industrial labour, but who always cherished a compensating dream of the freedom they would enjoy in retirement. The play shows them living in the idyllic country house they have bought for the retirement, but they behave like zombies, having lost the ability to communicate with one another; the free time which held out so much promise to them has now become nothing but a burden. After his own production of the play in 1975, it was revived by Patrice Chéreau at the TNP in 1977 in a haunting Surrealist design by Richard Peduzzi, which emphasised the internalised aspects of the drama between husband and wife. Wenzel went on to do documentary research in Bobigny, one of the vast working-class dormitory suburbs which surround central Paris, and his next plays were based on interviews with people who lived there. In 1979 he joined with Jean-Louis Hourdin and Olivier Perrier to form a company known as Les Fédérés. Like others before them (from Copeau onwards), they first withdrew to a small village community in order to build up a team spirit and to develop a form of dramatic expression that would satisfy their ambition for a form of theatrical communication that is simple, direct, popular in the best sense of the word. In 1985 they felt ready to move back into urban surroundings and changed their base to Montluçon, where Wenzel and Perrier have remained, faithful to the ambition of making theatre relevant to contemporary society. As well as directing his own plays, Wenzel has put on work by other contemporary writers such as Arlette Namiand and Enzo Cormann.

It is not only the authors of the Everyday who have written plays combining a bleakly realistic depiction of conditions in unglamorous social circumstances. This has also been the chosen territory of Tilly, an author-director of considerable power, who has produced a sequence of hyper-realistic 'slice-of-life' dramas depicting individuals of communities who are afflicted, like those of Deutsch, by a state of generalised schizophrenia. Where the Everyday plays were staged with minimal sets and costumes, Tilly takes enormous pains to recreate on stage an entirely believable image of the life lived by his working-class characters, so that their manner of boiling a kettle, for example, carries as much conviction as their language. Tilly's *Les Trompettes de la mort* (first staged 1985; revived 1996) takes the true story of a provincial girl whose move to Paris in search of the bright lights resulted in a such a sense of overwhelming loneliness and alienation that she took her own life. The production lovingly recreates every last detail of her spinster flat but scrupulously avoids drawing any conclusions about the social or psychological causes for her state. Because of this, his work is in danger of appearing intensely patronising, pretending to give a value-free, objective picture of the girl's life while condemning its humdrum nature by implication. In fact, this pseudo-objectivity is a feature of much Theatre of the Everyday as well.

It can be seen as one consequence of the disillusionments which grew in the decades following 1968. The events of that year had left many theatre people with the optimistic belief that they could build a bridge between themselves and the 'non-public'. But they soon discovered that the task was complex and not amenable to instant solutions; nor did it fit the simple slogans of 1968. Euphoria quickly gave way to a sense of fragmentation and of a daily life which could no longer be made sense of according to the old categories; one in which the behaviour of both individuals and public bodies seemed beyond rational control. The very language of social or political discourse seemed to be unreliable and that is why it became a focus of dramatic investigation. Unlike the politically committed authors of the 1950s and 1960s, the post-1968 generation did not see theatre as a suitable vehicle for promoting a philosophy, political or otherwise. Because they explore the social alienation of their characters, authors such as Deutsch and Wenzel must be classed as political dramatists, although they would never claim to be *'engagés'* in the way that Sartre claimed. It is particularly ironic that fifteen years of Socialist government subsidy for theatre has resulted in a drama that rejects the explicitly didactic left-wing plays of earlier decades.

Michel Vinaver

The outstanding playwright of the Everyday is Michel Vinaver, although much of his long career (his first play dates from 1955) extends beyond it. As the managing director of Gillette in various European countries during the 1960s he was also deeply involved in the corporate structures of the multinational business operations which have come to dominate world trade since the Second World War. His response to the upheavals of the late 1960s was an immense Rabelaisian epic farce, entitled *Par-dessus bord (Overboard, Plays I*, Methuen, 1997), which depicts an old-fashioned French toilet-paper manufacturer struggling to fight off hostile bids by an American paper products giant. The play includes a character whose position reproduces that of its author: both a manager with the firm and, at the same time, the author of the play. As the play unfolds, this character, in passages of direct address to the audience, develops a meditation on the problem of his dual position, as he struggles to integrate his two perspectives on the firm: that of employee, with a stake in the company's success, and that of outside commentator, with a critical overview of the company's activities and the economic situation in which they took place.

Since *Par-dessus bord*, Vinaver has written a dozen further plays, most of which are set in the world of business, and all of which exploit the uncomfortable contradictions that are occasioned by the varying roles or identities each one of us assumes in different situations. His first play after *Par-dessus bord*, *La Demande d'emploi* (*Situation Vacant, Plays I*, Methuen, 1997) exploits this method by exploring the relationships between a small family – father, mother and daughter – who are going through a crisis as a result of the father's loss of his executive job. He has 'lost his place' and as he tries to negotiate a new 'place' in the world, his relationships with wife and daughter also go through a series of surprising variations. Even more successful in this respect was *Les Travaux et les jours* (*A Smile on the End of the Line, Plays I*, Methuen, 1997), set entirely in the after-sales office of a small manufacturing firm, in which the audience sees how each of the five employees who make up the characters of the play presents one face in the office, another outside, one for certain colleagues, another for others. These different 'faces' may be in contradiction with one another, but that does not stop them from coexisting; as Brecht often said, it is their contradictions which bring characters to life. The plays Vinaver wrote during the 1970s and early 1980s all exploit a rich thematic material: the contradictory relations existing between late-twentieth-century human beings and the economic environment they inhabit. The globalisation of markets, the rapid developments of new technology and the spread of ever more intrusive marketing practices have lead to a situation where even those parts of our lives we are accustomed to think of as entirely private are contaminated with the values and priorities of the business world.

After a further decade managing S. T. Dupont, a subsidiary of Gillette (1970–9), Vinaver decided to retire from business and devote all his energies to theatre and literature. His managerial skills soon found a new outlet when, in 1982, he was appointed chairman of the new theatre committee of the Centre National des Lettres (a wing of the Ministry of Culture responsible for literature) and embarked on an ambitious report into the crisis of playwriting and the collapse of French theatre publishing that had taken place in the 1970s. This survey led to the publication of an influential report in 1987 under the title *Le Compte rendu d'Avignon*. The report provided statistical evidence to demonstrate the excessive power wielded by directors and the financial difficulties encountered by professional dramatists. It also made a number of suggestions for reform, most of which were adopted by the theatre directorate of the Ministry of Culture (see below, pp.73–80). During the same period he began a new career as a university teacher. At first his courses focused on the analysis of dramatic texts but in 1984 he took the highly original step (in the context of the French Academy) of introducing a creative playwriting class. This proved to be a success and was followed by a further series of six similar workshop courses over the remainder of his teaching career.

The dramatic techniques employed by Vinaver are best described as 'juxtapositional' and his inspiration is drawn from poetry, painting and music rather than from other playwrights. The translation he made of T. S. Eliot's *The Waste Land* at the age of twenty convinced him of the value of a method which juxtaposes disparate elements, not integrating them, but challenging readers to relate them in their own imaginations. Among the many painters he admires, he has been especially inspired by the Cubists, by Dubuffet and by Rauschenberg. Just as the pictures of Rauschenberg juxtapose images of different kinds, playfully allowing for happy coincidence, or the surprise of the unexpected, so Vinaver juxtaposes different linguistic registers, from high culture to low, from learned to familiar, from mythical to modern. In the texture of the completed dramatic dialogue they do not lose their quality of difference, but acquire new resonances by virtue of other uses of language against which they reverberate.

The thematic material from which he builds up his plays is as vast and, initially at least, as shapeless as everyday life. This central concern with 'the Everyday' was reflected in the title of Vinaver's first play *Aujourd'hui* (later renamed *Aujourd'hui ou les Coréens*) and he has described his relationship with the Everyday as follows:

> My relationship with the Everyday is one going back unchanged to my infancy and which is at the very centre of my creative work. I recall that as a child I was astonished when permitted to do the simplest things, such as open a door, run, stop running, etc. I was both astonished and enraptured at being given these rights; I was always afraid that they would be withdrawn and that I would be thrust back into non-existence. In this way the Everyday was something highly charged, on the brink of transgression, at all events precarious, undeserved.[3]

Because he had a sense of standing somehow *outside* reality, creative writing became, for him, not an exercise in imitating reality, but rather a constant attempt to capture or penetrate a domain never perceived as given in advance: 'In other words, for me, as a writer, nothing exists before I begin to write, and the activity of writing becomes an attempt to give consistency to the world and to myself within it.'

The experience of the world as something not given in advance, but constituted in and through the act of writing, provides an essential key to understanding Vinaver's work. Almost obsessively, he insists upon the banality, the absolute flatness of the material from which he begins the compositional process. The situations depicted are intensely *ordinary*: a man looking for a job (*La Demande d'emploi* and *L'Emission de télévision (The Television Programme, Plays II*, Methuen, 1997), the routine workings of a secretarial office (*Les Travaux et les jours*). Even

---

[3] Vinaver, M., *Ecrits sur le théâtre*, Lausanne: L'Aire, 1982, p.123.

where the situation is exceptional (as in *L'Ordinaire – High Places, Plays II*, Methuen, 1997 – depicting the aftermath of a plane crash in the Andes, with the survivors turning to cannibalism), Vinaver emphasises the ordinariness of daily life, underlined by the play's title in French: *L'Ordinaire*. Vinaver sees the work of the playwright as being to empty all these situations of their dramatic potential in the common sense of the word, to prevent the usual presuppositions and interpretative grids from falling easily into place.

Writing, for Vinaver, is thus a process of *composition* not of *interpretation*. The result aims to surprise, stimulate and question its readers/spectators, not to teach them a lesson. Like other dramatists of the Everyday, the author does not claim to know something which he can then pass on through his writing. In fact, his intention in composing the play is to create a work that will, to some extent, resist interpretation, in the sense of not being easily expressed in different terms, not reducible to paraphrase or to a 'message'. Writing is a process of research and discovery. It is (as for Vaclav Havel) a journey, starting from an attempt to penetrate the terrain of the Everyday and discovering along the way points of articulation between experiences of different orders.

Because of the political nature of much of the action in his plays, and because all French theatre was subject to a very strong Brechtian influence when he was beginning to write in the 1950s and 1960s, Vinaver has sometimes been criticised for not coming out with clear ideological statements. In reply, he argued that the writer's commitment must be of a different kind: 'It is sufficient for the creative artist to apply himself to his work, to avoid being distracted by what he wants to say, to dare to commit himself (or abandon himself) completely to his material.[4] The nature of this material is, in the first place, linguistic, and he is fond of describing language as his 'raw material'. The playwright's job, he considers, is to assemble the building blocks of our everyday speech in such a way as to reveal how we construct our images and understanding of the world.

[4] Op. cit., p.12.

In his plays different linguistic idioms confront one another, shift, break up and re-form, attuned to the characters and the situations in which they find themselves.

Because he refuses to submit the events of his plays to a single narrative line of causal links, but is constantly breaking them up into discontinuous fragments, his dramatic technique clearly has points in common with the Brechtian epic. Like Brecht, Vinaver strongly rejects the Aristotelian unities. But he rejects the didactic element which is present, to a greater or lesser extent, in most of Brecht's work. He shares Brecht's concern to demystify and show up the contradictions of the social structures generated by capitalism, but believes that the playwright must always remain a marginal figure, like a court jester, paid to say the unsayable, to expose the cruelties and absurdities of the system that are taken for granted, rather than to identify himself with a given political philosophy.

Unlike most of his contemporaries, Vinaver has never been tempted by the Beckettian monologue: in his theatre, speech is always part of a process of action and reaction between characters. Here again, a fundamental duality or multiplicity can be seen as the underlying principle of his creative vision. The layering of many different voices, which drama inevitably entails, is fundamentally congenial to him. He welcomes the fact that the playwright, unlike other writers, cannot speak with his own voice, but only through the orchestration of other voices: 'Dramatic writing suits me because in it I make others speak, and because its language does not describe, nor comment, nor explain, but acts.'[5] The absence of punctuation in the written texts of his plays only serves to reinforce the active quality of this language, which is not tied to a static, fixed form on the page, but asks for a reader to give it life, rhythm and, hence, meaning.

This makes for plays in which the audience is never able to settle back into a comfortable emotional identification with any given character, since the perspective is constantly shifting. The viewpoint of one character is contradicted by that of a second, or a third, often overlapping in the same scene. A similar tension

---

[5] Vinaver, M., '*Mémoire sur mes travaux*', *Les Cahiers de Prospero*, No.8, July 1996, p.17.

characterises his use of dramatic situation. Every one of his plays can be seen as an ironic exposure of the gap between the expectations of the characters and the situation in which they are placed. This is where the social and political dimensions of Vinaver's work emerge most clearly. The plays restlessly explore the discrepancies between the characters' own limited appreciation of their situation and the realities of that situation. The author has gone so far as to suggest that such irony is the necessary condition for the emergence of meaning: 'Irony – that is to say the brutal discrepancy between what is expected and what occurs – is the equivalent in writing of an electric discharge: all at once the current flows. A current of meaning.'[6]

Vinaver's achievement lies in his having abandoned a theatre of linear narrative for one of multiple perspectives: he suggests that it may be impossible to make sense of our lives as linear sequences, but that we can at least get a partial grip on them by establishing connections between ordinarily discontinuous situations. In this way a new form of epic theatre is created, opposed to the Aristotelian theatre, but differing from Brecht's in that the 'distancing effect' is obtained by a continuous stream of microtextual fractures rather than by the systematic discouragement of empathy. It is the first authentically modernist theatre, succeeding in 'transforming the most uninteresting raw material into an object of enjoyment and knowledge'.[7]

His last two plays to date are *L'Emission de télévision,* directed by Jacques Lassalle with Comédie-Française actors at the Odéon theatre in 1990, and *Le Dernier Sursaut,* a short farce commissioned by Antoine Vitez for the traditional celebrations of Molière's birthday at the Comédie-Française in 1990, but judged too sulphurous for performance in that context. *L'Emission de télévison* is a major play, developing his reflection on contemporary life, on human beings' relationships to one another and to social institutions in the television age. In it Vinaver deals with the role of spectacle in society, dramatising some of the themes raised two decades earlier by the Situationist

---

[6] Vinaver, M., *Ecrits sur le théâtre,* op. cit., p.125.
[7] Ibid., p.132.

writer Guy Debord, in his seminal work *The Society of the Spectacle* (1967). As with all his plays, its fascination lies in the author's ability to suit the dramatic shape of the work to the raw material of the drama, and its structure represents yet another new departure. It is based around a murder investigation and so has the 'suspense' interest of a 'whodunnit'. But although this provides the mainspring for the action, the play subverts the drive towards closure and resolution of the classic detective story, since its scenes alternate between events just *before* and events just *after* the murder. The motives for the murder become more and more open to doubt as the play progresses; by the end the question of the motive and identity of the criminal have ceased to be the main focus of the audience's attention. Instead it is more interested in seeing how the event is 'digested'; how powerful social institutions such as law courts or television companies absorb individual tragedies, feed off them and make them seem almost normal.

Vinaver's most recent work for the theatre was his translation of Botho Strauss's play *Time and the Room*, directed by Chéreau in 1991 with Anouk Grinberg in the central role for the Odéon-Théâtre de l'Europe (while Chéreau was waiting to begin filming *La Reine Margot*). Productions on the French stage of works by Strauss and Heiner Müller have helped to strengthen the influence of postmodernist techniques in *mise en scène*. To the fragmentary, juxtapositional methods of Vinaver's plays are added the eclectic intertextuality of plays by writers such as Enzo Cormann, or the devised productions of Jean Jourdheuil and Jean-François Peyret, in whose work fragments of European history and culture are brought into collision with violent present-day realities without any attempt to provide framing explanations or messages (see below, section on playwrights of the 1990s).

The Status of the Playwright

Vinaver's influence on recent developments in French theatre is second to none. Not only is he acknowledged as the leading dramatist of the 1970s and 1980s, but he also had an important role in articulating policy as chairman of the Theatre committee of the Centre National des Lettres (1982–7). His personal experience of marketing techniques on the one hand, and of the difficulties facing creative writers on the other, made him uniquely suited to the job of assessing the nature of the crisis in play publishing. In the course of the 1970s, the major publishing houses had cut their drama lists and a number of specialist drama publishers had gone bankrupt. Vinaver decided to undertake a full-scale report into the conditions in which playwrights worked and the state of publishing in France. The report came out in 1987 under the title *Le Compte rendu d'Avignon* (The Avignon Report), reflecting the fact that Vinaver had given the first presentation of his findings at the Avignon Festival the previous summer. The major conclusion of the report, backed up by surveys and statistical data, was that the condition of the playwright had undergone a change of status since the 1960s. Before that, the report argued, an author would turn to the theatre as naturally as to the novel. In fact the major authors of the postwar period, like Sartre and Camus, were as active in the theatre as in publishing novels or essays. In this they were simply carrying on a tradition of literary life which dated back to the beginning of the century and before, when authors as various as Claudel, Gide, Giraudoux, Cocteau, Mauriac, Montherlant, experienced no necessity to choose between poetry or novels or plays, but spread themselves across genres.

Vinaver's report made out a strong case that the rise of the all-powerful director and the consequences of 1968 in the theatre had, between them, resulted in the playwright coming to be seen as a specialist kind of author and the craft of play construction as something which only theatre professionals could undertake successfully. This was a result, he argued, of the combined administrative and aesthetic conquests of theatre directors. Not only had they established themselves as the recipients of public subsidy, they had also identified a specific 'scenic writing' as their peculiar aesthetic domain. As a result, the playwright had come to be seen as a specialist and 'dramatic writing' as something that could only be supplied by those who had chosen it as their exclusive vocation. He pointed out that dramatists were never invited to speak on the popular and controversial intellectual talk-show on television, entitled *Apostrophes*, which, for two decades, has been the arbiter of taste and fashion in the world of literature and the arts. He discovered that very few bookshops bothered to stock play texts, considering them to be a poor financial investment. In short, he concluded that the drama had ceased to be accepted as part of the mainstream of the nation's intellectual life, becoming marginalised and confined to a specialist ghetto.

The tendency identified by Vinaver's report was reinforced by the new practice, copied from the German theatre, of employing a dramaturge in many large theatres. This term (roughly synonymous with the German *dramaturg*) conveys a person whose job is to act as literary manager to the theatre and also to supply background research on an author whose work is to be produced in the theatre. Tasks include tracking down any variant editions of the play if it is a classic, reworking the translation if it is a foreign text and even reordering the play, inverting scenes or inserting new material, like a surrogate author. The fashion for staging adaptations rather than new plays which swept through the French theatre in the late 1970s (see above, p.50) meant that there was plenty of work of this kind for aspiring playwrights who could get themselves taken on as dramaturges. In fact many young writers have learned their craft as dramatists in this way and have gone on to establish themselves as fully fledged playwrights. This arrangement clearly offers excellent training opportunities, but at the same time it encourages the writer to become even more specialised in the dramatic field and few authors who began in this way have been successful in other genres as well.[8]

Not content with analysing the situation as it stood, Vinaver's report went on to recommend a number of measures, some immediate, some long-term, for the revival of the French theatre text. It was necessary, he maintained, for his ideas to be carried out *en bloc* and simultaneously, in order to overcome

[8] For a hilarious send-up of the dramaturge, see the character Hervé Ladance in *Nefs et naufrages (sotie)* by Eugène Durif, Paris: Théâtre Ouvert, 1996.

current difficulties and create a change for the better. His suggestions ranged from those specific to theatre publishing to more general recommendations about theatre practices and the place of the play text within French culture.

To resolve the crisis in publishing, he urged publishers and theatres to start co-operating with one another in a concerted effort to promote the sale of play texts, and suggested that theatres and publishers work together on developing the sales outlets. He also considered it essential that the play once more become treated as a form of literature alongside other genres such as novels or poetry. In order to achieve this, recognition within the educational establishment, both at school and at university level, was a prime consideration, with contemporary plays to be encouraged on syllabuses wherever possible.

Happily, the last ten years have witnessed positive developments on both fronts. Contemporary play texts now appear on some *baccalauréat* syllabuses, as well as on university study programmes,[9] while there are more companies publishing plays than ever (see Information Section below). While they still face financial constraints and it is still difficult to make a play text profitable, prices for plays are very comparable to those for novels or collections of poetry. Published plays are now a regular sight on sale in theatres (both private and public) before and after performances. Actes Sud (the largest theatrical publisher) regularly adds titles to its catalogue which tie in with current programming in major theatres. Many of these also have a specialist bookshop, either in the form of permanent retail space (like that in the new Comédie-Française Studio Theatre) or tables displaying relevant texts which reflect the current season's repertoire and/or the particular interests of the theatre. Other books relating to the subject matter of the play being performed are frequently offered for sale alongside the play texts.

Published theatre texts are, in addition, contributing to the promotion of new writers' work among directors, believes Rodolphe

---

[9] Vinaver has played his part in this development by editing a volume entitled *Ecritures Dramatiques* which aims to develop a new scholarly method for the analysis of play texts (see Further Reading).

Fouano, who took the issue to task in an article entitled '*Y-a-t-il un lecteur dans la salle?*' ('Is there a reader in the house?') in 1993.[10] He pointed out that in the 1990s publishers now play a vital role in getting plays staged by making them more widely available to directors as well as to prospective spectators. There is a demand for contemporary texts, too, which can be demonstrated by the example of Philippe Minyana's complete works: these needed to be reprinted in 1993 to keep up with demand, 1500 copies having been sold over the previous four years, and his plays continuing to be performed both in Paris and in the provinces.

However, it is not only the independent theatre publishers who have helped to disseminate new theatre texts among directors and decision makers, hence promoting new authors who might otherwise remain unnoticed. Today there are a handful of active organisations in France whose job it is to make sure that plays are distributed and recognised in the theatre community. In his report Vinaver noted the need for measures to be taken to promote the published play as a work of art in its own right. For example, he mentioned the need for the Centre National du Livre to work closely with the SACD (Société des Auteurs et Compositeurs Dramatiques) on issues brought up in his report: this provoked the setting up of regular meetings between the two organisations.

As a result of such encounters, and of a general change in the climate of cultural opinion, the need to promote the French playwright has been widely accepted and a number of different organisations have been set in place to achieve this. Firstly, Théâtre Ouvert, founded in 1971 and promoted to the status of Centre Dramatique National in 1987, continues to publish numerous '*tapuscrits*', or working texts, each year, sending them out to theatre professionals and organising regular workshops. The purpose of these workshops is to empower authors and a number of different strategies have been devised to this effect. For example, an author may be given the studio space in which to workshop an as yet unfinished play. He or she has the choice of actors (and director, if so desired) and is given *carte blanche* to

---

[10] Fouano, R., in Laville, P. (ed.), *Théâtre 1992–3*, Paris: Hachette, 1993, p.269.

work in whatever way seems best with the aim of bringing the play to its conclusion. The studio at the Jardin d'Hiver in Clichy is also used to stage the occasional full-scale productions.

Concurrently, Théâtrales/l'association, set up in 1991, organises play readings and discussions around new writing for the theatre. The Association was created in order to promote new plays, both unpublished and published; it maintains a resource centre and library of new play texts in Paris, containing some 500 new plays, and also has a dozen branches spread around different parts of France and in Francophone countries. It promotes the work of all publishers, not just those of its sister company Editions Théâtrales. Entr'Actes, a division of SACD, does similar work, but concentrates mainly on promoting new French plays abroad. It publishes an extremely handsome and informative bilingual booklet every six months, in French and English, entitled *Actes du théâtre*. This describes new plays that have been published, productions of new work, international gatherings of theatre people, especially playwrights, and gives lists of productions, publications and other useful information. The Maison Antoine Vitez at Montpellier collaborates with the above organisations; its role is as a translation centre facilitating the availability of foreign texts in French. The establishment of La Chartreuse in 1991 as a National Centre for Playwriting (Centre National de l'Ecriture du Spectacle) has also helped to promote the position of the playwright: the Centre's role is largely to provide a place for residencies, readings and colloquia, though it also publishes a limited number of texts in its *Premières Impressions* series. Its position, in a beautiful old monastery just across the river from Avignon, lends it a special attraction, and it organises 'Les Rencontres de la Chartreuse' in conjunction with the Avignon Theatre Festival every year. These include full productions of new plays, as well as numerous workshops and play readings. It also publishes a journal, *Les Cahiers de Prospero*.

Because most of these associations are funded by public money there is less of a temptation for them to feel that they are in competition with one another than there would be if they were trying to sell their services. They appreciate the need for concerted action and meet regularly to discuss their individual activities, as well as to share information and resources, in a committee known as CRAC (Collectif de Réflection sur les Auteurs Contemporains). This is a welcome development where promotion of authors is concerned and can be seen as evidence that the author's contribution is once again highly valued in the French theatre today. For more details on these associations and how to get in touch with them, see the Information Section beginning on p.187.

While in some ways a confirmation of Vinaver's affirmation that writing for theatre has become a specialised domain, requiring first-hand knowledge of the theatre world, some theatres have begun to encourage writers to work closely with them, recognising their importance for the future development of theatrical art. The practice of appointing dramaturges in certain theatres has contributed to this development of relationships between theatres and local writers, which continues to be important in some of the CDNs. At the Théâtre National de Strasbourg, for example, a new scheme was started in December 1995 to train writers from many different backgrounds in the workings of theatre. Activities ranged from sitting in on rehearsals to working with designers, actors and directors. The aim was to open these writers' eyes to the possibilities afforded by theatre, as well as to train them in the specific genre of playwriting. Other theatres, such as the Scène Nationale de Poitiers, encourage new writing through putting on an annual festival, in this case entitled 'Coups de Théâtre'.

Vinaver's report drew attention to the lack of financial support, either direct or indirect, for writers whose work *is* regularly performed. Their situation, too, has improved since 1987, though many would argue that there is still a long way to go. Nevertheless, it was welcome news in 1995 when Jacques Toubon, then Minister of Culture, announced changes to the 'Aide à la Création Dramatique' scheme, granted at that time to publicly funded theatres, to encourage new '*créations*'. The term '*création*' is profoundly ambiguous as a result of the success of directors in claiming the status of '*créateurs*' for themselves (see above, pp.47–53) and so is the reform attempted to distinguish between the work of directors and that of writers who were not at the head of a theatre institution. Given that the money for the Aide à la création had previously gone to the director of the theatre or CDN in question, the scheme had too often been used to fund work devised or adapted by the director without calling on the services of a playwright at all.

The two priorities of the reforms were stated as being not only to facilitate the discovery and presentation of new texts, but also to ensure that authors whose work was staged were actually paid for their work. The changes mean that authors can now receive money in several forms from the Aide à la Création scheme. Subsidy can now be paid directly to a writer or adapter, even if they do not belong to a company or theatre and even if they have had no previously performed work. As before, money for research towards a play or to assist the revival of a play is still available and aid may be paid in one of two ways: either to the company staging the production, in which case 10 per cent of the subsidy is withheld so that it can be paid directly to the author, or in the form of a grant paid directly to the author. This money can be used either to finance the writing of the play, or the author may use it to ensure the staging of his play. A new clause was also added to the 1991 legislation of subsidy agreements between the Ministry and the directors of CDNs (see 'Institutional Developments' below, pp.149–55), actively limiting the scope for them to stage their own works under the heading of '*créations*'. Now they must produce at least three works by a francophone living author (other than the director) and give at least ten performances of each play, within the period of their contract (normally three years). Directors of CDNs must also appoint a text reader who is responsible for reading every text received by the Centre.

It is encouraging, too, to note that despite the fact that subsidies have been at a standstill under the Chirac regime, the amount allocated to playwrights under the Aide à la Création in 1997 rose from 2.6 million francs in 1996 to 5.14 million francs in 1997 – still not as high as the 7.8 million francs allocated in 1991, but nevertheless a significant increase. In addition to this government funding, writers can also obtain grants from the 'Beaumarchais' association of the SACD in the form of bursaries, aid for production, translation and writing. The Centre

National du Livre also offers bursaries and sabbaticals for published writers which are open to playwrights. Thus it would be
fair to conclude that while further funding for playwrights
would still be welcome, the situation of the French playwright
has certainly changed for the better, both financially and artistically, since the publication of Vinaver's report.

Among actors and directors of the younger generation, however, there is still much to be done to promote the work of
contemporary playwrights. There are exceptions, such as the
thirty-year-old Stanislas Nordey, who declares himself fascinated
by the work of Jean-Luc Lagarce because of the directorial challenge posed by its linguistic complexity (see below, pp.106–7), but
there are also many youngsters graduating from the training
schools who have been brought up on a diet of the classics and
know little of contemporary writing. They are wary of showing an
interest in challenging new forms and have not been encouraged
to do so in the course of their training. Nordey (who studied acting at the Paris Conservatoire) made the following comments on
the attitudes of students graduating from theatre schools in 1996:

> It is true that, apart from some who are mad about Koltès,
> young actors often know very little about contemporary
> authors. A certain form of militancy should nevertheless be
> taught in schools. I had the opportunity, thanks to theatre
> workshops which I did with my mother before entering the
> Conservatoire, to be aware of new authors. And within the
> Conservatoire I was free to choose: I decided to present some
> work by Michel Deutsch, Bernard Chartreux, Jean Genet, in
> my final showcase. In general, apart from rare exceptions, no
> account is taken of contemporary authors in these institu-
> tions. The exemplary course of action taken by Théâtre
> Ouvert should not be unique. In France there should be
> twenty, or even a hundred, places like Théâtre Ouvert,
> which defend contemporary writing, without necessarily
> having this as their mission.[11]

[11] Interview published in the press dossier for Nordey's production of *J'étais dans ma
maison et j'attendais que la pluie vienne* by Jean-Luc Lagarce, at Théâtre Ouvert,
March 1997.

Bernard-Marie Koltès and Patrice Chéreau

One of the few generally acknowledged major playwriting talents to emerge during the 1980s was Bernard-Marie Koltès, first promoted by Théâtre Ouvert in the 1970s and brought to international acclaim through his collaboration with Patrice Chéreau in the course of the following decade, until his untimely death in 1989. Koltès sums up better than any other playwright of recent times the paradoxes and contradictions of contemporary French theatre. His instincts and life-style were deeply anti-establishment, yet his work has been seized on eagerly by the established French theatres. His tastes were anti-theatrical: he adored reggae and Kung-Fu, cinema and blues music, and went so far as to proclaim that he detested theatre. 'I have always rather detested theatre because theatre is the opposite of life; but I always come back to it and I love it because it is the one place where you say : this is not life.'[12]

This statement reveals his rather schizophrenic attitude towards theatre: on the one hand saying he detested it, yet always coming back to it. Because the plays he wrote have become so successful (both within France and world-wide) his paradoxical attitude towards theatre has become fashionable; it sometimes seems as though many of today's French playwrights hate the theatre and only write plays despite their better instincts. This attitude naturally influences the kind of plays they write, which are similar to those of Koltès in that they are quite unlike the Theatre of the Everyday. They present characters who confront one another in long, formal exchanges of the kind that one would seldom encounter in everyday life. Their language is cool, almost classical, and they tend to speak in long monologues. Koltès's first successfully performed play (at the Avignon Festival in 1977) was a dramatic monologue, *La Nuit juste avant les forêts*, which owed a great deal to Faulkner and to the unquenchable stream of monologue that pours out of so many of Beckett's characters.

Most paradoxical of all was Koltès's success in a theatre which seemed to have abandoned new writing in favour of

---

[12] Koltès, B-M., 'Un Hanger à l'ouest' in *Roberto Zucco*, Paris: Minuit, 1990, p.120.

spectacular re-creations of the classics. At the time when Planchon's re-creations of Molière and Racine, or Chéreau's spectacular restaging of Marivaux, were leading the fashion in 'scenic writing' Koltès's work came as a reminder that lively theatre is ultimately impossible without new dramatic writing. Racine is often evoked by the critics when speaking of Koltès, and his dramatic dialogue contains something of the formal perfection and luminous clarity of the classical French theatre. He himself spoke of Marivaux as the playwright who had had the greatest influence on him. Yet his language is also uncompromisingly modern, almost, but not quite, the language of the street.

Like Chekhov before him, Koltès was convinced that the plays he wrote were comic and wanted them to be performed lightly, eliciting laughter. Yet the subjects dealt with in his published plays are anything but light; they are those of general concern to Europeans living in the last decades of the twentieth century: the state of our cities; the disparities between rich and poor, natives and immigrants; the relationships between first and third worlds and the commercial realities that bind us all together, whether we like it or not; racism, crime, violence; fears of things falling apart set against myths of utopian wholeness. He presents these subjects with a rawness and urgency rarely matched in the theatre today.

Koltès never aligned himself with a particular political standpoint, but his plays all deal with realities viewed in a political perspective. He was always interested in the economic links that hold people together and the way that they affect even the most private relationship. He once wrote that: 'I have never liked love stories. They tell you so little. I don't believe in the love relationship . . . If you want to tell a story with any subtlety you have to take a different route. For me the "deal" is a sublime means. It really encompasses everything else.'[13]

In line with this vision, Koltès saw human relations as a series of *deals* (he always used the English–American word and did not

---

[13] Cit. Bataillon, M., in '*Koltès, le flâneur infatiguable*', *Théâtre en Europe*, No.18, September 1988, p.26.

try to translate it). He explained what he meant by the term in the epigraph he wrote for *Dans la solitude des champs de coton*:

> A *deal* is a commercial transaction concerning values that are banned or subject to strict controls, and which is conducted in neutral spaces, indeterminate and not intended for this purpose, between suppliers and consumers, by means of tacit agreement, conventional signs, or conversations with double meanings – whose aim is to circumvent the risks of betrayal or swindle implicit in this kind of operation – at any time of day or night, with no reference to the regulation opening hours for officially registered trading establishments, but usually at times when the latter are closed.[14]

All of Koltès's characters use words in this way and all find themselves embroiled in conflictual relationships. Every one of his plays presents struggles of an intensely dramatic kind, which take place not only between individuals, but also between societies, cultures, world views. *Le Retour au désert (Return to the Desert, Bernard-Marie Koltès Plays: 1,* Methuen, 1997), for example, enacts a conflict that is essentially to do with ownership. It is set among the upper bourgeoisie of a French provincial town recalling the Metz of Koltès's own childhood. Here Adrien and Mathilde (brother and sister) fight about who can lay claim to the family property, but their struggle also suggests a deeper conflict about which section of society will inherit France. Will it be the colonial mentality, the civic values enshrined in the local mayor and corporation, the escapism of youth or the values of North Africa sweeping away the tired and compromised ideologies of northern Europe? In his last play the main conflict pits the outlaw, Roberto Zucco, against the whole of law-abiding society; but the play also depicts struggles within the family unit, evoking the conflictual nature of relationships between parents and children, brothers and sisters.

Most powerful of all, perhaps, *Combat de nègre et de chiens (Black battles with dogs, Bernard-Marie Koltès Plays: 1,* Methuen

---

[14] Epigraph to the text of *Dans la solitude des champs de coton*, Paris: Minuit, 1986.

1997) evokes whole cultures and economies in conflict. The play is set on a building site somewhere in Africa, where a multi-national construction company is engaged in a public works project financed by European capital. The expectations and assumptions of the engineers who run the site, and of a girl-friend on a visit from Paris, are brought into conflict with those of the African villagers who live nearby. The play tries to come to grips with the major disparities of the late-twentieth-century economic order, in which one part of the world is condemned to a life of drudgery and hunger, often labouring on projects imposed by the other part, the so-called developed world. It undermines the alibi of the developed world by showing how, despite its claims to protect the rights of the individual and extend human freedoms, its first aim is to increase its own wealth. Different attitudes towards the value that can be placed on a human life are dramatised through a simple story, in which a labourer has been knocked down and killed by a truck on the site. The play opens with Alboury, a villager, saying: 'I have come for the body.' Horn, the site manager, tries to strike a deal with Alboury: he offers him compensation and promises that the body will be returned to the village in the morning, but Alboury refuses to be put off by this and settles down to wait. Through-out the play he will be there, half hidden by the shadows, but always present, waiting and watching. The other two characters are: Léonie, a woman whom Horn has met on a recent trip to Paris and has persuaded to come out to visit him, and Cal, a young engineer working on the project. It slowly emerges that Cal is responsible for the death of the worker and, in a fit of panic, has dumped the body.

The play's twenty short scenes are made up, almost exclus-ively, of encounters between two out of these four characters. In the course of their encounters the characters speak not only of themselves, but also of the other two characters who are not present. In this way the audience gradually comes to know the characters, as much through what is said about them as through what they themselves say. The form in which they express themselves is a mixture of dialogue and extended monologue. The style is strongly reminiscent of Faulkner (a writer to whom

Koltès acknowledged his debt). Like the monologues of Faulkner's characters, they focus on concrete, closely observed details, and employ a language that is not remote from that of ordinary speech, yet they have the complex, condensed quality of language in dreams and lack the realistic patina of banal, everyday talk.

Patrice Chéreau, who directed the premières of four plays by Koltès in the 1980s, stated that for Koltès the monologue was primary: it was his way of getting to know his characters and, until he was able to write a monologue that satisfied him, he did not feel he had found the character's true voice.[15] The French publication of the play contains, as a postscript to the text under the heading 'Notebooks', a series of supplementary monologues by each of the characters: e.g. 'My firm, by Horn'; or 'Léonie sees someone beneath the bougainvillaea'. In the course of these monologues the characters define their position *vis-à-vis* the world as they imagine it, just as they do in many of the monologues included in the play.

Ultimately, the strength and originality of this play lies in its manipulation of language. It would be a mistake to take any of the characters too literally, as if they were depictions of real people one might meet on a West African building site. Koltès's whole approach to theatre, at once very formal, very violent and very down-to-earth, has a lot in common with that of Jean Genet. Genet considered the theatre as a '*de-realising* space'. Like Koltès, he considered it to be the opposite of real life. For him, the theatre's special property was to deny the reality of everything that appears on stage. Archibald, the master of ceremonies in *Les Nègres* (*The Blacks*, Faber, 1960), states this idea when he declares: 'An actor . . . A black . . . if he tries to kill, destroys the reality of even his knife.'[16] Archibald is deliberately insisting that blacks have no more reality than actors: they are condemned to see themselves in the roles assigned to them by the whites who define what it is to be black. In this way, Genet was emphasis-

[15] Chéreau, P., 'Staying Alive' (Public interview at the Edinburgh Festival, August 1995), *Theatre Forum*, No.9, Summer/Fall 1996, pp.12–18.
[16] Genet, J., *Les Nègres*, Décines: L'Arbalète, 1958, p.164.

ing that the blacks in his play were not to be seen as 'real' blacks, but as the imaginary projections of white Europeans at a time when the old dreams of empire were collapsing around our ears. His play was quite specifically designed to disturb white audiences by first confronting them with their image of the blacks, then showing these imaginary blacks threatening to break loose through their use of theatrical games, or clown shows, as Genet subtitled his play. Speaking of the play, Genet said: 'When we see Blacks, do we see something other than the precise and sombre phantoms born of our own desire? But what do these phantoms think of us then? What game do they play?'[17]

In *Combat de nègre et de chiens*, Koltès shows us not mimetic images of the real world, but the sombre phantoms that we try unsuccessfully to externalise and impose on others, but which, ultimately, are bound to return to haunt and possibly to destroy us. The battle takes place, in the last analysis, at the imaginary or ideological level, and re-enacts those mythic forces that condition the way we think about our surroundings. Like Genet before him, Koltès uses the freedom that this view of theatre implies in order to develop a meditation on subjectivity and point of view. The audience is constantly being made to see how one point of view conditions another and how the construction of subjectivity is a constant struggle. Linked to this is his insistence that the right question to ask of a play is not *why* the characters do what they do, or say what they say, but *how*: 'People too often tend, when you tell them a story, to ask the question "why?" whereas I think the only question worth asking is "how?"'[18]

Taking his cue from this attitude, Chéreau quoted Brecht's preface to *In the Jungle of the Cities* for the programme of *Dans la solitude des champs de coton*: 'Don't worry your heads about the motives for the fight, concentrate on the stakes. Judge impartially the technique of the contenders and keep your eyes fixed on the finish.'[19] The vocabulary used here (stakes, fight,

---

[17] Cit. White, E., *Genet*, London: Chatto and Windus, 1993, p.494.
[18] Koltès, B-M., 'Un Hangar à l'ouest', op. cit., p.115.
[19] Brecht, B., *Collected Plays: One*, London: Methuen, 1994, p.118.

contenders, etc.) recurs frequently in Koltès's own statements about his plays. The technique of the contenders is as much verbal as physical and, as they fight to the finish, they reveal to us how our ideas are constructed through the many-layered texture of the linguistic and imaginary reality we inhabit.

As well as tackling the world economic order, Koltès wrote about recent French history. *Le Retour au désert (Return to the Desert, Bernard-Marie Koltès Plays: 1*, Methuen, 1997) is set in November 1960 and depicts the struggle between a brother and sister in their early fifties. They are the last survivors of a bourgeois family which had made a fortune from the expansion of the Lorraine steel industry in the early years of the century. Because he considered his sister Mathilde to have let down the family, Adrien has victimised her: after the liberation of France in 1945, he made sure she was accused of sleeping with the enemy and paraded through the town with her hair shaved off. She fled to Algeria, where she lived throughout the late 1940s and 1950s. Now she is once again fleeing from hostilities (in Algeria) and comes back to confront Adrien in the family home.

In this play, Koltès returned to the main theme of much of his early work: the family, its conflictual relationships and its links with property, inheritance, ownership. In ways that recall both Faulkner and Salinger, Koltès presents individuals who may feel alienated within the family structure, but who return to it as the only environment in which they can discover self-definition. The saga of the family dynasty is not new, but the linking of a provincial industrial family to the Algerian war has considerable originality. For while the Second World War and German occupation of France have provided material for hundreds of plays and films, very few dramatists have been bold enough to deal with the equally disturbing material of the Algerian war. Yet this conflict, which lasted from 1954 until 1962, cost over 100,000 dead or wounded and affected the lives of everyone living in France or in French North Africa.

Koltès did not write issue plays in the straightforward sense. His method of handling social and political concerns was always oblique. Just as he wrote that *Combat de nègre et de chiens* was not a play about neocolonialism, so *Le Retour au désert* is not directly about the Algerian war. Rather, it deals with attitudes and social realities which both explain and are explained by the conflict in Algeria. It concerns itself with the mentalities current in the early 1960s in a provincial town such as Metz, and the action of the play develops a rich interweaving of the characters' dreams and aspirations, their behaviour in the private spaces of the home and their actions in the society outside. In fact, a principal theme of the play is how the French managed to deny the reality of the war going on in Algeria.

Koltès's last play, *Roberto Zucco (Roberto Zucco, Bernard-Marie Koltès Plays: 1*, Methuen, 1997) which was completed just before his death (aged only forty-one) in 1989, was given its première by Peter Stein in Berlin, although it has subsequently been per-formed in many different theatres in France. Koltès's Roberto Zucco is a character whose mythical dimensions are more outsize than any of his previous dramatic characters. He walks free over the roof of the high security prison in which he had been held; he quotes passages from Victor Hugo; his death is heralded by a hur-ricane and an explosion in the heavens 'as blinding as an atomic bomb'. In other words, he has heroic qualities and was described by the author as 'a mythical character, a hero like Samson or Goliath, monsters of strength, finally struck down by a stone or a woman'. And yet, paradoxically, this is also the most realistic of Koltès's plays, in which the dialogue seems closest to everday speech (while nevertheless retaining a certain poetic density).

Koltès first became interested in the case of the real murderer, Roberto Succo, in 1988, when he saw a 'wanted' poster in the metro, which carried photographs of him. Succo had murdered both his parents and had been sentenced to life imprisonment in Italy in 1981. After five years he had been given parole, had broken it and had been on the run for nearly two years, com-mitting other murders. The first thing that struck Koltès about the 'wanted' poster was that it included four different portraits of Succo; 'each one showed a face that was so different from the others that you had to look several times before you could be sure it was the same person'.[20] The play is prefaced by an extract

---

[20] Cit. Froment, P., in *Alternatives Théâtrales*, No.35–6, June 1990, p.41.

from an ancient ritual of the cult of Mithra, quoted by Jung in the last interview he gave to the BBC, and it manages to combine, throughout the action, resonances of mythical and psychoanalytical kind, as well as the brutal realities of the Succo murders. In common with some English playwrights such as Edward Bond, for example, Koltès clearly felt that violence is one of the defining features of our society (and one that we try not to see). The play concerns itself as much with the attitudes towards violence in society as with the monstrous nature of Zucco's actions.

At the opening of the play, Zucco has already killed his father; in the second scene he strangles his mother. In the most graphic way possible, he has thus destroyed his own origins. His three further crimes are rape (destruction of innocence), murder of a policeman (destruction of the law) and, finally, the murder of a child (destruction of the future). Zucco is beyond the understanding of an audience: he incarnates the cosmic cruelty that has a quality of indifference to it, referred to by Artaud. He never succeeds in establishing contact with another character in the play: his desperate monologue on the telephone (in scene viii), with no one at the other end, is an emblem of his situation. The text encourages us to think of him in a mythical light, with constant references to the labyrinth and to the myths of Theseus and of Icarus. His wanderings around the city suggest the search for a way out of the labyrinth; his encounters with a character called Le Balèze (the Bruiser) suggest the combat with the minotaur; and his final appearance on the roof and fall from sight in a blinding light suggest the escape and death of Icarus, from flying too close to the sun.

The crimes committed by Zucco are not 'investigated'; rather, they are taken as read and set in the context of a society where violence is the norm. This is presented at first in a family setting, then in a larger, more public space. At first we meet the family of the teenage girl whose virginity is taken by Zucco. It is a family in which every relationship is based on violence: husband to wife, parent to child, brother to sister. The brother's attitude towards his sister is especially instrumental. For him, there are only two options: either he protects her virginity or (once she has lost it) he sells her to a pimp. Her relationship with Zucco, by contrast, has a different quality: they meet as equals, each putting him- or herself in the hands of the other. She gives herself to him, but he also places himself at her mercy, and it is in fact she who, later on, betrays him to the police.

The public consumption of violence is dealt with in the longest scene of the play, which takes place in a public park. Here Zucco takes two hostages, a woman and her young son. The dramatisation of the episode lays emphasis on the role of the bystanders, their voyeuristic fascination with the events enacted before their eyes, their desire for a juicy crime and their need to demonise Zucco as the young hooligan. 'Explanations' for Zucco's behaviour are offered by a comic duo who appear in the first scene as prison warders and in scene xiv as policemen. Their bumbling discussions remind one of the two identical detectives, Dupont and Dupond, in the Tintin stories, who always get the wrong end of the stick. Their fixation on psycho-sexual explanations reveals nothing and blinds them to what is really going on in the situation facing them.

The structure of the play is far more episodic and open than anything Koltès had written before. It suggests that he was, at the time of his death, beginning to develop in a new direction. The play relies more on dialogue and less on monologue than his earlier work, and it moves freely from one location to another. The titles he gave to the scenes suggest what happens in them rather than their location. For example, the scene in which the girl betrays Zucco is headed 'Delilah' and the one in which her brother sells her to the pimp is headed 'The Deal'. The play's time-scale is vague: it covers the period between Zucco's first escape from prison and his final, fatal fall from the prison roof, but the number of days involved is unclear: it could be as little as two or three, or it could be a matter of weeks.

Although Koltès had to wait thirteen years between the writing of his first play and the 1983 production of *Combat de nègre et de chiens* which made him famous, he enjoyed an extremely productive relationship with Chéreau during the remaining five years he had to live. Chéreau committed himself to directing each new play Koltès wrote and also commissioned a translation of Shakespeare's *A Winter's Tale*. Knowing that he had the unconditional support of a director such as Chéreau undoubtedly gave Koltès a certain freedom to experiment and made it possible for him to write plays with large casts which would otherwise have remained unperformed. Perhaps even more important was Chéreau's ability to attract actors of the calibre of Michel Piccoli, who took the role of Horn in *Combat de nègre et de chiens* and of Adrien in *Le Retour au désert*. His ability to speak Koltès's complex monologues, together with his masterly physical presentation of ageing men who are both desperate and sensual, contributed greatly to shaping those roles. Actors in France love to perform Koltès, as English actors love to perform Pinter or American actors David Mamet. This is for the same reason: their plays may be rather stiff and formal, certainly not naturalistic, but they are always centred on powerful conflicts between characters who fight to the death and their language simmers with dramatic tension.

The qualities in Chéreau's production work which were appreciated by contemporary critics were his manipulation of a vast stage space, his originality (as when he set Wagner's *Ring* cycle in the industrial revolution) and the visual brilliance of his designer, Richard Peduzzi. But it may be that the lavish production values which became associated with Koltès's plays as a reult of Chéreau's elaborate productions did him a disservice. Recent revivals of his plays have shown that they work as well, if not better, in small-scale, relatively intimate productions, and Chéreau's three stagings of *Dans la solitude des champs de coton* have become progressively simpler, with a corresponding gain in power. His 1995 production of the play was for the Odéon-Théâtre de l'Europe (staged at the Edinburgh Festival, then at the Manufacture des Œillets at Ivry as part of the Festival d'Automne). Designed by Richard Peduzzi, it was suitably bleak and pared down, staged in an empty warehouse, with the audience seated on two sides of a large expanse of untreated concrete floor. In this space Chéreau, playing the dealer, and Pascal Greggory as the client stalked each other in carefully choreographed movements, lit by cold spotlights with contrasted sequences of strobe-lit, desperate dancing from one end of the 'stage' to the other. The minimalistic nature of the staging only served to emphasise the formal beauty of the language and the contained human passions simmering beneath the attempts to strike a 'deal' (see above, p.83) emerged in the unrestrained frenzy of the dance sequences.

Ariane Mnouchkine's Shakespeare Cycle

The recent history of theatre in France is marked by two exceptional collaborations between writers and directors; one is that between Chéreau and Koltès, discussed above, the other brought together Ariane Mnouchkine and Hélène Cixous, whose first play, *Portrait de Dora*, had been staged by Simone Benmussa (see above, p.57). After the successes of the early 1970s Mnouchkine had temporarily abandoned live theatre to make a film about Molière. Rather than focusing on Molière the man, the film is centrally concerned with the life of his theatre troupe. In a series of spectacular virtuoso sequences, it develops a meditation on one of Mnouchkine's central preoccupations: the utopian life that may be achieved by a group of artists with a shared vision, however repressive the society in which they live and work. A key sequence of the film depicts the carnival at Orleans and its suppression by the newly established local branch of Jesuits. The sequence lasts for some fifteen minutes of action in which hardly a word is spoken. It shows the narrow streets of seventeenth-century Orleans being filled with an irresistible stream of masked and costumed carnival dancers. The boys of the town's college, Molière among them, escape from their locked doors into this world of misrule, both frightening and appealing. Soon, mounted soldiers appear who charge and scatter the crowd. Escaping from the violence of the streets, the young Molière finds himself in a barn where a company of travelling players is performing. He is spellbound and feels as though he has discovered a new world: a community not goverend by the hierarchies of authority, like the family and church within which he has grown up, but by mutual interdependence based on a shared vision of festive play.

When Mnouchkine returned to live theatre in 1979, it was

with an adaptation she had made of Klaus Mann's novel *Mephisto*. This, too, offered a meditation on the relationship of a theatre company to the political life of its times. She used Mann's story about an actor sacrificing his soul for success under the Nazi regime in order to comment on the dangers facing France at the time and the need for the Left to unite. The production was successful, both artistically and commercially, but the company's debts had been increasing for some years and Mnouchkine conducted a forceful campaign for improved funding. The company was saved from bankruptcy by the victory of the Left in 1981: one of the first actions taken by Jack Lang, on becoming Minister of Culture, was to double its grant. With renewed optimisim, Mnouchkine held a series of open workshops, from which she recruited many new young actors, including the man who was to take over the mantle of Philippe Caubère: Georges Bigot. She embarked on a cycle of Shakespeare plays, turning towards Eastern theatre traditions for her inspiration, and the result was a series of productions that once again dazzled her audiences and astonished them with a new vision of Shakespeare's world. It is a mark of Mnouchkine's greatness that she was able, at this time, to make a fresh start with a new company and achieve such extraordinary results.

The underlying principle in this work, as it had been in the work of the 1960s and 1970s, was the centrality of the actor to the art of theatre. When asked why she had recourse to the theatre traditions of Japan, or China, or India, she explained that, in them, the art of the actor was the link to the oldest sources, not, as in Western theatre, the written text. Pursuing her search for the most truthful, subtle and complex language of gestural communication, she was therefore bound to encounter these traditional forms, as Artaud had done before her. Working on the Shakespeare plays, she adopted a method similar to that of *la création collective*, despite the existence of a text, in that she used a great deal of improvisation, and kept the casting of the plays open until the last possible moment, so that all the actors would, at some stage, try out all the different roles and thus learn to build on one another's strengths. This led once again to an atmosphere of tension and competition in the company, and resulted in the noisy departure of Philippe Hottier in 1984, making accusations very similar to those that had been made by Caubère seven years earlier.

The Shakespeare productions were universally acclaimed. The use of the enormous thrust stage, the introduction of music played by Jean-Jacques Lemêtre accompanying every moment of the action, the shimmering silks and rich fabrics, not to speak of the physical dexterity of the actors, all of these things were a feast to the eye and ear. The effect was well captured by Gilles Sandier, one of the most respected and most demanding of French theatre critics, when he wrote:

> Into this sublime arena comes rushing a dreamlike caval-cade of Elizabethan samurai; they freeze for a moment in front of the spectators, still wild though motionless, like strangely sumptuous bronze beasts, their faces painted like masks, their ruffs an added reminder of characters from Rembrandt . . . And what a stream of lyrical images! – Visions which are among the most dazzling that I have experienced in the theatre: the challenges in the lists, the stylised cavalcades, the two tortured favourites of the king turning in a great wheel, and Richard restrained by immense ropes, and the adventurer who has won the throne kissing the naked body of the young murdered king draped across his knees as in a *pietà*.[21]

For the audience the experience was once again enhanced by the transformation of the Cartoucherie and the process of enter-ing into the spirit of the performance began from the moment one stepped inside the building. Gone was the rather rumbus-tious, popular atmosphere of the early 1970s and in its place was a quiet hum of concentrated activity. Long tables were set out on the floor, with low-level lighting, and at them the actors were putting on their elaborate make-up and changing into cos-tume. This was taking place in the same space as that occupied by the seating and the stage, so that the audience could move around among these preparations and appreciate their stillness

---

[21] Sandier, G., *Le Matin*, 19 December 1981.

and concentration. When the show was about to begin the audience took their places on tiered benches facing the stage and remained in this frontal relationship to the action throughout.

The practice of changing the environment for each new production became a permanent feature of Mnouchkine's work from 1981 onwards: for the Sihanouk play in 1985, for example, the space resembled a Cambodian temple; for *Les Atrides* in 1990 the audience reached the performances via an archeological exploration of the Ancient Greek theatre and the playing space carried suggestions of the bullring. But during the same period the arrangement of seating remained, essentially, unaltered. The large, open stage was faced by a bank of tiered benches and, once installed, the audience remained static throughout. The experiments in audience mobility that made for some of the excitement of the productions of the 1970s have been abandoned. This appears to have been in order to create an atmosphere in which the audience would pay closer attention to the text and corresponds to a period when Mnouchkine entered into a partnership with the writer Hélène Cixous to attempt to develop a theatre form large enough to deal with the experience of twentieth-century life.

Ariane Mnouchkine and Hélène Cixous

The Shakespeare cycle had been undertaken, according to Mnouchkine, in order to learn how to produce a theatre that could speak about the contemporary world in all its complexity. During their work on Shakespeare the company had benefited from the advice of Hélène Cixous, a noted Shakespeare scholar as well as a writer. Mnouchkine encouraged Cixous to write a play for the company that would enable them to confront the late-twentieth-century world; in fact she wrote three, over a ten-year period, the first two dealing with colonialism and its legacy, and the third with recent government scandals in France. The importance of this determination to speak of and to the world we live in should not be underestimated. Yet the plays themselves have proved disappointing. Everything that made for the excitement and originality of the plays on the French Revolution, or of the Shakespeare cycle, seemed to have been abandoned in these productions. The actors no longer expressed themselves primarily in physical terms, but resorted to wordy speeches; the stage space was no longer filled with movement and life, but was, for most of the time, left empty, while the actors lined up along the front to deliver their speeches across a row of footlights. Most damaging of all, the account of political reality had lost the multi-layered quality that so distinguished *1789* and *1793* and had become, instead, unilinear.

This is doubly surprising in the light of the avowed aims of the writer, Hélène Cixous, who has frequently affirmed her opposition to unilinear discourse in favour of a more open, pluri-vocal structure. The first two plays examined the struggles for independence in Cambodia during the 1960s and 1970s, and in India during the time leading up to and after partition: *L'Histoire terrible mais inachevée de Norodom Sihanouk, roi du Cambodge* (1985) and *L'Indiade, ou l'Inde de leurs rêves* (1987). In these plays both Cixous's text and Mnouchkine's production attempted to undermine Western colonial attitudes by emphasising the femininity of some of the characters, for example, King Norodom Sihanouk. Here was someone who accepted the qualities ascribed to colonised peoples by the West – childishness, wayward behaviour, passivity – and turned them into a strength. But in so doing, they created a new set of binary oppositions, between aggressive, devilish Westerners and serene, saintly Orientals. Precise historical analysis of the period examined was lost in the process, as Jennifer Birkett has argued:

> What becomes of history in this play [Sihanouk] is what becomes of the feminine subject in patriarchal discourse. Colonized, expropriated, made up and made over into the mirror of more powerful others, Cixous's Cambodia is waved away to the margins before it has a chance to open its own mouth. Turning the death of a nation into an anatomy of passions, a theoretical model of the human condition, produces not living drama but an academic exercise.[22]

[22] Birkett, J., 'The limits of language: the theatre of Hélène Cixous', in Dunkley, J., and Kirton, B. (eds), *Voices in the Air: French Dramatists and the Resources of Language*, Glasgow: University of Glasgow French and German Publications, 1992, pp.183–4.

Because the saintly figures of Sihanouk or Gandhi were con-trasted by a number of devil-figures (most notably Kissinger in the Sihanouk play), the result was to present the contemporary political process in Cambodia and India in terms of an over-simplified set of binary oppositions.

These first two plays written for the Théâtre du Soleil emerged from a process that had begun with work on Shakespeare's history plays, so it is not surprising that their struc-ture, their approach to characterisation and the appeal to feudal values of the Sihanouk play all conform to a Shakespearian model. Before Cixous wrote the last play, however, a new burst of creative theatrical energy had illuminated the work of the company in their experiments with Ancient Greek tragedy. In the four productions that went to make up *Les Atrides*, Mnouchkine rediscovered some of the strong ritual images that had imbued her earlier productions. Especially remarkable was their use of the chorus, where it was the strength of the phys-ical, gestural work that Mnouchkine can elicit from her actors that made these performances so moving. The combination of chant, movement, dance, that characterised the chorus in these productions gave spectators a sense of rediscovering for the first time something of the impact that the Ancient Greek chorus might have had in fifth-century Athens and the music of Jean-Jacques Lemêtre really came into its own. Following on from her experience with the Shakespeare cycle, Mnouchkine looked to Eastern theatre traditions, and especially to Kathali, for inspi-ration in the search for how to unite the musical and gestural elements of the performance. The result managed to convey both a sense of the representative group speaking for a whole community and something of the mystery of the Dionysiac forces erupting at the centre of that community. This use of the chorus mirrored, to some extent, the use of the crowd scenes in earlier productions such as *1789* and restored the voice of the people to the stage. This is what had been missing in the plays on Cambodia and India, where the historical and political expe-rience was reduced to the struggles between a small number of eminent characters.

In writing *La Ville parjure, ou le réveil des Erinyes*, c 1994,

Cixous benefited by the experience of the company's work on the four Greek plays in the early 1990s. Her play is designed to echo various themes and techniques of one of them – *The Eumenides*, which she had translated. The central action of the play brings back the Erinyes, the fearful representatives of matriarchy neutralised at the conclusion of Aeschylus' *Oresteia*, and this seemingly archaic device enables her to enlarge the focus and to offer alternative visions of reality in a way that had eluded her earlier on. The chorus of *La Ville parjure* is composed of down-and-outs who live in the cemetery, on the outskirts of the town. They are brought together by the arrival of the Mother, who has left the city and is seeking justice for the deaths of her two children, killed by transfusions of contaminated blood. They arrange a trial of the city authorities in which all the hypocrisies of modern governing élites are exposed and the Mother cries in vain for just one word of apology from them. The different characters of the play are conceived and performed in such a way as to emphasise the symbolic resonances with the deepest layers of our myths and memories. This produces some of the most moving and memorable images of the play, and at last succeeds in offering roles of real power to the women in the company. Nevertheless, there is a price to be paid for this mythologising approach: precise political points of reference (the real French scandal of contaminated blood, for example) are effaced in favour of a vision that becomes progressively more generalised until the audience is left, at the end of the play, with a manichean-feminist view of a world forever divided between manipulative men and merciful mothers.

Nevertheless, the Mother's denunciation of the male-dominated professional establishment is powerful and carries echoes of Genet's Mother in *Les Paravents* (*The Screens*, Faber, 1963). There were other elements in this powerful performance that recalled Genet: the choice of marginalised setting and characters; the undermining of familiar figures of authority. Yet the subversive power and poetry of Genet's theatrical vision eludes both Cixous and Mnouchkine. Where Genet shows how every revolt carries within it the seeds of its own betrayal, the Soleil is fuelled by a fierce determination to prove that revolt can lead to the realisation of utopia. Mnouchkine's insistence that true theatre must be essentially childlike contributes to building up a polarised world in which good and evil confront one another in pure, essentialist terms. *La Ville parjure* concludes on an evocation of a better world beyond the heavens; the play recalls *L'Age d'or* in its nostalgia for an impossible golden age.

There is a natural affinity between Mnouchkine's view of theatre and Cixous's construction of a space for feminine writing freed from the constraints of patriarchy. Although ostensibly dealing with history and politics, it may be more frutiful to read the plays Cixous wrote for Mnouchkine as commentaries on the writer, her role in modern society, and her struggle to communicate her vision when this meets with hostility.[23] Gandhi and Sihanouk should perhaps be seen as standing essentially for poetic identities. They are attempting, not so much to intervene in the historical process, as to articulate a vision which is rejected or misunderstood by all the parties involved in the political process. Although *La Ville parjure* appears to centre on a fight for justice in the modern state, maybe its central concern is really the poet's struggle to speak for the oppressed. This interpretation emerges most clearly from two other recent plays by Cixous, *Voile noire, voile blanche* and *L'Histoire (qu'on ne connaîtra jamais)*. The first was performed in Britain by the Actors' Touring Company in 1994 as *Black Sail, White Sail*, but has not yet been seen in France; the second was staged, also in 1994, at the Odéon by Daniel Mesguich. Both plays place poets centre-stage: in the first it is Anna Akhmatova and Nadezha Mandelstam; in the second, Snorri Sturlusson, the Icelandic author of the tales of the Nibelungen. When told to recount the story of Siegfried and Brünnhilde, he finds himself caught in the very tale he is telling. The poet wishes to achieve a closed narrrative but can never do so – he has to give in and accept

[23] This interpretation was first put forward by Julia Dobson of Wolverhampton University, in a paper read to an international conference, 'Women give voice to Women', in London in 1997. Dobson's paper, 'The Scene of Writing: The Representation of Poetic Identity in Cixous's Recent Theatre', is due to be published in *Theatre Research International*, Vol.23, No.3, autumn 1998. The remainder of this paragraph is a paraphrase of her ideas.

participation in the fluid, continuously creative process of writing that is narrative (or theatre).

This play, which would seem to share so much with Mnouchkine's methods and ideology, nevertheless marks a break in Cixous's exclusive ties with the Théâtre du Soleil. Mnouchkine went on to present a *Tartuffe* set in an Islamic society, in which the religious hypocrite is a ruthless fundamentalist (1996). In the mid-1990s Mnouchkine occupies a position of singular authority in the French theatre. After the untimely death of Antoine Vitez in 1990 (coinciding with Patrice Chéreau's retirement from the theatre at Nanterre) Mnouchkine has come to be seen as the natural heir to the great tradition of director–teachers, going back to Jacques Copeau in the early years of the century. It is now the ambition of every young French actor (and many from other countries as well) to be picked for one of her training *'stages'* and then perhaps to be invited to join the Soleil for a while. Like Peter Brook, she has shown that by liberating the actor, and by moving outside the spaces traditionally allotted to theatre, it is possible to challenge and revitalise the most profoundly held beliefs of our society: beliefs in justice, democracy, loyalty to the truth and to ideals of world peace and solidarity with the oppressed. Moreover, she has always practised what she preached: the company still operates a policy of equal salaries for every member and she never shrinks difficult personal commitments, such as her 1995 hunger strike for peace in Bosnia. However, a life of action committed to utopian ideals does not free one from criticism, nor from the contradictions of our age. But even if the gap between particular political concerns and utopian mythologising sometimes threatens the very integrity of her enterprise, there is no director working today who can match the liberating effect that her process has on actors, nor the lasting power of the images she creates, images which continue to resonate in the hearts and minds of spectators long after the show is over.

Playwrights and Directors in the 1990s

In the 1970s, as we have seen, the playwright was marginalised.

Directors succeeded in establishing their claim to be the major creative force in creating new theatre and in introducing new forms. Practitioners such as Vitez were seeking to 'make theatre from anything' (see above, p.38), rejecting the notion that the text was a necessary prerequisite or blueprint for their work. It was more commonly the designer who enjoyed a close collaborative relationship with the director, since the qualities on which production work was judged came to be primarily visual rather than verbal. Planchon's work with Luciano Damiani and Ezio Frigerio, Chéreau's with Richard Peduzzi and Mnouchkine's collaboration with Guy-Claude François marked an era of highly pictorial production values.

Even in the mid-1980s, when both Mnouchkine and Chéreau developed close working relationships with particular authors, Mnouchkine with Cixous, and Chéreau with Koltès, the collaborative relationship they enjoyed was the exception rather than the rule. Many young writers were not so lucky, receiving a far more lukewarm response to their attempts to infiltrate the closed shop of public theatre. Indeed, until recent years the view was widely held that, since so few authors could match Koltès's success in getting plays produced on the major stages, the reason was that they were, at best, inept. In 1986, for example, Pierre Laville had the following to say of contemporary French playwrights: 'Nearly all authors are inept in the way they communicate with theatres, and so little informed about who is who, not knowing which person to target or choose. The result: they are little known (no one reads them), ignored (no one replies to them), treated lightly (when someone does respond); authors have a hard life.'[24]

The attitude from the critics was no more positive: in 1987, for example, Bernard Pivot, presenter of *Apostrophes*, a leading arts programme on French television (who might be compared with Melvyn Bragg on the *South Bank Show*), blamed authors for their own fate. He claimed that what they wrote was just not of a sufficiently high standard. As quoted by Vinaver in *Le Compte rendu d'Avignon*, he condemned the whole state of

[24] Laville, P., in *Acteurs*, No.38–9, 1986, p.1.

modern writing for the theatre: 'If writers wrote superb plays, they would be staged, published and talked about in the media . . . But it is impossible to quote a single author of thirty or forty years old . . . Let's not dream. There are neither interesting plays nor theatre texts at the moment. There is thus no problem of play publication . . . Currently, today, I'm not aware of the slightest sign of change.'[25]

This pessimism also extended to celebrated directors, including Chéreau, who, after Koltès's death in 1989, became disillusioned with theatre and what he saw as a dearth of playwriting talent. This attitude resulted in his abandonment of theatrical pursuits, for the main part, in favour of a career in cinema. In an interview given at the Edinburgh Festival in 1995, he went so far as to say that after Koltès 'there are no authors'.[26] The kind of partnership illustrated by the example of Chéreau and Koltès is nevertheless still considered desirable, even essential, by many working in French theatre, if the era of the dominant director is to give way to more evenly balanced creative collaborations. Conferences and pronouncements on the need for directors to nurture new writers have become commonplace in recent years. Olivier Py, one of the most talented of the new generation of writer–directors, has expressed very clearly the need for the director to be seen as just one player in a much larger team:

> I deeply despise the job of direction. I prefer by far the work of the costume cutter or lighting expert. Once you have lined up the work of the author, the actors, the lighting, costume and stage designers, the musician, the assistant and the tea boy, I wonder what is left for the director to do. I defy anybody to tell me what direction consists of, once you've taken away everything done by the other members of the team, including the dramaturgy.[27]

The tone of Py's comment is representative of a widespread

---

[25] Op. cit., p.54.
[26] Chéreau, op.cit., p.18.
[27] In the programme for *Nous, les héros* by Jean-Luc Lagarce, staged by Olivier Py at the Ferme du Buisson, Marne-la-Vallée, April 1997.

Les Bonnes by Jean Genet

Les Voisins by Michel Vinaver

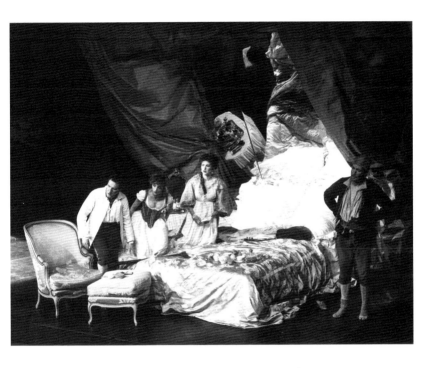

Le Mariage de Figaro by Beaumarchais

L'Ile des esclaves by Marivaux

Terra Incognita by Georges Lavaudant

Le Libertin by Eric Emmanuel Schmitt

Le Jeu de l'amour et du hasard by Marivaux

Dans la solitude des champs de coton by Bernard–Marie Koltès

desire to see theatre production as a team effort. This is an approach which suits some writers better than others. At a conference designed to bring writers and directors together ('Les Rencontres Charles Dullin' in February 1996) the writer Philippe Braz, for example, stated that the experience of workshopping his plays with actors and a director had provoked confrontation and dialogue, both of which he had found enriching. Michel Azama, on the other hand, explained that he found this kind of encounter constricting rather than liberating: he needed to distance himself from the team effort of producing the play, if only for self-protection. Writing a new play with a specific director in mind was not something he relished, as it compromised the sense of isolation necessary to his creative process.

A common cause of agreement in such debates is that the French theatre must attract new playwrights if it is to renew itself. But despite changed attitudes on the part of some directors and theatre managements, there are still many professionals who are reluctant to experiment with new work, preferring the comparative safety of the classics. Micheline Attoun of Théâtre Ouvert points to this as the one major obstacle in the path of young playwrights (see Interview on p.166) and many of them echo her opinion. Noëlle Renaude, for example, has complained that 'hardly any directors are interested in living authors. On the pretext that it is difficult to fill a theatre, they always prefer to stay with Molière or Shakespeare, rather than to take a risk on a contemporary author.'[28]

Even with younger directors, there is still a tendency to feel that they must build their reputation by stamping their own creative vision on a play from the classic repertoire. This is especially true when it comes to plays they are invited to present at prestigious festivals, such as the Festival d'Automne, which has become a major showcase for directors to display the best of their previous season's work. In 1996, for example, the one living French playwright to be featured was Novarina. His play *Le Repas* was staged by Claude Buchvald at the Centre

---

[28] Interview by Hervé Guay in *Le Devoir*, 4–5 January 1997.

Pompidou. But most of the other prestigious shows in the Festival were new productions of classics by acclaimed directors. Peter Brook, for example, staged his first Beckett: *Oh les beaux jours* with Natasha Parry; Luc Bondy chose to present Strindberg's *Playing with Fire*, starring Emmanuelle Béart; and the young star director Stéphane Braunschweig opted for an epic (and highly acclaimed) production of Ibsen's *Peer Gynt*. The 1997 French Theatre Season in London also features Brook's Beckett production. Bondy was invited to bring his Strindberg to Nottingham in May 1997. Stanislas Nordey, who in France has been active in promoting the work of young authors, has been invited to bring his production of *La Dispute* by Marivaux to London for the French Theatre Season in 1997.

The alternative between 'safe' classics and 'risky' new plays is not always as easy as it might seem, however, and Nordey rejects the making of such simple distinctions. Whether he is directing a play by Marivaux, or the recently discovered *Splendid's* by Genet, or a new play by Jean-Luc Lagarce, Nordey seeks to discover what will speak to our age and seem relevant to a young audience. He specifically rejects the notion of the director as supreme creative artist, seeing his function more as that of mediator between playwright and public:

> I don't imagine theatre as a place apart from the world. It's a place in a town and it's important that we're not demi-gods whom people come to visit for the evening with religious devotion. Some consider the theatre a sacred place. Not me. It's more a place for conviviality and exchanges. As I work with taxpayers' money, I take public opinion into account, unlike those of the generation before me (Vincent, Chéreau, Mesguich, Lavaudant) who deviated from an idea of public theatre which I find very beautiful. One must not simply impose an ego without explanation before or after.[29]

Nordey's view strikes a note of combined realism and idealism, or yearning for a renewed ideological purpose, which is wide-

[29] Interviewed by Hervé Guay in *Le Devoir*, 4–5 January 1997.

spread among young theatre workers today. This contrasts interestingly with the view expressed by Koltès a decade earlier, considering theatre as something apart from the real world, a place which is 'not life' (see above, p.81).

One obstacle standing in the way of young practitioners who seek to make theatre more relevant to contemporary society is the increasingly abstract nature of much playwriting. Authors like Philippe Minyana, for example, prefer to talk about characters in an abstract, psychological sense rather than in terms of a concrete social setting. Burning issues, such as AIDS or homelessness, certainly do make an appearance in contemporary French texts, Cixous's *La Ville parjure* being the clearest example, but it is the way they are dealt with which is of particular interest (see p.98). Cixous distanced her subject by giving it a timeless setting reminiscent of Aeschelean tragedy. Minyana, Azama, Lagarce, among others, seek to achieve a similar distancing effect by writing dreamlike, unlocated actions, in which issues such as drug abuse, homelessness or street violence are dramatised through impressionistic, fragmented dialogue. These are emotional mood-pictures, deliberately leaving loose ends and building up an air of mystery. They draw attention to their own artistry rather than facing their audience with a realistic depiction of a given problem. Even Durringer, who may at first glance seem to be writing gritty realist plays, is equally interested in experimenting with language and dramatic structure (see below, p.113–4).

Michel Azama's works provide examples of plays springing from and dealing with social issues in experimental form. Speaking at a public debate entitled '*Ecriture théâtrale et fracture sociale*' in April 1997 (organised by Théâtrales/l'association and La Maison des Ecrivains in their regular 'Les Lundis du Théâtre' series of debates), he explained how his play *Le Sas*, first staged in 1989, came out of the research he conducted by talking to twelve women prisoners in Rennes. Describing himself as '*un auteur militant*' at that time, he explained how he combined the experiences of these women into one 'voice', a monologue, recounted by a woman on her last night in prison, but in fact featuring many facets and viewpoints on the issue of women in prison taken from the experiences of the group of women he interviewed. In his work *Contes d'exil*, the issues of war and exile are dealt with through the story of three generations of Vietnamese women in exile in France, and how their situation has affected each of them. Time spans and memories of all three women are mixed together, at times almost seeming to merge into the same person: all three are haunted by ghosts from the past. In this play, as in *Le Sas*, therefore, Azama attacks social issues, but uses the medium of multi-perspective and different levels of reality to explore his subject matter (see his views on form and structure in the interview with him on p.184). As he says himself in the introduction to the British edition of his play *Croisades (Crossfire,* Oberon Books, 1993), 'A central image of our time might be zapping. Theatre cannot change anything. May it long continue to interrogate a few consciences.'

The stress many contemporary playwrights place on experimental structure, form and language is proving an interesting challenge for young directors who are happy to recognise the role of the writer, and find it exciting to work with texts which give a director scope to add structure and shape. A good example of this is Stanislas Nordey, who in spring 1997 staged his version of Jean-Luc Lagarce's *J'étais dans ma maison et j'attendais que la pluie vienne*. In this play five women, three generations of the same family, await the return of the prodigal son who is coming home to die. Previously voiceless, they are provoked into speech and expression of emotion by the return home of the young man they have all been waiting for. The difficulties in the text proved a positive attraction to Nordey. He went on to stage another Lagarce play requiring similar directorial versatility to overcome linguistic obstacles, *Le Pays lointain*. His production of the former play at Théâtre Ouvert (which had originally commissioned the play from Lagarce) was bleak. On a virtually empty stage with spotlights on the five women, now singly, now as a group, he sought to highlight the disparity and yet the unity between their five voices, in a bid to give structure to Lagarce's poetic but unstructured text. In the programme Nordey states the main reason why he was attracted to Lagarce's two latest plays: 'It seems to me that these long incoherent sentences which go on and on until the last gasp, testing the limits of what is bearable, pose a formidable challenge for the stage. It's for this reason that I've chosen to stage consecutively two plays by the same "poet", to dig deep into this language, which is furthermore very varied from one work to the next.'[30]

In the production, Nordey's explorations into the power of Lagarce's language resulted in a tirade of verbal images spilling out of the various characters at a speed and pitch which the director sought to vary and control. Nordey wisely adapted his staging to give scope to the text itself, which in performance, like many other contemporary works, became an example of the 'word' or 'parole' as an object to be admired from a distance, rather than the tool for expression or functional communication of information, either emotional or factual.

In the interview on p.178 of this book, Philippe Minyana describes a play text as having more in common with a painting or piece of architecture than with other literary forms, to be admired as a "structure" in its own right: this was very much the impression given by this production, which demanded an ear attentive to the power of the verbal pictures being painted. The audience was encouraged to stand back and admire Lagarce's choice of words, rather than to identify or respond on an emotional level. Similar demands are made on the audience in Jean-Louis Bourdon's play *Scènes de la misère ordinaire*, in which each member of a working-class family (father, mother and two children) comes forward, one at a time, to give his or her version of the family tragedy befalling them all. The picture they slowly build up is of a disastrous marriage, the father's suicide and the mother's ensuing unhappy life in a relationship with an oppressive female lover.

While the interest of directors such as Nordey in linguistically challenging texts is helping to redress the balance in favour of the writer within the theatre arena, playwrights are also seizing

---

[30] Taken from the programme of Nordey's production of Lagarce's *J'étais dans ma maison et j'attendais que la pluie vienne*, staged in March 1997 at Théâtre Ouvert.

the initiative themselves, taking their own works directly to audiences rather than waiting for a benevolent director to declare an interst in their work. More and more of them are staging their own plays, hence side-stepping the need for an independent director. Philippe Minyana, Catherine Anne, Valère Novarina and Olivier Py are just four of many authors (some with a background in the theatre business, some not) who have taken the creative power into their own hands. For example, Catherine Anne staged her play *Surprise* at the Théâtre de l'Aquarium (1996); Minyana directed his own *Drames Brefs 1* at the Menagerie de Verre (1996); Valère Novarina his *La Chair de l'homme* at the Théâtre du Rond-Point (1995), and *Le Jardin de reconnaisance* at the Théâtre de l'Athénée (1997), and Olivier Py achieved huge success with his five-play epic cycle *La Servante I* at the 1995 Avignon Festival, then at the Manufacture des Œillets, Ivry sur Seine (1966).

The advantages of being able to direct their own work for writers are clear: like Beckett, they can ensure that the rhythms of their language are respected and that stage effects appealing to the eye do not distract the audience from *hearing* the text. The playwright Joël Jouanneau believes, for example, that:

> One of the possibilities is getting away from the spectacu-
> lar, centring on the 'word', limiting and mastering every
> image, as we're working in a minefield. In this sense
> Sophocles and Aeschylus seem more relevant to me than
> Shakespeare. For them, violence doesn't take place on the
> stage, but through their words. Oedipus remains immo-
> bile. And it is this immobility which produces the violence
> offstage. Thus we need to return to a proliferation of
> words. I would like the quasi-immobility of characters to
> be what is *spectacular*.[31]

Jouanneau's words demonstrate that the classical heritage is never far from the mind of French playwrights. The struggle for renewal is expressed as a need to rediscover in a modern world

[31] Jouanneau, Joël, 'Comment résister au spectaculaire?', *La Revue du théâtre*, No.5, Actes Sud, 1994, p.13.

the secret of Racine, or of the Ancient Greek theatre, in which violent acts were kept offstage, but the words spoken onstage achieved such dramatic force that they could bring events to life before the spectators' eyes.

Playwrights in the 1990s: Fragmented Text and the Monologue

Today's experimental playwrights are thus rediscovering a traditional preoccupation of French theatre: finding new forms and structures which can give body to abstract ideas. Psychological states, emotions and themes are being used more and more frequently in place of character, and dramatic action is often internalised and verbalised, rather than being expressed in external activity. Mireille Davidovici of Théâtrales/l'association (see p.192) attempts to pin-point this tendency by relating it to the nature of the world we live in today, which writers are reflecting in their work: 'There exists a fragmentary kind of writing, material where there are no longer really characters nor plot, which reflects the fragmented world we live in.'[32]

The main influences for this emphasis on non-narrative text are clear. First, the experimentation with language in the work of writers such as Beckett and Ionesco is still as influential as ever in France. Second, the 'stream-of-consciousness' style of dialogue inherited from authors such as Duras and Sarraute also exerts a strong influence. Linked to this is the tendency away from what might be considered traditional theatrical language towards a new kind which borrows from the novel or poetry, which is then adapted to the theatrical genre. As Claude Confortès points out in his article 'Un Théâtre de poètes', published in 1996, Vilar's vision of a *théâtre de poètes* still lives on today: 'The theatre of poets is that of authors inventing their own language . . . They have their vision of the world to communicate. They cannot do otherwise.'[33] This reinvention of language is also due, in some part, to the growing use of non-

---

[32] Interviewed by Hervé Guay in *Le Devoir*, 4–5 January 1997.
[33] *Théâtre et Compagnie*, No.1, July–August 1996.

theatrical text to make theatre practised by leading directors such as Vitez during the last twenty years.

A prime example of an author who owes the origins of his texts to non-dramatically rooted language is Valère Novarina, whose *La Chair de l'homme* was a theatrical adaptation of his poetry by the same name. Others, meanwhile, have gradually developed a theatrical language of their own, by learning from their experiences within the theatre world. As Micheline Attoun points out on p.167, Noëlle Renaude's work at the Théâtre Ouvert set her on the road which spurred her on to write the expansive (four-hour-long) monologue *Ma Solange, comment vous écrire de mon désastre, Alex Roux*. In this play Renaude uses language from everyday life to paint verbal images of country existence. Recognisable speech patterns presented in an unusual form lend the work its humour. Neither Renaude's nor Novarina's plays rely on any realistic plot-based action, event or storyline to propel the work along, simply linking ideas by theme, emotion and almost 'musical' linguistic shape. Characters, as Minyana explains on p.177, are often no longer necessarily well-rounded identifiable personalities in plays today, but may be representative of a mood or type in a much more abstract way than has previously been seen.

In many contemporary works, there is also a reallocation of balance betweeen narrative, action and theme. This overall pic-ture may simply paint a mood, rather than seeking to develop it or bring it to a point of crisis. Koltès's plays may be thought of as setting the trend for this kind of writing, but, in contrast to much recent work, they contain a strong narrative thrust. In his *La nuit juste avant les forêts*, for example, dramatic monologue is used to relate the story of a homeless young Arab on the streets of Paris with immediacy and urgency: we want to know *what happens next* to the character. By contrast, in plays such as Nöelle Renaude's *Petits Rôles,* or Minyana's *Drames Brefs 1,* the authors are content to paint unrelated fragments of mood, linked by a common theme, which is not developed through a storyline, but explored from a variety of viewpoints. Azama's *Croisades* is another case in point. It deals with the atrocities of war in the form of a prologue followed by a series of self-contained scenes, or numbered sequences, which mix monologue and dialogue and poetic tone with everyday conversation. Rather than telling a story, the play presents a series of vignettes of the horrors of war through a collection of characters, switching viewpoint and focus from scene to scene.

Taking this principle one stage further, Olivier Py's *La Servante*, created originally for the 1995 Avignon Festival, consists of a series of self-contained plays, rather than scenes, linked together into a twenty-four-hour cycle, which was performed continuously and for the first time at Avignon 1995. *La Servante*, the title of the first play as well as the cycle as a whole, refers to the 'night-light', or ordinary light bulb on a simple stand which is left 'on guard' overnight on the stage of French theatres. This is a symbol which runs through the cycle of plays, and refers metaphorically to a young woman who in the first play sets up a contract with four male friends, asking them to go out and see the world, while she waits for them at home. Each of the subsequent plays tells the individual story of one of the men, who returns at the end to recount his story to her. The plays are designed cyclically, so that the end of the last play leads back to the beginning of the first, hence the play's full title, *La Servante, Histoire sans fin*. While each one play may be given independently, it is by the juxtaposition of one after the other that the full message of *La Servante* can be appreciated.

In terms of form, the monologue has been one of the most well-used options in the French theatre of recent years, owing its popularity to the opportunity it provides for both writers and actors. To the writer wishing to develop a theatre of '*la parole*', long virtuoso speeches offer the opportunity for elaborating a poetic idiom unrestrained by the needs of characterisation or day-to-day trivia. To the actor it provides plenty of scope for expressive use of voice, gesture, movement, even opportunities for playing against the text and, occasionally, for gross overacting. The prevalence of performed monologues emphasises the trend away from character and plot-led plays. Instead of the conflict between characters provided by traditional drama, these monologues rely on developing a linguistic landscape of sufficient power and fascination to hold the audience's attention through a whole evening of performance by a solo actor.

For a monologue to be a successful piece of live theatre, as playwrights Azama and Schmitt point out (see Interviews on pp.184 and 172), it needs to develop its own internal dramatic tension, either by implying conflict with other characters (as in Koltès's *La Nuit juste avant les forêts*) or by evoking events which occur as the monologue unfolds. Good contemporary examples of effective dramatic monologues are Eugène Durif's *Le petit bois* and Adel Hakim's *Exécuteur 14*, discussed below. Others, such as Renaude's *Ma Solange*, successfully feature a number of voices adopted by the performer within the extended monologue. But many other monologues written in recent years lack tension, conflict, or any other dramatic devices, attempting to replace these with heightened poetic language or emotional outbursts and lacking coherent dramatic structure. Such monologues give rise to confused performances in which verbose outpourings are unrelieved by visual variety of any kind. Their continued existence on so many French stages testifies to the logocentricity of French culture, always pulling against the love of spectacle. The influence of classical drama, in which the stage was seen as a place for high-flown discussion rather than for violent action, remains surprisingly powerful (see Joël Jouanneau's comment, p.108).

Contemporary French critics frequently cite poetic language as being a necessary quality for plays that are to succeed in the theatre. Eugène Durif's work provides a good example of an essentially poetic tone, which is particulary effective in works such as his dramatic monologue *Le petit bois*, written in 1985. In this monologue, the cruelty and incomprehensibility of the adult world is retold through the eyes of a child, isolated in his own world, within the society around him. Another essentially poetic monologue is Adel Hakim's *Executeur 14,* a shocking exposé of the nature of hatred and extremes of war and what it drives the human spirit to do. A man firmly set against war and bloodshed watches himself and his actions transformed, as war touches him personally and the murder of his child leads him to kill in return. It is Hakim's exploitation of this in strong, uncompromising language which provides a markedly chilling edge to the play.

Experimental Form and Social Issues

The works of Hakim and Azama discussed above show that concern for experimental form in contemporary French writing for the stage does not necessarily deny concern with social issues. Durif, too, has tackled major political issues of our time, notably the Algerian war (1954–62), which was the subject of *Tonkin-Alger* (1988) and *B.M.C.* (1991). The first is a fragmentary series of scenes depicting young French servicemen in a working-class district of Lyon on the eve of their departure for Algeria. *B.M.C.* is set in Algeria – the intitals B.M.C. stand for Bordel Militaire de Campagne – in a military brothel where a prostitute is awaiting her evening consignemnt of soldiers. This latter play consists of two monologues, one by the prostitute at the time of the war, the second by a young man of Algerian origins living in France a generation later. Through these monologues, Durif gives a voice to individuals who suffer the consequences of war but are seldom asked their opinion about it.

Another experimental author to have dramatised the consequences of the war is Daniel Lemahieu whose play *Djebels* (1988) consists of thirty-seven short fragmentary scenes in which French and Algerian perceptions of the war are contrasted. The Algerian author Fatima Gallaire has written movingly of the situation in Algeria today, her most successful play being *Princesses* (1988), which depicts a French-educated woman returning to her home village in Algeria where she meets death at the hands of religious and cultural fundamentalism.

Xavier Durringer is a popular young writer whose work confronts social issues, in his case combined with realist plot and recognisable individual characters with names, in plays such as his *Bal Trap* (1990) or *Une envie de tuer sur le bout de la langue* (1991). Both are notable for their very colourful use of the slang spoken by the streetwise youth of urban France today. They deal specifically with problems of unemployment and alcoholism, and develop an atmosphere of hard-hitting cynical despair. These two plays are conventional in structure if not in their language. More experimental is *Chroniques, des jours entiers, des nuits entières* (1996), a series of sketch-like pieces of monologue or dialogue featuring snippets of everyday life from various angles and viewpoints, with different voices or characters, some in monologues, some in dialogue form. The unifying threads between these short scenes are the theme of disillusionment with everyday life coupled with a richly colloquial use of language and situation; Durringer is especially observant of the nuances of relationships between men and women, neither of whom derive much satisfaction out of their lives of circumstances. It is this acute observation of human behaviour and speech patterns which makes his works and words recognisable to the audience, and accounts in some part for his popularity with young audiences.

Catherine Anne is another example of a playwright whose interest in experimental form has been applied to a social issue: child abuse. In *Agnès* (1994), she depicts a woman in her twenties coming to terms with the experience of having been sexually abused in childhood by her father. The play's five acts, divided into forty-five short scenes, are spread across the span of her whole life, with three actresses playing the part of Agnès (as child, teenager and mature woman). The chronological order is disrupted to give a sense of the heroine's obsessive return to painful scenes in her past, and her gradual ability to face her experience.

Most of Catherine Anne's plays employ a more conventional structure than *Agnès* and she has also written light-hearted comedies, such as her recent *Surprise*, which she directed at the Aquarium in 1996. She undertook this play with the express aim of writing something funny about the relationships between men and women. 'After *Agnès*, I got the urge to write and stage a light, fun play, a comedy . . . a comedy bringing into play, words and actions – failed and successful – romantic relationships today,' wrote Anne in the programme of *Surprise*. The play tells of two women, fed up with their dealings with men, who go on holiday to a house in Provence to escape for a while. The only problem is that the other side of the house has been let to two men, who are equally exasperated by the opposite sex and have also gone there to escape. Needless to say, romance between the two inevitably ensues.

Eugène Durif has also begun to develop a comic vein in his projected trilogy: *Via negativa, Nefs et naufrages* (both 1996) and *Les Tigres en papier* (in progress). *Via negativa* takes as its subject a group of former hippies from the 1960s – now an engineer, an executive in the communications business, a salesman for a pharmaceutical laboratory, a psychiatrist and a therapy addict – who are gathered together to try a new miracle anti-depressant drug. Instead they are forced to face up to the failure, or shallowness, of their philosophy and dashed hopes. *Nefs et naufrages* is a satirical look at the state of French theatre today, which builds up a hilarious image of the various power games played by workers in the French cultural industry.

Both Anne and Durif are examples of playwrights who are attempting to address the issues of the day through a variety of dramatic techniques. The thread running through all their work is a close observation of human relationships. Other examples of sensitively observed human dramas include Enzo Cormann's recent play *Ames Soeurs* (1996) which also explores a close relationship, in this case the love–hate relationship between a man and a woman who cannot live with each other, yet seem unable to live without each other. Natacha de Pontcharra's monologue *Mickey la Torche*, on the other hand, deals with loneliness and lack of close relationships, a situation which the author expolits for comic effect by clever use of language. The friendless and lonely Mickey is constantly facing disappointments both at home and at work. His obsession with his female neighbour involves him stooping to examine the contents of her rubbish bin to find out more about her private life; she, meanwhile, remains unaware of his existence, a situation which is strangely endearing and amusing as well as sad, thanks to Pontcharra's style of language and humour. As the programme of the most recent Paris production of the play (Guichet-Montparnasse, September 1996) explains, it is this use of language which gives the play its shape and meaning: 'Language is bastardised to his [Mickey's] image. It breaks with all usage and rules of rhetoric and grammar and causes more meanings to emerge, and casts light on Mickey's personality, which stands somewhere between blindness and lucidity, fear and daring, reality and fantasy, the lost and the found.'

Jean-Claude Grumberg is an excellent example of a playwright whose work since the 1970s has combined sociopolitical themes with an acute ear for dialogue and an experimental attitude to dramatic form. His first play, *Amorphe d'Ottenburg*, premièred at the Odéon in 1971, was the first of many works to centre on historical periods of violence or anti-Semitism, in this case drawing on Absurdist techniques with a strong influence of Jarry in its display of cruelty, systematic distortion of the truth and unrelieved egotism of most of the characters. His later play, *L'Atelier*, first staged at the Odéon in 1979, is based on his own family experiences. Born in 1939, he hardly knew his father, who was deported during the Occupation and never returned. His mother was obliged to work as a seamstress to support her family and Grumberg took her life in the post-war years as the subject matter for his play. While *L'Atelier* is classically Naturalistic in style, in contrast with the Absurdism of *Amorphe*, both plays demonstrate Grumberg's ability to turn any chosen style to good account when dealing with subjects of urgent human and political dimensions, such as anti-Semitism. Another characteristic of his plays, which he shares with other dramatists who have been commercially successful such as Anouilh, is his frequent exploitation of self-conscious theatricality as a way of commenting on character or situation. An early example of this is *En r'venant d'l'Expo* (1975), which considers the function of the popular cabaret-style of entertainment known as *le café concert* as a focus of nationalist sentiment in the years leading up to the First World War.

These tendencies are also evident in his more recent plays, and again he illustrates his ability to switch adeptly from style to style. *Maman revient pauvre orphelin* (1994), for example, is an autobiographical piece, dealing with the same early experience of life as in *L'Atelier*, but in a much more dreamlike, less Naturalistic manner. *Rêver peut-être* (1996 – the title is a quotation from Hamlet: 'perchance to dream') also uses dream sequences with such success that it becomes very difficult to draw the line between what is 'reality' and what is 'dream'. The play centres on an actor who is in the process of rehearsing the role of Hamlet for a production of Shakespeare's play. He wakes up one morning to a knock on the door from a strange police-woman who accuses him of murder. In the plot which follows, it emerges that he committed this 'murder' in a dream and his attempts to clear himself become as convoluted and elusive as those of K in Kafka's *The Trial*. The play rings the changes on the theme of identity without losing sight of the pain at the heart of the actor's dilemma, and Grumberg uses dream techniques with a lightness of touch and considerable humour.

These same qualities also ensured the popularity of his play *Adam et Eve*, directed by Gildas Bourdet in February 1997 at the Théâtre National de Marseille – La Criée – and later at the Théâtre de Chaillot, April 1997. Adam and Eve, two middle-aged Jews, who used to frequent the cafés of Paris's tenth *arrondissement* in the years following the war to discuss the communist ideologies and hopes for the future, return to one of their former haunts, for old times' sake. Now settled in the unradical suburbs, with Adam confined to a wheelchair, returning here forces the couple to confront the fact that everything has changed, from the café's ownership to their vision of the future. Against a backdrop of pre-millennium and middle-aged angst, they discover that their relationship is perhaps the only thing of which they can be entirely certain. The closely observed characterisation and humorous light touch Grumberg employs in this play, as in others, means that he is able to combine complex cultural references with entertaining dramatic action. His ability to appeal to a wide audience perhaps explains why he is one of the few authors whose plays are frequently staged in the subsidised theatres but then may transfer to enjoy successful second runs in private theatres.

CHAPTER 4

PRIVATE THEATRE
IN THE 1990s

According to the French understanding of the term, *Théâtre privé* implies a self-governing and self-funding structure, usually with a theatre practitoner at the helm, even if the building itself is let by a disinterested party (insurance companies or other businesses are often the landlords of private theatres). The term applies to a specific group of theatres which should not be confused with the large number of 'independent' theatres operating in the capital, such as the Théâtre de la Bastille or the Rond-Point. The latter receive money from the government or the city of Paris for productions in grants which may be paid directly to the theatre, or come indirectly through the company performing there. True 'private' theatres referred to here do not have this advantage, although they organise their own self-help scheme through which theatres can recoup losses (see Fonds de soutien below). Few private theatres are owned by those directing them; the Poche, Variétés and Palais Royal theatres are the best-known exceptions. Most pay a rent which is fixed according to the number of seats the theatre holds.

Private-theatre seat prices are usually higher than in state-run theatres, reflecting higher rates of value-added tax on private-theatre seats and the small amount of financial aid available from public sources. In 1995 the fifty-three private theatres in Paris received a total of 52 million francs from the Direction du Théâtre, while the five national theatres alone received 317.5 million francs and the CDNs 305.9 million francs from the same source (see statistics quoted below, pp.152–3). The city of Paris also helps to subsidise certain private theatres and gives general encouragement to theatre-goers with its annual two-for-the-price-of-one ticket deal for many productions in the capital.

Many Parisian private theatres also subscribe to the Association pour le soutien du Théâtre privé, set up in 1964 and financed by a tax on ticket revenues from participating venues, as well as by voluntary contributions and allocations from state and city funds (the city of Paris allocated it 17.4 million francs in 1996). This association, open to any theatre of over 200 seats, is designed to help private theatres balance outgoings with receipts on a given production, 200–500-seaters usually receiving the most help. Aid may be provided from its Fonds de soutien for help with staging productions or promoting them, for structural improvements or equipment required to put on a particular play. The amount given varies according to the play: premières of new French work attract more help than classics or one-man shows. The Fonds de soutien also allocates money to help any of the first three plays by a new French playwright, and to help a production that has been slow to get an audience, but where the attendance figures are picking up, under a scheme known as L'Aide au second souffle (Aid for a second wind). Fourteen smaller private theatres have recently grouped together to form the Fédération des petites scènes de Parisiennes, which also attracts funding from the city of Paris (130,000 francs in 1996). Its goal is to fight for a place for smaller theatres, claiming that these are essential if unknown actors, directors and playwrights are to emerge.

Since 1945, the private theatre sector, which today accounts for half the total theatre-going in France, has faced increasing competition from the public theatres, which can produce elaborate shows while still being able to keep ticket prices at reasonable levels, thanks to government subsidy. Like all commercial theatres, the French private theatres need plays which can guarantee a long run in order to cover production costs. The trend in British commercial theatre, of housing transfers from the subsidised sector, has not yet become common practice in France, where private theatres usually prefer to mount their own productions, chosen carefully to appeal to a particular middle-class and fairly conservative public.

Private Theatre and the Star Actor;
Theatre and Cinema

A long-standing tactic for attracting audiences to the private theatre is to cast star actors whose names alone will guarantee a flurry of attention in the press. This is not a recent trend, nor is it limited to private theatres, though in France today such crowd-pulling actors have usually made their reputation in films before they return, sporadically, to the stage. Almost fifty years ago, when Gérard Philipe attracted record attendances at his performances of Corneille's *Le Cid* and Kleist's *Prince of Homburg* (Avignon Festival, 1951), the public flocked to see a film star who had begun his career as a stage actor and had never lost touch with the theatre. Recent examples are mostly stars who have been discovered by the cinema. In autumn 1996, for example, the film star Emmanuelle Béart played opposite the experienced stage actor Pascal Greggory in Strindberg's *Playing with Fire* at the Bouffes du Nord; Pierre Arditi took time out from films to perform with Marcel Maréchal and Robert Hirsch in *En attendant Godot* at the Rond-Point; and Alain Delon and Francis Huster helped to make Eric Emmanuel Schmitt's philosophical play *Variations énigmatiques* the hit of the season at the Marigny theatre. The success of the latter was in no small part due to the rarity value of seeing Delon on stage for the first time in twenty-eight years. Standing ovations, colour splashes in magazines and plenty of air time on French television made a star of Eric Emmanuel Schmitt, too, with press and television interviews about the production.

In general, it would be true to say that closer links exist between theatre and cinema in France than is the case in English-speaking countries. In France, actors, writers or directors who want to work in films do not have to travel to Hollywood, but can remain in Paris, where both theatre and film careers can be developed concurrently. Success in both art forms is recognised by the award of prestigious annual prizes modelled on Hollywood's 'Oscars'. The awards made by the French film industry are known as 'Césars', while the theatre awards are called 'Molières'. The latter are sponsored by an independent body, L'Association professionnelle et artistque du théâtre, and recognise commercial as well as artistic success. Actors are not the only ones to enjoy the flexibility offered by being able to work in both media: many dramatists work for the cinema as well as writing stage plays. Even directors find it relatively easy to cross over to the cinema and return to theatre. The most notable example of this in recent years is Patrice Chéreau, whose film career began in the early 1980s with art movies such as *L'Homme blessé* (1983) and who went on to enjoy commercial success with *La Reine Margot* (1994). To a certain extent Chéreau can be seen as the natural heir of the New Wave film directors of the previous generation and he enjoys a similar prestige.

Plays and Playwrights in the Private Theatres

In terms of repertoire, the private theatres of Paris today are a far cry from the pocket theatres of the Left Bank in the 1940s and 1950s where the Theatre of the Absurd was launched. The tradition which they inherit is that of the 'boulevard comedy', which had its heyday in the boulevard theatres of the Parisian Right Bank in the nineteenth century. The major playwrights of that period who were responsible for honing the genre of French Farce – Georges Feydeau, Eugène Labiche, Georges Courteline – remain staples of the private theatres to this day, while their milder colleagues who wrote light romantic comedies are largely forgotten. A significant number of twentieth-century playwrights have made successful careers writing 'boulevard comedies': Sacha Guitry, Marcel Aymé, André Roussin, Marcel Achard, Félicien Marceau were all prolific writers of light comedies which, while centring on a romantic plot, provided witty comments of a gentle kind on their life and times. Their plays use many of the devices of nineteenth-century French Farce, but lack the obsessive frenzy and acerbic cruelty of some of the best plays by Feydeau or Labiche. In the last twenty years few playwrights have continued in this tradition and those who have, such as Marc Camoletti, have turned more towards the genre of sex comedy. An outstanding exception is Françoise Dorin, who continues the tradition of earlier years, supplying the private sector with witty comedies which view contemporary society with a detached, sardonic smile.

In addition to light comedies, private theatres will, from time to time, put on plays with greater literary pretensions. Most of Jean Anouilh's works were originally staged in such venues, and his successors today are Eric Emmanuel Schmitt, Yasmina Reza and Jean-Marie Besset. In the interview on p.170, Schmitt explains that many authors find they must tailor their work to the expectations of the audience they will attract in a private theatre. Like other writers whose work is performed in both public and private theatres, he has to decide for which sector a new play is more suitable, both in tone and in subject matter. In this sense, therefore, there is as much a creative divide between public and private theatre as there is in terms of funding and audiences.

Yasmina Reza's '*Art*' provides a good example of the kind of play which is successful in private theatre. It opened at the Comédie des Champs-Elysées, directed by Patrice Kerbrat, in 1994, where it enjoyed a long run. Staged in 1996 at Wyndham's theatre in London by Matthew Warchus, translated by Christopher Hampton, it was dubbed 'the quintessential West End play' by Robert Butler, drama critic of the *Independent on Sunday*. It charts developments in the relationship between three friends, Marc, Serge and Yvan, through their reactions to the purchase by Serge of a piece of modern art. Their responses to the abstract painting (an entirely white canvas) provide the catalyst for Reza's characters to come out with hitherto unvoiced jealousies, confusions and other strong emotions. The plot is minimal and in this sense Reza employs a similar approach to many of her more poetic contemporaries. But the discussions between the characters remain well within the limits of what might realistically be probable in a relationship between comfortably-off professional-class characters. Some interesting insights into male bonding and some witty comments are made in passing, but the overall impression is of a rather lightweight vehicle for three virtuoso actors, owing a certain amount to Pinter, but lacking his dangerous edge. Likewise, in her play *Conversation après un enterrement* (1986) the backbone of the play is a complex web of family relationships which surface after a family tragedy. Here, too, character study is to the fore, as Reza explores the feelings of each member of the family towards the others, using the situation as a catalyst. It is interesting to note that her play *L'Homme du hasard*, staged by Patrick Alexsandre at the Théâtre Hébertot in 1995, did not enjoy the same success and features a different approach. In this play there are two characters, named simply '*la femme*' and '*l'homme*', whose conversation face to face in a railway carriage forms the basis of the play. The fact that Reza does not name her characters, and that both setting and action are more static than in her other plays, may explain why it was not successful in the private theatre. In many ways it is more characteristic of work by authors staged in public theatres such as Minyana or Renaude.

Eric Emmanuel Schmitt's plays are similar to those of Reza in that he too enjoys character and relies on well-tried dramatic structures, as he explains in the interview on p.172. A philosopher by background, having written a doctoral thesis on Diderot, he introduces a philosophical theme to all his plays, although their elegantly phrased, witty dialogue ensures that they remain accessible, flattering their audiences' sense of their own cleverness. In *Le Visiteur*, for example, Schmitt's protagonist is Sigmund Freud and the location specified is Vienna in the spring of 1938, when Hitler had just annexed Austria, and Freud was facing the prospect of exile. Against this grim background Schmitt allows whimsical dialogue to develop. A character named '*L'inconnu*' comes, uninvited, to Freud's apartment, claiming to be God. Freud, who is in a nervous state, vacillates between believing him and dismissing him as simply a madman on the run from the Gestapo. As they discuss religion, Judaism, Fascism and the difficulties of political commitment, Schmitt preserves the enigma as to the real identity of the visitor. In *La Nuit de Valognes* (translated by Jeremy Sams as *Don Juan on Trial* for an RSC production at The Other Place in 1996), Schmitt imagines Don Juan as an old man, summoned to an eighteenth-century chateau where he is confronted by the women he has betrayed. They place him on trial and oblige him to admit that the failure of his life was when he fell in love with a young man who did not return his affection and whom he failed to seduce.

Schmitt's recent play *Le Libertin*, staged by Bernard Murat at the Gaîté Montparnasse in 1997, again takes eighteenth-century morals for its subject. Denis Diderot is the central character and his web of amorous affairs and casuistic moralising forms the mainspring not only of the plot, but also of the humour in the play, supplying ample scope for farcical hide-and-seek and libertine romps alongside philosophical musings. Diderot ponders on such subjects as hypocrisy, love and family values as he attempts to put together the entry on 'Morality' for his encyclopedia. Again, Schmitt combines conventional dramatic structure with well-crafted dialogue and witty philosophical discussion, blending comedy with thematic depth, which the audience is free to appreciate on several levels. As Schmitt says on p.170, his intent is to write plays for everyone to enjoy, from his grandmother to his intellectual friends. In pursuit of this aim he will occasionally write specifically for a star actor, as in the case of *Variations énigmatiques* (Marigny, 1996), written for Alain Delon. The play enacts a psychological duel of words, pitting a reclusive writer (played by Delon) against a journalist who tries to come and reawaken memories of a past love affair. Their battle of wits is conducted through elegant dialogue which enables Schmitt to pass comments on the state of Europe today.

Jean-Marie Besset is a young playwright whose first play was performed in the subsidised sector, but whose subsequent works have enjoyed success in private theatres. *Villa Lucco*, staged at the Théâtre National de Strasbourg in 1990, presents an imaginary encounter between de Gaulle and Pétain after the liberation of France in 1944. Through this device, Besset is able to comment on the way circumstances may have as much to do as political beliefs in the line dividing the traitor from the hero. His recent plays, which have enjoyed critical as well as commercial success, are calculated to appeal to the audiences of the private sector. They present plot-led scenes of modern French life at the top end of the social spectrum, with recognisable characters and realistic settings.

Ce qui arrive et ce qu'on attend (Gaîté Montparnasse, 1993) combined a caustic examination of the power games played in government circles with a sensitively handled love affair between two men – not a subject frequently dealt with in modern French drama. *Un Coeur français* (Hébertot, 1996) develops further Besset's jaundiced view of corruption among the French ruling élite, and *Grande Ecole* (Théâtre 14, 1995), which won him a 'Molière' prize for best playwright, investigates the pressured lives of the students training to join that élite at one of the selective training academies for high-fliers. These are elegant and witty plays, which rely on developing complex characters through a coventional dramatic structure, building to a moment of crisis in which characters confront one another and reveal themselves in a new light. In *Grande Ecole*, for example, the fragile harmony among the students sharing a flat is disrupted when one of them, Paul, brings home a boy-friend, Mécir, who comes from a deprived background, worlds away from that of the students. The disruption is used to suggest the divisiveness of a system which encourages a small class of young people to assume a privileged position, separated from the majority of the population. But critical comments of this kind are not hammered home, still less do they proceed from an overt ideological position. Rather, they are hinted at, while the emotional confusions of the characters remain firmly in the foreground.

As this brief examination has shown, the best contemporary works in the private sector have much in common with mainstream commercial Anglo-American notions of what is theatrically effective and this may explain why Reza, Schmitt and Besset have all enjoyed success in the UK, USA, Germany and elsewhere in the world, while the less commercially successful playwrights have won contemporary French drama a reputation for being rather verbose:

> French authors have difficulty finding takers outside France. Sabine Bossan, of Entr'Actes, whose task is to promote them, recognises that contemporary French theatre has the reputation of being wordy. It's a difficult reproach to refute, inasmuch as fewer and fewer foreigners are capable of reading French authors in the original, given the

decline of French as an international language. In other respects, contemporary French theatre is equally disconcerting because it often emphasises the musicality of the word, because of its fragmentary nature, because the destruction of character is common currency and because of the absence of dramatic progression which sometimes distinguishes it.[1]

The plays which have done well in the UK, such as Grumberg's *L'Atelier* or Reza's '*Art*', are those which have employed traditional plot, structure and characterisation, rather than experimenting with form and language like much of the work to be seen in French public theatres today. But through events such as the 1997 French Theatre season in London, assisted by Entr'Actes and AFAA, it is to be hoped that more of the diversity of contemporary French theatre will be brought to foreign audiences, and that collaboration between theatre professionals in France and other countries will continue to develop.

---

[1] Hervé Guay in *Le Devoir*, 4–5 January 1997.

CHAPTER 5

AVIGNON AND SUMMER FESTIVALS

Although the summer months see many of the urban theatres closing their doors for their *'fermeture annuelle'*, or annual break, the French theatre scene continues all year round, thanks to the many arts festivals up and down the country during July and August, when there is a mass exodus from the cities to the countryside. The festival bonanza owes its creative and idealistic origins to the success of the Avignon Festival, the biggest and by far the most important in theatre terms, which held its fiftieth birthday celebrations in July 1996. The Festival was begun in 1947 by Jean Vilar, whose philosophy of popular theatre grew and developed at the same time as the Festival. The ideas he formed through his experiences at Avignon over the years were to be influential on French political thinking concerning decentralisation of the arts.

At the time of the Festival's founding, in the midst of a post-war mood of renewed idealism in cultural and political terms, Vilar set out to bring the classic repertoire to new audiences in such a way as to expose them not only to great theatre, but also to broad issues concerning society and the world they lived in. He aimed 'to renew theatre and collective forms of art by providing a more open space, to bring a breath of fresh air to an art form stifling in antechambers, cellars and salons'.[1] Following the success of the Avignon experiment, a plethora of festivals have been set up all over France, often with mixed motives. Many provincial towns realised that the benefits of a festival would not only be cultural, but also bring a source of financial prosperity.

The number of arts festivals in France each year recognised by

---

[1] Avignon Festival official publication, 1996.

the Ministry of Culture now stands at around 600 (for details of the main theatre events, see the Information Section). Alongside theatre festivals, the gamut of events includes dance, music, opera, performance art, street theatre, puppet theatre, circus arts, cartoon drawing and design. Some events have come to represent the annual mecca for performing arts professionals in a particular field. For example, while Avignon is the pre-eminent meeting place for theatre workers, particularly those in the public sector, so Chalon-sur-Saône provides the annual point of congregation for street theatre performers, and Aix-en-Provence is the home of opera and music theatre.

As well as festivals organised by a local council, there also exist a number of events hosted by individual theatres, many of which are reputed for the quality of their work: Enfantillages or children's theatre at the Théâtre Gérard Philipe, Saint-Denis; Coups de Théâtre, a week-long festival of work by new play-wrights at the Scène National in Poitiers; Rencontres Théâtrales de Hérisson at Les Fédérés in Montluçon and Théâtre en mai at the Théâtre National de Dijon are just a few examples.

Since the early days of decentralisation, the funding for festivals has been provided by state, regional and local authorities. However, the explosion of festivals in recent years has put serious strains on the funding available from such sources. Even the Avignon Festival is facing a drop in real terms in the funding it receives from the town, as Bernard Faivre d'Arcier, the current director of the festival, explains in the interview on p.182. Although sponsorship from private companies, such as Perrier at Avignon in 1996, helps to make up for shortfalls from official sources, there is a distinct possibility that cuts in public funding will reduce the number of festivals in years to come.

In artistic terms, the variations in size and quality of theatre festivals across France is enormous. After Avignon, the festival with the greatest prestige is doubtless the Festival d'Automne held in Paris every autumn. This was founded in 1972 by Michel Guy, who went on to be Secretary of State for Culture under President Giscard d'Estaing (1975–6). Guy secured funding from both the state and the city of Paris, which he used to bring directors of international standing to Paris, but also to encourage young playwrights and performers. Among the former, invited in the course of the festival's twenty-five years, have been Robert Wilson, Giorgio Strehler, Tadeusz Kantor, Peter Stein, Klaus Michael Grüber and Peter Brook, while the young playwrights and performers have included Jean-Marie Patte, Jérôme Deschamps, Valère Novarina, François Tanguy and Catherine Anne. Guy's vigorous direction (until his death in 1990) and his real enthusiasm for international avant-garde work led to the Festival's gradual expansion, to the point where it is now spread over three months and ensures that top-quality international work is seen in the capital during the early part of the theatre season every year. In 1996, under the direction of Alain Crombecque, the Festival included productions by Robert Wilson, Peter Brook, Stéphane Braunschweig, François Tanguy, Robert Lepage and Carmelo Bene, as well as dance events by the Merce Cunningham Dance Company and other major companies.

Paris also has its summer festival. The Quartiers d'été Festival has proved a successsful response to those who claimed that no public remained in Paris during July and August, and the organisers have been able to counter the claim that Paris theatre is 'dead' during the summer months. Nevertheless, the majority of festivals take place away from Paris during this period. The first festival of the summer is Théâtre en mai, which has been situated in Dijon since 1991, promoting the work of young companies from France and abroad. The Festival International des Francophonies at Limoges is an important event featuring plays written in French from francophone countries all over the world, and also takes place in May. In June, Strasbourg's Turbulences follows; then the regional troupe-based Festival de Saint-Herblain (near Nantes); the Printemps des comédiens Actors' Festival in Montpellier; and the Lille Festival du Prato for clowns and other performance artists. These lead up to Avignon in July, although this is not the only festival to take place during this month. Others include the *Festival d'Alès*, organised by Les Amis du Théâtre Populaire and based around the local Scène National, Le Cratère, Grenoble has acted as annual host to the Festival de Théâtre Européen since July 1985, welcoming companies from all over Europe for performances and debates, while Blaye, a relative newcomer since its beginnings in 1990, focuses on encouraging the emergence of new talent, especially in the region of Aquitaine. Festivals at Aurillac and Sarlat also take place in July, together with the mime festival at Périgueux.

Despite the large number of such festivals, more details of which are included in the Information Section, Avignon remains by far the most important and its history provides useful material for reflection on French theatre in society during the second half of the twentieth century.

The Avignon Festival

For three weeks every year, this ancient Provençal town is taken over by theatre troupes of every kind, from major international companies to experimental or student groups. The official festival offers some thirty productions, many of which are given on open-air stages in different parts of the town and its environs, as well as concerts, lectures and music theatre performances. Hundreds more companies perform in the 'Off' festival, Avignon's answer to the Edinburgh fringe, and the narrow medieval roads are constantly crowded with street performers, artists and parading actors touting their companies' productions. The management of the Festival is a full-time operation, with permanently staffed offices in Paris and Avignon (see Information Section for addresses).

Its story began in 1947, when Vilar was invited to put on his acclaimed production of T. S. Eliot's *Murder in the Cathedral* in the courtyard, or Cour d'honneur, of the Papal palace, to tie in with an exhibition of modern art. At first he refused, finding the vast expanse of the courtyard intimidating, but he was persuaded to change his mind and proposed three other plays to be performed alongside the Eliot: Shakespeare's *Richard II*, Paul Claudel's *Tobie et Sara* and Maurice Clavel's *La Terrasse de midi*. The setting and the simple open-air stage lent the productions an atmosphere of ritual solemnity, which also helped to establish the reputation of Avignon and the Cour d'honneur as a performance space. Vilar's work at Avignon began to attract well-known actors, drawn not only by the atmosphere and excitement, but also by the timing in July, when most theatres were closed. His productions of Corneille's *Le Cid* and Kleist's *The Prince of Homburg* in 1951, both with the charismatic young Gérard Philipe in the lead, were outstanding successes. Both remain classic reference points in French theatre to this day, illustrating the mythical spirit of Avignon during the exciting period of its first few years.

The public appreciation shown in audiences of over 10,000 for these 1951 productions was taken by Vilar as evidence that his vision of '*théâtre populaire*' really could work. This vision involved bringing the classics to new audiences in an exciting contemporary style which underlined their continuing relevance to modern society. It was a vision that continued to influence his direction of the Festival after 1951, the year when he was also appointed director of the Théâtre National Populaire at the Théâtre de Chaillot in Paris (see p.13). Approaching the vast space of the Chaillot theatre stage in the same spirit as the open-air space in Avignon, he continued to pursue the same goal of making theatre available to a mass audience. Each year Vilar's TNP company would put on a new production in the Cour d'honneur, which it would then perform in the Chaillot theatre the following season. Particularly memorable examples of productions which achieved a relevance to contemporary events were Brecht's *The Resistible Rise of Arturo Ui* in 1960, when it seemed as though de Gaulle might be willing to compromise with right-wing forces in the army, and Giraudoux's *La Guerre de Troie n'aura pas lieu* in 1962, the year of the peace negotiations to end the Algerian war.

In the early 1960s the Festival had grown to the point where it was attracting 50,000 spectators a year and it was no longer possible for it to revolve around a single company. Vilar resigned from the TNP in 1963 and devoted his time to enlarging the artistic scope of the Festival, inviting productions by younger directors – Roger Planchon, Jorge Lavelli, Antoine Bourseiller – and introducing new performing-arts disciplines, notably modern dance, with Maurice Béjart's company, Les

Ballets du vingtième siècle, performing in the Cour d'honneur. He also opened up a number of new venues, exploiting the possibilites for performance offered by former monastic buildings such as the Cloître des Carmes and the Cloître des Célestins. This expansion made it possible for the Festival to include contemporary work alongside the popular revivals of the classics. Antoine Bourseiller, for example, was responsible for staging works by François Billetdoux and Philippe Adrien.

By 1967, audience figures had doubled to 100,000, two thirds of this number being young people under the age of thirty. In 1968 Avignon became the focus for the revolutionary spirit aroused during the near-revolution of May. When the American Living Theatre Company arrived to rehearse their productions for the festival, their 'hippy' and provocative behaviour was sufficient to upset the conservative local community. Relations between actors and locals became progressively worse when the Préfet du Gard banned a production by the young local company, Théâtre du Chêne Noir, called *La Paillasse aux seins nus*, which they were planning to present alongside the official Festival. The Living Theatre, joined by youngsters fresh from Paris and filled with revolutionary fervour, protested vehemently, demanding that all events in the Festival should be free, or it should cease at once.

While providing a forum for debate and attempting to allow all sides freedom of speech, Vilar came in for violent criticism when he refused to let the protesters bring the Festival to a halt. He was branded 'fascist' for his insistence that events should proceed according to the programme and that spectators should not be admitted unless they had paid for tickets. Deeply shocked and wounded by such attitudes, Vilar attempted to defend his vision of the Festival. A few months later he suffered a heart attack from which he never recovered, dying in 1971. In his wake, Paul Puaux, who had been his assistant, took over the running of the Festival, determined to continue and build on Vilar's work.

During the 1970s the Cour d'honneur, no longer the preserve of the TNP, welcomed many major companies. These included the Comédie-Française in 1972 with Shakespeare's *Richard III*,

Benno Besson's production of *The Caucasian Chalk Circle* by Brecht and Otomar Krejca's *En attendant Godot* by Beckett, both in 1978. However, still more famous to this day are probably Robert Wilson's *Einstein on the Beach* from 1976, Antoine Vitez's four Molière productions in 1978 and the Théâtre du Soleil's *Mephisto*, adapted and directed by Ariane Mnouchkine in 1979. Modern dance, first introduced by Vilar, was expanded with invitations to Carolyn Carlson, Merce Cunningham and others, while new writing was promoted by Lucien and Micheline Attoun, who founded Théâtre Ouvert at the Festival in 1971.

In 1979 Paul Puaux handed on the direction of the Festival to Bernard Faivre d'Arcier. He proceeded to take a new look at how the Festival was run. He considered that it was time to rethink the organisational set-up and to renew the funding base. Helped by the election of Mitterrand and the Socialist government in 1981, he was able to secure a fresh injection of funds and to restructure the Festival's administration, welcoming Jack Lang, now Minister of Culture, on to the board of directors. He also renewed the staging in the Cour d'honneur, so as to allow more flexible production arrangements and more comfortable seating. Young, relatively untried directors were encouraged to present their work there, including Georges Lavaudant, Daniel Mesguich and André Engel. In 1983 the Cour d'honneur saw the staging of two contemporary works directed by Jean-Pierre Vincent, followed by Mnouchkine's memorable Shakespeare cycle in 1984: the new generation of directors had well and truly arrived.

In 1985 Alain Crombecque arrived to take over from Faivre d'Arcier. His term in charge saw the introduction of poetry, music and non-European arts to the Festival. He implemented a plan of focusing on the culture of a different civilisation each year. India, for example, was the focus in 1985, when Peter Brook's and Jean-Claude Carrière's adaptation of *The Mahabharata* was performed in a quarry at Boulbon, which spectators could reach by taking a boat along the Rhône from Avignon. Crombecque's years in charge are also remembered for Vitez's staging of Paul Claudel's great epic *Le Soulier de satin*,

Patrice Chéreau's *Hamlet* in 1988, as well as numerous contemporary productions of work by authors such as Robert Pinget, Aimé Césaire and Valère Novarina. In 1983 Crombecque left to direct the Festival d'Automne and Faivre d'Arcier returned to Avignon, where he is still director today.

Avignon since 1993

Faivre d'Arcier's aim for his second period of office has been to develop Avignon as a centre of European theatre, as well as to ensure a number of new productions are created specially for the Festival each year, including at least one newly written work. Under the increasing pressure of having to reconcile financial stringency with artistic merit, the Festival now works on co-productions with Centres Dramatiques from all over France, which are launched at Avignon. The Cour d'honneur continues to attract 'star' directors and large-scale productions which make the most of the extensive stage space, as well as the venue's unmistakable atmosphere and cachet: Alain Françon's staging of Edward Bond's *War Plays* in 1994 was one notable example. New writing still finds its place: in 1997 Olivier Py has been invited to stage his new play *Le Visage d'Orphée* in the Cour d'honneur, following the critical success of his *La Servante* which played twenty-four hours non-stop in 1995.

Although the Cour d'honneur remains a central part of the Festival, a large range of other venues has now become established, offering complementary programmes. The Festival has other large open-air auditoria, for example the Lycée Saint-Joseph seating up to 800, or the Cloître des Carmes, and it also makes occasional use of other sites in and around the town, including the quarry at Boulbon, where *The Mahabharata* was performed in 1985. There are, too, some enclosed theatre buildings, used when flown scenery or special staging requires it: the Municipal theatre, the Salle Benoît XII, and the Chapelle des Pénitents blancs, as well as various gymnasia and deconsecrated churches. In 1996 the official festival took in twenty-nine venues, with fifty productions in total to celebrate its fiftieth anniversary, selling some 109,200 tickets over three weeks. In

1997 the Festival comprises only half this number of productions, in order to concentrate on quality rather than numbers, especially in the light of reduced funding from the town of Avignon (see Faivre d'Arcier, p.182).

Funding currently comes from the Ministry of Culture (whose subsidy remained unchanged between 1996 and 1997), as well as from the town of Avignon (5 million francs in 1997) and from the region. To this is added money from ticket sales and a range of sponsors. In 1995 these included three new names: Perrier (giving support for dance productions); the French Post Office and the Franco-German television station ARTE.

Alongside the official festival there have been alternative or fringe productions since 1966, when the local author André Benedetto staged his play *Statues* and founded La Nouvelle Compagnie d'Avignon. He was soon followed by other local troupes, the Chêne Noir, for example. By 1971 the number of unofficial events had developed to such an extent that the phrase 'Off' was coined by an American journalist, comparing it to the 'Off-Broadway' scene in New York. The name stuck and is still in current use to refer to the body of independent productions going on at the same time as the official festival, sometimes referred to as the 'In'. In 1983 the Avignon Public-Off association was formed by Alain Léonard with the aim of offering support to independent companies, providing advice and promoting plays through its programme of 'Off' events for member companies. Venues around Avignon come in all shapes and sizes, ranging from small theatres to barns, basements, converted warehouses and outdoor courtyards.

In terms of content there is no real qualitative difference between the best of the 'Off' and the 'In', with many actors and other theatre professionals having worked in both. The main difference is in the vast range of performing arts covered by the 'Off' programme, including comedy, cabaret, stand-up, mime and acrobatics. The 'Off' is open to anyone having the wherewithal to mount a production, while the 'In' consists of a specifically selected and invited programme. In 1996, 482 shows were presented 'Off', drawn from all over the world, in ninety-five different performance spaces and at times ranging from 10 a.m. to 2 a.m. Undoubtedly the parades, paraphernalia and general liveliness of the 'Off' adds to the festive mood throughout the town and attracts large audiences of its own. It has also taken up the cause of contemporary authors, promoting them by publishing a list of writers present at the Festival in the programme. In 1996 over 80 per cent of the plays performed 'Off' were by living writers. While the official festival continues to attract the vast proportion of critical interest in national papers, the 'Off' is popular with the local press, although critics from the national papers can sometimes be persuaded to attend its productions. Most important, however, is that the 'Off' is tremendously popular with the public, a fact that remains a major determinant of the Festival's success and adds to the popular and festive mood in Avignon, an achievement which vindicates the original enterprise of Jean Vilar.

CHAPTER 6

INSTITUTIONAL
DEVELOPMENTS 1968–1997

The Comédie-Française

The radical questioning of all accepted practices in the French theatre provoked by the events of May 1968 had its effects on the old-established institutions, as well as on avant-garde companies such as the Théâtre du Soleil. The first and most famous casualty of the events was the Odéon theatre in the heart of the Latin quarter. Under Jean-Louis Barrault in the 1960s, this had been the site of some of the most exciting and challenging theatre available, including the premières of Ionesco's *Rhinocéros* in 1960 and of Genet's *Les Paravents* in 1966. Genet's play had provoked riots, both in the theatre and in the streets outside; perhaps a flavour of political dissidence had rubbed off on this venerable old edifice. Whether for this reason, or rather because it was close to the centres of student unrest, it was the Odéon that was occupied, on 15 May, by the student *contestataires*, and which served as forum for impassioned debates which continued around the clock for the next four weeks. When the theatre reopened, nearly a year later, it was without a permanent company and there was a plan to make it into a showcase for the best of the provincial companies. But by the end of 1971 the Comédie-Française had taken over control of the theatre (which had once been its home before the French Revolution). For part of the year it served as a second house for Comédie-Française productions, and for the other part it housed guest productions by foreign or provincial companies visiting Paris.

The Comédie-Française itself appeared relatively untouched by the events of 1968. It continued to perform its classic repertoire as before and was able to persuade the government to devote a large slice of the reduced spending on theatre to a much-needed overhaul of its main theatre, the Salle Richelieu (1974–6). It did not entirely escape the commotions of the time, however, suffering repeated disruptions by strikes among the technical staff. In 1973 these disputes closed the theatre. To show that the company was not out of touch with the liberated spirit of the times it set up a circus tent in the Tuileries gardens, where performances took place until a settlement was reached. Meanwhile, at the Conservatoire (the training ground for new recruits to the Comédie-Française) far-reaching changes had begun to take place with the appointment, in 1968, of Pierre-Aimé Touchard. For the first time, he introduced work on the contemporary repertoire into the school which had hitherto concentrated exclusively on the classics. He also made a number of inspired appointments, including Antoine Vitez, who, for the previous three years, had been teaching at the Lecoq school. In 1974 Touchard was succeeded by Jacques Rosner, formerly Planchon's assistant at Lyon, and the changes accelerated. Symptomatic of the new spirit was Rosner's abolition of the '*concours de sortie*' (passing out competition). Previously, all the students had competed for a 'placing' in the last year of their studies and the results were published in the form of a graded list. Rosner insisted on the need for a more collaborative attitude towards actor training, reducing the tendency of young prodigies to see themselves as stars and stressing the need to learn how to work in a company.

Pierre Dux, who headed the Comédie-Française from 1970 to 1979, resisted these changes, arguing that student actors should be made to concentrate to the acquisition of specialist skills and that it was dangerous to allow guest directors to work with them as if they were a repertory company (by now this has become the standard practice in all acting schools). Resistance of this kind led to the establishment, for a short period, of two different courses under the same roof, one led by Vitez and the new young firebrands, while the other desperately tried to cling on to the traditional training in technique alone. But students voted with their feet and after a couple of years the old guard had to give up the struggle to resist the new methods. The demand for new plays to be performed at the Comédie-Française also grew during this period and was able to be satisfied because the company had use of the Odéon with its 'Petit Odéon' studio theatre. Here, a large number of younger authors had their work put on during the 1970s and 1980s. Getting new work on to the main stage of the Salle Richelieu was an altogether more difficult matter. Only after the appointment of Jack Lang to head the Ministry of Culture in 1981 did the theatre begin to be seen by some as having a mission similar to the British National Theatre (i.e. to perform plays drawn from the whole range of the repertoire, including new work). Before that it had been proud to see itself more as a museum of the classical theatre traditions. But in 1983 Lang appointed Jean-Pierre Vincent to the post of artistic director and he endeavoured to bring a new spirit into the house.

Vincent's appointment was seen as revolutionary in a number of ways. First because he was one of the young generation of directors who had established themselves in the decentralised theatre. He had begun by working with both Chéreau and Jourdheuil; for the previous eight years he had been in charge of the Théâtre National de Strasbourg. He had never worked at the Comédie-Française, still less been a *sociétaire*, and had no previous connections with it. Second, because his early productions had been anything but classical, depending rather on a reinterpretation of works by Brecht and other left-wing dramatists. This was not at all the kind of pedigree expected of a director of France's first theatre. With the backing of Lang, he attempted to introduce a number of new authors into the repertoire of the main house, but encountered strong resistance from the more conservative *sociétaires*. After three years he left, saying that it was an impossible theatre to run unless one had the backing of the company. He was succeeded by a senior company member, Jean Le Poulain, who died unexpectedly in 1988 and was followed by Vitez, who was, in his turn, struck down in 1990. Jacques Lassalle, who took over in 1991, benefited from the financial generosity of Mitterrand's and Lang's last few years, and was able to secure the renovation and reopening of the

Vieux-Colombier theatre as the Comédie-Française's theatre of contemporary writing. It opened in 1993 with revivals of early plays by Sarraute and Vinaver. But the political climate was changing. Like Vincent before him, he found that his mandate was not renewed after his first three-year term and Jean-Pierre Miquel took over in 1993. Under his direction the Vieux-Colombier has ceased to be principally a stage for contemporary writers. However, the funds available to the theatre have not sensibly diminished and 1996 saw the opening of a new studio theatre within the Carrousel du Louvre complex, in the gallery beneath the Louvre pyramid. The Studio Theatre aims to present a mixture of small-scale classic and modern productions, as well as programmes of literary discussions. It also provides the opportunity to see films of classic theatre productions screened in the 'Théâtreothèque' video theatre run in association with the television station ARTE.

One of the arguments for renovating the Vieux-Colombier and placing it under the control of the Comédie-Française was that the Odéon, traditionally the second home of the Comédie-Française, had been removed from its control in 1990. For the previous seven years, since 1983, its programming had been divided: half the year for the Comédie-Française and the other half for the newly created Théâtre de l'Europe, under the leadership of Giorgio Strehler. It cannot have been easy for Strehler, dividing his time between Paris and his own theatre company in Milan. At all events, he only did one new production at the Odéon during his period as director. This was Corneille's *L'Illusion comique* in 1984. Apart from this he brought productions in Italian from Milan and invited a number of guest directors. In 1990 Lang decided to make the Odéon over entirely to the European ideal and appointed the Catalan director Lluis Pasqual to run it. His mission was to produce the great works of the European repertoire, both classic and modern, and he succeeded in doing just that, staging Romanian, Hispanic, Russian and British seasons, as well as bringing to the Odéon the work of major European directors (Klaus-Michael Grüber, Giorgio Strehler, Stéphane Braunschweig, Patrice Chéreau, Deborah Warner) and dramatists (Botho Strauss,

Frank McGuinness, Bernard-Marie Koltès, Alexander Galin, Ramon Valle-Inclan).[1]

The Maisons de la Culture and Decentralised Theatre

Perhaps the most far-reaching effect of 1968 on the institutional infrastructure of French theatre was to be seen not in the capital, but in the provinces. Malraux's vision of Maisons de la Culture had set up expectations that every provincial centre should possess its own well-equipped stage, capable of housing the best in drama, dance and music. Many provincial towns had only just opened their brand-new theatres when the wave of 'contestation' broke over them. The questions posed in the upheavals of 1968 – what theatre? for what purpose? serving whose interests? – acquired a special urgency in places not used to having a theatre at all. Then, with the return of normality in the shape of another Gaullist government and the prolonged economic crisis of the 1970s, these questions appeared to have lost their urgency. But they re-emerged when the Socialist tide began to flow at the end of the decade and were once more hotly debated in the 1980s. A keenly felt scandal was the existence of state-of-the-art new theatres in which no productions took place because the buildings themselves were too costly to run. The Maison de la Culture at Bobigny provided a high-profile example: built in the course of the 1970s, completed in 1979, it remained closed to the public for more than a year because the funds available to it were only just enough to cover the salaries of administrative and technical staff. There was nothing left over to fund productions. In the course of the 1970s, for similar reasons, the idea of the Maisons de la Culture fell out of favour, although this was the period when many were completed and commissioned. The reason for this was not only that they proved so costly to run but also that they failed to tempt the most vigorous and talented of the young theatre directors (see above, p.51). Nevertheless, Malraux's vision had set up an initial network and this was ready to be expanded and rationalised after 1981.

[1] See Delgado, M., and Heritage, P. (eds), *In Contact with the Gods? Directors talk theatre*, Manchester: University Press, 1996, p.203.

The period from 1968 to 1981 was one of stagnation as far as the attitudes of government towards the theatre were concerned. A successful damage limitation exercise was conducted by Guy Brajot, who remained as Director of Theatres at the Ministry of Culture for most of the period (1970–9). Government funding for culture remained roughly static, at 0.5 per cent of the national budget. There was a rapid turnover of ministers, none of whom was tempted to take a high profile role as Malraux had done. Pronouncements about the role of culture in society were largely negative, reflecting the shock that 1968 had administered to right-wing forces in France. In 1973 Maurice Druon, on his appointment as Minister, declared that he would not tolerate theatre people who came 'with a begging bowl in one hand and a Molotov cocktail in the other'. This accurately expressed the mood of the Gaullists, but was the first in a series of gaffes which gradually turned public opinion against a centralising right-wing government. A similarly provocative statement was that of Jean-Philippe Lecat, the last Minister under Giscard d'Estaing, who announced in 1979 that decentralisation was an idea whose time had passed. In the run-up to the elections of 1981, in which Mitterrand was voted President and the Socialist party took power, decentralisation became one of the main issues. Not only in cultural matters, but in all areas of public life, the Socialists were able to make much of the dead hand of centralism under Giscard and to promise a greater degree of decentralisation if they were elected.

In campaigning for more resources to be put into theatre outside Paris, three associations took the lead. One was the SYNDEAC, which grouped all the directors of CDNs (see above, p.51). Another was the AJT (Action pour le Jeune Théâtre), founded in 1971 when a number of young companies (many based in the provinces) came together at the Cartoucherie in order to campaign against negative attitudes by the Ministry. Their demands were for a system of formal guarantees to be extended to young companies. These were to include a greater share of national subsidies, approved and well-maintained touring circuits throughout France and access to an officially recognised progressive career structure. The association's aims were gradually adopted by the SYNDEAC, which many of the 'young' directors joined, and AJT was wound up in 1980. The third organisation was ATAC (Association technique pour l'action culturelle). Set up in 1966, ATAC published a regular journal which, as well as giving details of productions in all the decentralised theatres, became a forum for discussions about how to retain and strengthen the original left-wing orientation of the decentralisation movement. This did not please the Ministry of Culture in the 1970s, who tried, but failed, to suppress it and established a new organisation, ONDA (Office National de Diffusion Artistique), which it hoped would replace ATAC. In this it was partially successful, but only because ONDA began to promote some of the aims of ATAC.

The election of Mitterrand in May 1981 was of enormous significance for the theatre because it inaugurated more than a decade of stability at the Ministry of Culture under Jack Lang, a man with a strong theatrical pedigree. As a doctoral student in Law, Lang had written a thesis on the relationships between State and Theatre in France,[2] and he was the founder of the Nancy Festival of Young Theatre, which, under his vigorous direction, had invited a number of influential foreign companies to perform in France for the first time. These included Peter Schumann's Bread and Puppet Theatre, Tadeusz Kantor's Cricot 2, Robert Wilson's production of *Deafman Glance*, Pina Bausch's Wuppertal Tanztheater and many others. Although Lang's reign was interrupted for two years (1986–8), when a right-wing legislature temporarily replaced the Socialist government, François Léotard did not attempt to change Lang's policies and it would be true to say that the development of the Ministry of Culture from 1981 until 1993 was an expression of Lang's vision. His main enthusiasm was for breaking down the barriers between 'high' and 'low' art. He ensured that greatly increased subsidy went into the cinema, and he supported a wide range of activities, including pop groups and circus performers, which earned him the hostility of many in the Establishment. But his great achievement was to raise the profile

---

[2] Lang, J., *L'Etat et le Théâtre*, Paris: Librairie Générale de jurisprudence, 1968.

of culture within government priorities, putting an end to the negative thinking of the 1970s and doubling the Ministry's financial allocation to just over 1 per cent of the national budget by the end of the decade.

He also ensured that the key post of Director of Theatre was filled by men who had a real expertise in and commitment to the development of new work in the French theatre. The first was Robert Abirached (1981–8), a published playwright as well as a professor of theatre studies, who presided over the re-invigoration of the decentralisation movement. Abirached, a man respected within the profession, was able to push through a number of reforms in the way money was distributed. While ensuring that the decentralised theatre companies received increased subsidies and the official career structures demanded by the AJT were implemented, he was also able to channel new funds directly into the pockets of playwrights, thus beginning the slow swing back of the pendulum, away from the all-powerful director and towards a more even spread of responsibilities in making theatre (see above, pp.72–117).

One result of the Socialist victory at the polls in 1981 was a new law concerning the decentralisation of administrative processes, which delegated certain powers to the twenty-two regions. This affected every area of life; where theatre was concerned, it boosted the importance of the DRACs (Directions Régionales de l'Action Culturelle – Regional Directorates of Cultural Action). The first of these had been established in 1977, before the change of government, but the Socialist programme led to them being strengthened and standardised across the country. Each DRAC was given authority to administer subsidies to independent companies in their region, and to develop its own policy for the encouragement and support of local theatre. Their authority did not extend to National Theatres and CDNs, but Abirached did his best to encourage local participation in the support and subsidy of these as well. Collaboration between theatres in the State-funded sector, and touring arrangements between them, were greatly assisted by the strong development during this period of ONDA under the direction of Philippe Tiry. Tiry, like Abirached, is an example of the professionalism that is found in government arts services. Before becoming director of ONDA he had been head of both a CDN (at Aix-en-Provence) and a Maison de la Culture (at Amiens). By the end of the 1980s his budget had reached 18 million francs. The willingness of the Ministry to appoint people of this calibre and to ensure adequate funding for their tasks is one key to understanding the success of the subsidised sector of decentralised theatres in France.

New Theatre Buildings

The increased priority given to cultural spending under Mitterrand found its most visible expression in an ambitious building programme. Out of this emerged such landmarks as the Bastille Opéra and the new National Library building, criticised by many for their over-ambitious scope and their disproportionate share of the cultural budget. But just as important was the theatre-building programme; funds for this leapt from only 10 million francs in 1981 to 100 million in 1983, and the public works programme approved under Lang resulted in the building of over 400 new theatres and the renovation of over 300 more.[3] The vast majority of these new buildings were situated in the provinces, thus strengthening the Ministry's commitment to decentralisation. Their construction reflected the cultural policies of the Ministry in other ways as well: many of them were of modest size and designed with local needs in mind. The emphasis Malraux had tried to place on artistic interdisciplinarity no longer seemed feasible, or even desirable, and most of the new buildings were designed specifically with theatre in mind. Abirached took advantage of the fact that the main stage of the Rennes Maison de la Culture needed redesigning (because of bad acoustics) to change its status to a 'Regional National Theatre'. He also ensured that work finally began on the last of the planned Maisons, at Chambéry, which opened in 1987 with a beautifully equipped new theatre.

In their design, many of these new theatres reflected a change

---

[3] See Chollet, J., and Freydefont, M., *Les Lieux scéniques en France 1980–1995*, Paris: Editions AS, 1996.

in attitudes among the theatre profession about the status and purpose of civic theatre. In the 1960s, when so much avant-garde theatre had been concerned with throwing off inherited constraints, the fashion had been for 'found' spaces, not normally used for theatre performance. This was epitomised by the Théâtre du Soleil, performing first in a disused circus building and then, from 1970 onwards, in the Cartoucherie de Vincennes. In line with such developments, new theatre buildings were designed to be '*salles polyvalentes*' or '*salles modulables*' – flexible spaces that could be rearranged in any shape or form according to the needs of each new production and could also be used for different purposes altogether. The inspiration behind such thinking was not only the current practice of groups such as the Soleil, but also the theories of thinkers such as Artaud, who questioned the very nature and role of theatre in society. In *The Theatre and its Double*, Artaud suggested an ideal theatre in which the action could surround the audience, who would be seated on pivoting stools. This idea became reality with the construction of the Maison de la Culture at Grenoble which included a theatre whose stage encircled the audience. A further influence on architectural and design thinking was the Théâtre Populaire movement, which had stressed the social divisiveness of the old 'Italianate' theatre, whose audience was separated into different strata, reproducing the class system, with the poor condemned to the most uncomfortable seats in the gallery, often with a restricted view, while the bourgeoisie showed off in the boxes or the 'dress circle' (see Vilar's comments above, p.14).

An answer to this seemed to be the 'black box' – an empty space within which seating, staging, etc. could be arranged in any configuration, and many such theatres were built in the course of the 1960s and 1970s. A good example is the Théâtre des Quartiers d'Ivry, a communist suburb of Paris where Vitez was director during the 1970s. This is a flat-floor space with a grid covering the whole area at a height of eight metres and flexible seating for up to 400. When Jack Lang was appointed as director of the Chaillot theatre in 1973, he insisted on a total reconstruction along similar lines, so as to make it completely flexible. But although this kind of design has its advantages, it can also be very limiting. Its main disadvantage is that it prevents the use of a fly-tower (by means of which scenery can be raised or lowered) and makes it difficult to install permanent electronic equipment. In addition, it necessitates seating which is light and often rickety: on one occasion the seats at the Cartoucherie collapsed. In short, it may provide a liberating environment, but does not favour continuity, nor does it provide for the needs of touring productions which may have been planned for technologically sophisticated stages.

The buildings which were designed and constructed in the course of the 1980s and 1990s tend to display a return to more traditional design: stages equipped with fly-towers and traps, the latest electronic systems for lighting and sound, and a permanent, fixed auditorium. The most frequent shape for audience seating is a horseshoe or semicircular arrangement, again displaying a return to more classical models along the lines of Greek or Roman amphitheatres. A key example of this change can be seen in the construction of the Marseille National Regional Theatre 'La Criée'. When Marcel Maréchal agreed to direct the CDN at Marseille in 1975, he said that is was partly because the old '*criée du chalutage*' (trawler fish market) on the harbourfront had been made available to him and he dreamed of installing a flexible theatre space similar to that of the Cartoucherie at Vincennes. But over a six-year period of planning, designing and building, his ideas changed, and the theatre which finally opened in 1982 has a fixed auditorium of 788 extremely comfortable seats, arranged in a single sweep facing the well-equipped stage. The idea of the flexible space has only been retained in the building's studio theatre, a small black box which can seat up to 240.

One of the chief causes of dispute over the years has been the joint funding (both central and regional) of cultural institutions. In theory, the CDNs and Maisons de la Culture were to be funded 50 per cent by the State and 50 per cent by the municipality in which they were situated. But it was often difficult to persuade both partners to fund at the same level. A number of municipalities, resenting any control by the State, went so far as to take over their local Maison, turning it into a municipal theatre. This was the case, for example, at Caen. The mayor of Caen used the 1968 events as a pretext to dismiss Jo Tréhard, director of the Maison de la Culture. Judging the dismissal to be politically motivated, the Director of Theatre maintained the Ministry's support for Tréhard. But the mayor refused to accept this and formally refused Tréhard access to the new building, so he withdrew with his company to a converted parish hall, leaving the theatre in the hands of the municipality. This continued to be an open wound for a long time and was only finally healed in 1987, with the construction of a new theatre for the Comédie de Caen (directed since 1972 by Michel Dubois) at the nearby suburb of Hérouville-Saint-Clair.

The potential for this kind of dispute remains as strong today as ever. In 1984, after the right had regained control of the municipality at Chalon-sur-Saône, the Maison de la Culture was appropriated and turned into a Théâtre Municipal in protest at what were seen as the excessively left-wing activities of its director. A recent example, uncannily similar to that of Caen in 1968, took place in 1996, when Jean-Claude Penchenat's company 'Le Campagnol' was locked out of its theatre at Corbeil-Essones by the mayor, Serge Dassault. This was a particularly flagrant case, since the theatre had only been open for three years, built (at a cost of 21.5 million francs) specifically for the use of the Campagnol. It is an attractive, semicircular auditorium seating 525, with up-to-date technical equipment (fly-tower and revolving stage). Penchenat, who retains the support of the Ministry, has converted his company into a Centre Dramatique National Itinérant (Travelling National Dramatic Centre) and, putting a brave face on his difficulties, claims that touring has always been one of his aims. A similar political battle divided the town of Toulon in 1997, when the National Front mayor evicted the director of the Centre Culturel de Chateauvallon.

At the same time as Abirached was encouraging the regions to take more responsibility for the development of live theatre in their area, an additional office for cultural development was established in the Ministry of Culture. Its director, Dominique Wallon, took on responsibility for establishing more CACs

(Centres d'Action Culturel). These had a similar aim to that of the old Maisons de la Culture, but were much more modest in size and were funded chiefly by the locality, with only a third of the subsidy coming from the Ministry. A second type of establishment, the CDC (Centre de Développement Culturel), was also set up, where the subsidy was almost entirely raised from local organisations. These efforts resulted in the opening of many new buildings in the course of the 1980s, but seldom created the conditions in which new companies could operate. As a reaction to this state of affairs, Abirached attempted, in his last years as Director of Theatre, to create a climate in which more of the independent companies would receive a permanent home in one of the new institutions. His success was only limited, and, when Bernard Faivre d'Arcier made a review of the whole theatre provision in 1990, he decided to link all these institutions together in a new network called Scènes Nationales, accepting that their function would be largely to house visiting productions.

Bernard Faivre d'Arcier, Director of Theatre

Before Faivre d'Arcier, Abirached's immediate successor was Bernard Dort, who appeared to be an inspired choice, since he had proved himself a theatre critic and professor of rare insight and consistency (both at the University of Paris and at the Conservatoire). Dort, however, found the demands of the job intolerable, and resigned after less than a year. In his place Lang appointed Bernard Faivre d'Arcier, a vigorous administrator, trained at the prestigious ENA (Ecole Nationale d'Administration), who had had the experience of running the Avignon Festival from 1979 to 1984, as well as working for the government's adminstrative service at the INA (Institut National de l'Audiovisuel) and at the Centre du Cinéma. Faivre d'Arcier made a public statement about the need to rediscover the sense of public service and proceeded to try to rationalise the whole theatre sector.

This was necessary because the priorities of the 1990s were different from those of the 1980s. During the time when Abirached had been Director of Theatre the budget had been expanding fast and so the principal need had been to make sure the new funds were spread across the whole of France, increasing the quantity of outlets for new work in the regions and developing the opportunities for the production of new plays. When Faivre d'Arcier took over at the end of 1989, austerity was already the order of the day. There was no chance of further expansion to the budget and the priority was to ensure better use of the resources already in place. One way of rationalising, which came naturally to someone of his background and training, was to identfy those institutions which were failing to balance their budgets, even within the generous State provision they received. In the first place, he discovered that the subsidised theatre sector had run up a colossal deficit of 80 million francs, most of which was the reponsibility of the Maisons de la Culture. His solution was to review the activities of all of them and to look for ways in which their administrative and technical personnel could be reduced. The result of his review was to abolish one Maison de la Culture altogether (Nevers) and to encourage others to focus their efforts on the particular art form which had proved to be their strong point. At Bourges, for example (one of the first Maisons de la Culture to be opened, in 1963), there is a permanent company and an 'Atelier Théâtral National' (National Theatre Workshop) whose mission is to be both a training ground for actors and a centre for devising, and experimental theatre work. At Amiens, on the other hand, the emphasis is on contemporary music.

At the same time, he created a new structure, Les Scènes Nationales (National Stages), whose mission he defined in terms which borrowed a good deal from Malraux's original vision: 'To establish themselves as centres of artistic production in contemporary culture at national level, to organise the dissemination and confrontation of artistic forms by prioritising contemporary new work, to participate in the development of culture within their region so as to assist the growth of new approaches to artistic creativity and to enhance its relevance to society.'[4] This new network brought together the seven surviv-

---

[4] Faivre d'Arcier, B., cit. Boselli, A-L., 'Le projet culturel et artistique des scènes nationales' in *Les Scènes Nationales, Revue du Théâtre* (Hors série, No.2), February 1995, pp.18–19.

ing Maisons de la Culture (Amiens, Bobigny, Bourges, Créteil, Chambéry, Grenoble, Le Havre), twenty-five Centres d'Action Culturelle and twenty-five Centres de Développement Culturel. The network continues to be strengthened: in 1997 it consists of sixty-three theatres spread across the whole of France, all equipped to receive touring productions, although a few also house permanent companies.

Faivre d'Arcier also drew up a new contract for the administration of the CDNs, specifying that they would be triennial and would require an explicit commitment to the goal of extending theatre to new audiences. Over a three-year period, the director must undertake to ensure at least six new productions (two per year), of which at least three must be directed by him/her. At least 20 per cent of the CDN's budget must be supplied from its own earnings (box-office and other sales) and not more than 50 per cent of the budget may go on administrative and technical salaries. At least a third of the salary bill must be devoted to actors or other artistic personnel and the centre is encouraged to draw on regional actors etc. wherever possible.[5] In this way, he attempted to ensure that subsidy would achieve the double goal of both encouraging new work and building up local audiences. This was important, since the analysis of trends from the previous decade showed that total audience figures had declined at the same time as subsidy had increased.[6] To anyone familiar with the funding of British theatre, the striking thing about this new contract is the low figure of 20 per cent required to come from the theatre's own earnings: in British subsidised theatres the figure is usually around 50 per cent. This, together with the relatively light cuts inflicted on cultural spending by the right-wing government in the years immediately following its coming to power, demonstrates the strength of feeling in France that theatre is still seen as a public service and deserves its current level of public subsidy.

[5] Temkine, R., *Le Théâtre en l'Etat* , Paris: Editions Théâtrales, 1992, pp.144–5. Reforms brought in by Jacques Toubon, when he was Minister of Culture in 1995, further modified these dispositions.

[6] Ibid., p.235.

The Situation Today

Cuts were bound to come, however, and in 1997 the SYN-DEAC claimed that the overall spending on culture had dropped from 1 per cent to 0.79 per cent of the national budget, despite a promise by President Chirac, made in 1995, that the 1 per cent level achieved under Mitterand would be maintained.[7] This was accompanied by much discussion of the role of subsidy in theatre; the 'Anglo-Saxon model' is often invoked as an example of how theatre *can* be made to pay its own way and theatre professionals are very alive to the dangers of relying on a concept of theatre as public service, when their levels of funding fluctuate according to the whims of the government of the day. But the fundamental instincts, even of right-wing parties in France, are to see cultural spending as a natural duty of the State, especially when this can be justified under the heading of preserving the French language from contamination by English or American slang. The structure of government-funded theatre in France has been described as combining 'Latin free-for-all and German institutionalism'.[8]

The institutionalism is evident in the remarkable efficiency with which the Direction du Théâtre issues statistics every year. The 1996 official publication of statistics for the previous year grouped the work of the government-funded theatres into three principal sectors: the National Theatres, the CDNs and the Scènes Nationales. The five National Theatres had received 317.5 million francs from the State and played to total audience figures of 883,000. This State subsidy represented 73 per cent of their total income: they earned 21 per cent of their revenue at the box-office and the remaining 6 per cent came from other sales. The 125 CDNs had received 305.9 million francs from the State and played to 1,859,000 people. The State subsidy represented only 40 per cent of their total income of 733 million francs: box-office receipts accounted for 26.5 per cent, with a further 8.1 per cent coming from other sales. The remaining

---

[7] See *Le Journal du Théâtre*, March 1997, p.4.
[8] Hordé, J-M., in *Le Journal du Théâtre*, March 1997, p.5. ('*En somme cela combinait le bordel latin et l'institution à l'allemande*').

25.4 per cent was made up by local subsidies, which broke down as follows: 15.6 per cent from the communes; 3.5 per cent from the *départements*; 6.3 per cent from the regions. The 63 Scènes Nationales had played to 1,650,223, receiving total income of 849.3 million francs, of which 26 per cent came from the State, 26 per cent from box-office and other sales, and 48 per cent was provided by the local and regional authorities. In addition, 1200 independent companies were registered with the Ministry, of which half received some subsidy, totalling 151.6 million francs, and a further 27.4 million francs went to subsidise sixty-nine theatre festivals. Finally, fifty-three 'private' Parisian theatres received a subsidy amounting to 52 million francs (about one ninth of their total receipts). The total State spending on theatre amounted to 1.3 billion francs for the year.[9]

Since the 1980s the efforts undertaken by Abirached to increase the amount of new work being produced on public stages have not been abandoned. A concrete sign of this was the opening, in 1988, of an impressive new National Theatre largely dedicated to new writing: Le Théâtre de la Colline. Its design is similar to that of the Marseille theatre (see above, p.147) with one large, fixed auditorium of 757 seats in a single sweep and a smaller flexible studio able to accommodate up to 214 seats. Until 1996 it was directed by Jorge Lavelli, who succeeded in filling the two auditoria with an eclectic mix of twentieth-century plays. He showed a natural bias for the work of Lorca, Valle-Inclan, Arrabal and Copi, who all share his own Hispanic background, while productions of work by Beckett, Berkoff, Bond, Friel, Kushner, Thomas Bernhard, Botho Strauss and Lars Noren have all helped to build up a wide-ranging and discriminating picture of the twentieth-century repertoire. He also directed a number of works by new writers, such as his acclaimed production in 1996 of the Belgian writer Serge Kribus's first play *Arloc*. In autumn 1996 Alain Françon was nominated as the new artistic director in succession to Lavelli;

---

[9] Schmitt, O., '*France: Esquisse d'un paysage théâtral*' in *Revue du Théâtre*, Hors série No.6, February 1997, pp.57–65. Schmitt's figures are taken from Cardona, J., and Lacroix, C., *Statistiques de la culture*, Paris: La Documentation française, 1996.

his first productions, announced for the autumn of 1997, were to be *Les petites heures* by Eugène Durif and *In the Company of Men* by Edward Bond.

The Colline is the newest of the National Theatres; the others are the Comédie-Française, the Odéon, the Théâtre National de Chaillot and the Strasbourg theatre with its attached theatre school. Since 1988 Jérôme Savary has been at the head of the Chaillot theatre; much criticised by some for his vulgarity and glitzy productions, he has nevertheless succeeded in filling this theatre which, since the departure of Vilar in 1963, had always had difficulty in justifying its existence. For eight years (1980–8), under the direction of Antoine Vitez, it had fulfilled something of the same function as the Odéon under Renaud–Barrault in the 1950s and 1960s. But Savary has no pretensions to becoming a high-culture icon and the position of his theatre, opposite the Eiffel tower, makes it the ideal house for attracting visitors and tourists rather than an audience of regular devotees. As for the Théâtre National de Strasbourg, it has succeeded in maintaining its pre-eminent position as the only national theatre outside Paris, with a mission to train the actors and directors who will go on to run the provincial theatres of the future.

In surveying the structural and financial developments which have affected French theatre since 1968, one is bound to be impressed by the generosity of the State funding that has been made available and by the intelligent planning decisions which have helped to reduce the universal tendency for institutions to gobble up subsidies to pay for running costs. Considerable imaginative and creative energies have gone into devising methods by which the application of government money can promote wider access to the theatre for the benefit of new audiences and new artists, playwrights, etc. The result is that France is endowed with a coherent and well-understood network of theatres, ranging from the large national or regional theatres through the CDNs and the Scènes Nationales, down to the hundreds of small independent companies. The regular publication of statistics concerning budgets, operations, etc., ensures that the system is transparent and accountable. This well-funded, well-organised system is only possible because of a cultural climate, with roots reaching back several centuries, which equates civilisation with a provision of opportunities for the arts to flourish.

CHAPTER 7

FRENCH THEATRE AT THE END OF THE CENTURY

The legacy of the post-war decentralisation movement, of idealists such as Copeau and Vilar, and of political visionaries such as Malraux and Lang, is a nation-wide network of theatre activity flexible enough to respond to every need. In France theatre is recognised as making a valuable contribution to life in society, and is funded and organised accordingly. The administrative organisation which underpins it strikes a healthy balance between the need to be accountable to the public on the one hand and the needs of artistic freedom on the other. Government policy over recent decades has been calculated, in similar fashion, to support and encourage the French cinema industry. These enlightened policies have created conditions in which outstanding artistic talents have been able to flourish.

Because French performers do not need to cross the Atlantic in order to make interesting films, the French theatre benefits from the presence of star actors such as Maria Casarès, Jeanne Moreau, Michel Piccoli, Daniel Auteuil, Isabelle Adjani, Emmanuelle Béart, Michael Lonsdale, Gérard Depardieu, Alain Delon, Anouk Grinberg. These and many others appreciate the chance to vary their work in films with regular stage appearances and, although these may often be in lightweight or 'boulevard' plays, star actors may equally well be found performing the most demanding contemporary work. Maria Casarès was a good example, since she had a key role in Genet's last great play, *Les Paravents*, in which she played the Mother,[1] and also inspired and acted in works by Koltès. One of her last stage performances

---

[1] Casarès performed this role in both the original production by Roger Blin, 1966, and the revival by Patrice Chéreau in 1983.

was as the Pope in Genet's posthumously published *Elle* (directed by Bruno Bayen in 1991 at the Gennevilliers theatre). Another is Daniel Auteuil, who gave a memorable performance as Woyzeck in a production by Jean-Pierre Vincent in 1993.

As well as such performers, who achieve a world-wide following because of their film work, there are large numbers of actors known and loved for their theatre work, often within a particular region in which they have chosen to work for most of their lives. The proud tradition of the Comédie-Française, going back over three centuries, has kept alive the dream of the ensemble, or company of actors; the continuing potency of this dream in our century is evident from the achievements of artists such as Copeau or Mnouchkine. There are even rare actors who manage to build a company around them, such as Laurent Terzieff, whose company dates back to 1961 and who has helped to make James Saunders better known in France than he is in Britain.

But it is true to say that these actors tend to be less well known than the star directors (many of whom, like Planchon or Chéreau, Vitez or Mesguich, are *also* actors). Although the conception of the director as creative artist practising 'scenic writing' has recently come under attack, the achievements of directors' theatre in France have been very considerable. Nurtured on Brecht and Strehler, and seeking to emulate Stein, the great French directors of recent years – Vincent, Lassalle, Lavelli, Mesguich, Lavaudant – have succeeded in astonishing and delighting audiences with productions of great richness and subtlety. The establishment in the 1980s of a Franco-German arts television station, ARTE, has ensured that many such productions have been filmed and preserved for the judgement of posterity.

The art of the director is one which is prone to galloping inflation, both economic and artistic. In the early 1990s the necessity for the theatrical equivalent of a devaluation was recognised and today a new spirit is abroad in the French theatre, one of modesty, minimal means and a return to the poor-theatre ideals of Brook's 'empty space'. The work of the previous decades had been torn between intense theatricality on the one hand and the banality of everyday life on the other. Those violent alternatives no longer appear necessary and many theatre productions of the 1990s have sought to strip theatricality down to its bare minimum. The example of Beckett has encouraged this trend and many new plays would be as effective on radio as on the stage. The old distinction between French theatre, which has *spectators*, and English theatre, which has an *audience*, has begun to break down: attentiveness to the individual voice of an author, and to intensified poetic language in general, is now a prerequisite for those attending new French plays.

Worries are sometimes expressed, however, about the quality of the creative work which goes into the state-of-the art circuits provided by the French theatre network. This unease is expressed by Jean-Pierre Thibaudat, whose thirty-page essay on French playwriting asks in its opening paragraph, 'who are the Becketts, Ionescos, Genets or Adamovs of today?[2] It is, of course, true that no single movement with the intensity and originality of the Theatre of the Absurd is currently lighting up French stages. But the preoccupation with language which characterised those plays continues to provide a fertile source of experimentation for playwrights in the 1990s, as is evident from the work of Minyana, Novarina, Renaude, among many others. Thibaudat concludes on another question: 'Who will be the Heiner Müllers, the Thomas Bernhards of our country?'[3] This seems an easier question to answer: the dark conflicts of Koltès and the modernist aesthetic of Vinaver offer work that is every bit as powerful as that of the two German-language playwrights. In some ways it might be said that Koltès's voice is a lone one, not much emulated, except that his example is partly responsible for the popularity of the monologue among writers and actors alike. Vinaver's juxtapositional method, on the other hand, has had a far-reaching influence.

In the 1990s many playwrights are set on exploring the processes of writing itself. This is not limited to outstanding

---

[2] *Le Théâtre Français*, Paris: Ministère des Affaires Etrangères, 1994, p.5.
[3] Ibid. p.31.

examples, such as that of Cixous, but is a common feature of much new work. This preoccupation can be traced back to Vinaver's monumental *Par-dessus bord* (*Overboard, Plays I*, Methuen, 1997) in which the author placed himself inside his own play in the character of Passemar, who struggles with the age-old problem of the writer: how to be both part of life, yet sufficiently detached from it in order to devise a generally valid commentary. This play, which deals at one and the same time with problems of economics, aesthetics, politics and artistic creativity, and all through the hilariously ironic perspective of how to market lavatory paper, can stand comparison with modern masterpieces of the stage from any country.

Another, more difficult question for the whole French theatre industry on the brink of the new millennium might be the one Brecht asked of the German theatre after the First World War: what *purpose* is served by all these fine theatres with their excellent heating systems and state-of-the-art technology? Many of the most active young playwrights and directors display a sophisticated grasp of theatre and its processes of representation, but appear less involved in the realities of the world around them. There are few equivalents, in France, of playwrights such as Edgar, Griffiths, Hare or Brenton, who seek to use the theatre as a means of responding to the major political conflicts of our time. Nor are their plays translated into French (apart from Hare's intimate *Skylight*). Translations of Bond's recent plays have had some success in the 1990s, perhaps because their situations are couched in general terms, not specific to a particular country or conflict. Berkoff's *Greek, Kvetch* and *Decadence* have also been well received in France.

Many analysts and commentators have shared Vinaver's uneasy sense that theatre structures which were expensively built with the express purpose of extending public access to the arts have lost that sense of purpose without finding anything to put in its place and that new audiences continue to be elusive. Perhaps the most inspiring example for the future will be that of Armand Gatti, who has never ceased to develop and change his creative methods, while remaining true to his initial determination to put the means of expression back into the hands of those who lack them because of educational or social deprivation. Political events in France in the course of 1997 have shown that many people are waking up to a concern about the strength of the Front National and the threat it may pose to civil liberties; artists have been in the forefront of public demonstrations against laws on immigration. Among many workers in the cultural field there is a hunger for a renewed sense of purpose and for the need to maintain the age-old function of art: to question and perhaps to disturb the powers that be.

Authors and administrators in France are very divided about the usefulness of government subsidy, as the interviews included in this book demonstrate. Some are painfully aware of the restrictions imposed by accepting Government money, where others believe that this need not impose undue limitations on creativity or on freedom to express political opinions. Clearly the danger of a system heavily dependent on the government of the day for its funding is that it will have to toe the government line. The legacy of 1968, however, is a strong and well-organised theatre sector, determined to retain its independence while at the same time accepting state funding. Admittedly, little can be done to limit the powers of a mayor within his own municipality, but at national level there is less evidence of central government bringing political pressure to bear on theatre in France than there is in Britain, despite the much-vaunted independence of the British Arts Council. In these circumstances the prospects are good for the theatre in France to develop once more a lively critique of society, as it did in the days of Molière, of Beaumarchais and of Vilar.

Another cause for optimism is the ever-growing number of groups whose work escapes the conventional definitions of theatre performance. The Jérome Deschamps – Macha Makeieff company is a good example of this tendency, situated midway between clowning, dance and acrobatics. Richly inventive in their observation of daily life in France, they nevertheless appeal to a universal sense of the comic which transcends national boundaries. Limitations of space have prevented us from investigating the work of these and other groups, such as Le

Théâtre du Mouvement, whose work is closer to dance than to theatre. A separate book would be required to do justice to the immense range of street theatre, *café-théâtre* and other manifestations of performance art which may be seen in France today. The establishment of a National Circus School, as well as the world-famous schools of Marcel Marceau and Jacques Lecoq, have ensured a constant stream of young artists trained to a very high level in performance techniques which can be turned to a variety of different purposes. One of the delights of living in France today is the inventiveness with which new sites and opportunities for performance are sought out by people for whom the established structures of theatre seem too constricting. By its nature, this kind of manifestation is ephemeral: that is its glory. But the vigour and quantity of such work is an indication of the liveliness of the whole range of theatrical performance in France today.

PART II

A GUIDE TO FRENCH THEATRE NOW

INTERVIEWS

In order to give the reader a sense of the main preoccupations, aspirations and issues in French theatre now, we have included the following excerpts from interviews conducted during the 1996–7 season with a representative group of theatre professionals. Chosen to give some idea of the breadth of opinion and concerns which exist, their attitudes offer surprisingly different viewpoints on issues such as the role of private and public money in developing theatre, the relationship between writer and director, and the public perception of the role of theatre in contemporary French culture. They clearly express the strengths and weaknesses of the current tendency towards poetic drama, for example, and help to fill out the differences in both theory and practice which separate Gallic and Anglo-American attitudes towards theatre.

Roger Planchon is included as perhaps the best-known of the directors responsible for the success of directors' theatre in the 1960s and 1970s (see pp.41–5), as well as in his capacity as a playwright. Interestingly, his views on the future development of theatre in France focus on the playwright rather than the director and he also stresses the importance of embracing the opportunities afforded to writers by film and television

Bernard Faivre d'Arcier has been director of the Avignon Festival since 1993 (see pp.134–5), a post he has already held once between 1980 and 1984. His background includes a three-year term as Director of Theatre at the Ministry of Culture, as well as training as a civil servant at the Ecole National de l'Administration, and his views give an interesting insight into the organisational aspects of French public theatres and festivals.

Micheline and Lucien Attoun are the founders and directors

of the Théâtre Ouvert (see Information Section, pp.193–4), the first and one of the most important organisations involved in encouraging new writing for the French stage. Over the course of three decades they have played a vital role in nurturing new talent and bringing it to the attention of the public and the theatre profession, and are thus in a key position to comment on the role of the playwright today and developments in play-writing practices.

The three playwrights interviewed are all widely respected figures within French theatre (see the chapter on playwrights in the 1990s for a fuller discussion of their plays). Eric Emmanuel Schmitt, for example, has enjoyed particular success in the private, commercial sector in Paris (see pp.123–4), as well as being internationally performed, and continues to adhere to fairly traditional notions of form, structure and tone in his writing. Philippe Minyana, meanwhile, has chosen to experi-ment with form and language in a new way which has much in common with music or art, painting pictures with language, as he explains on p.178. Michel Azama is well known for his playwriting (see pp.105–6), but his comments are also enlight-ened by his experience working as editor of La Chartreuse's *Les Cahiers de Prospero* until 1996, a journal for and about play-wrights in France today, which includes only playwrights on its editorial board.

Each of the above has valuable points to make about the French theatre as they see it; taken together, their comments reveal the vitality and vigour of the debates concerning theatre as part of French cultural life.

INTERVIEW – *Micheline Attoun and Lucien Attoun, directors of the Centre Dramatique National de Création, Théâtre Ouvert*

What is the relationship between writers and directors in France today?
MA: The situation has evolved enormously, for several reasons and in several directions. First, a number of authors have taken control themselves: there's been a completely new generation of authors who have decided that power should no longer belong to the director and who are willing to confront the work of the

stage directly. Directors may choose the plays, but the authors are closely linked to the production.

A good example of how things have changed is Noëlle Renaude. She used to work at home, locked away. Progressively, however, she plucked up the courage to take part in activities at the Théâtre Ouvert, i.e. a week of reading of her texts and working with actors; then a workshop which she led. Then one day she decided to write for an actor. The result was her play *Ma Solange*. . . . This play has been performed all over France. There's someone who had no knowledge of the stage at all, who has acquired it bit by bit. The relationship between director and writer is a question of distance. We think the author isn't necessarily best placed to notice the richness of what he's written himself. The director brings a new perspective to the play and most of the time, as long as everything goes well, this is more enriching than the view of the author alone. The real 'poets' of the stage (i.e. the writers) are well acquainted with theatre practices and at the same time know that the theatre is capable of anything, on the condition that you have the right director. One of the advances in theatre today is that authors are paid, something in which, I might add, the Théâtre Ouvert has helped. Ten or fifteen years ago, authors who received a proposition from a great director wanting to stage their plays would never have received payment. The director would have said yes, then things would have dragged on for several years and the play would either have been staged or not. What's changed in France in recent years is that you can't treat authors with the same offhandedness. The public powers have put into place a series of measures. There's the Centre National du Livre with its bursaries and encouragement for creation, there's the Beaumarchais Foundation, there's the SACD and bursaries from the Direction du Théâtre. These measures translate into a reality – which is that today the author can't be ignored.

Are there many authors who come from outside the theatre?

MA: There are many, many people living in the provinces who write for the theatre. Théâtre Ouvert receives 600 manuscripts a year, and it's crazy how many are unknown and aren't theatre people, but who throw their bottle into the sea with the hope of seeing some return one day. It's the role of an organisation like ours to encourage the assimilation of these people, when they have talent. There are texts which you can take right up to production, because they are very finished works: what's the point of putting them through the hoops? And then there are the texts where it's necessary to encourage the authors, to help them confront the stage head on. But there aren't many masterpieces.

What are the main tendencies you notice in playwriting today?

MA: It's difficult to say. There's a tendency to non-dialogue, to *récit*, to monologue, obviously because it's easier to do. There is also a tendency not to write realist dialogue – 'pass me the butter, I'll pass you the mustard' is finished. Today writing is a real literary task, spoken on stage, but a literary transposition, with carefully worked-out language. This is perhaps the main tendency and one which interests me greatly. There are many bad attempts. There's certainly not a tendency towards comedy – comedies are rare.

What makes a play work theatrically, in your view?

MA: The notion of theatricality has evolved enormously in recent years – perhaps differently in France from in England. Theatricality in France relies more on the 'word', made to be said, even if it's said alone, if there's no answer. It is poetic, but when you speak poetry, it remains a poem, whereas this kind of *'parole'* is made to be incarnated in a character, which gives the possibility of action.

LA: For some years we've had *texte à une voix* (one-voice text) – not monologue. Monologues up to now have been passive as far as action goes. A man stops, tells us his thoughts, tells us a story: there's nothing less theatrical than the traditional monologue. It's a convention. On the other hand, in contemporary writing, the monologue isn't monologue – it's *récit*. In the *récit*, there's action, i.e. a character who acts through what he's telling. We as the audience are obliged to participate. In the monologue there's a relative passivity, in the *récit* there's action in advance. In monologue we advance arbitrarily. In *récit*, we advance in the writing.

Is there a division between public and private theatre?

MA: Relations are very bad, which in my opinion is a result of private theatre being against the subsidy received by the public sector. The private sector is also subsidised in its own way. The theatres are private but most of the companies which play there aren't at all and receive subsidy from the Direction du Théâtre, the Ministère de la Culture. Private theatre also claims that it generates most contemporary authors, while public theatre doesn't play or discover them. That's completely false.

Should there be more subsidy in French public theatre?

MA: This year the subsidy of the CDNs was maintained. Of course, everyone knows that the cost of living has gone up. That means lower salaries in real terms for the permanent staff and the actors. But what's worse is that a part of the subsidy has been pulled, in actual fact – by being transferred from the creation budget to the structural budget. If you have structural work to do you'll get the money, on the condition that you find another local organisation like the town hall or *conseil régional* which will contribute the same sum. So for the actors and performance, the money's lost. Naturally we don't know whether our protest will be taken into account. Besides this, the City of Paris is threatening a cut of 20 per cent. We hope it's just a threat.

As far as the necessity of subsidy goes, the private theatre will tell you there's too much subsidy. Contemporary authors will tell you that without subsidy they would never have been staged, as a contemporary author is always a considerable risk. The duty of a country is to invest for the future, and subsidy allows people to emerge and become the classics of tomorrow. The work of Théâtre Ouvert, in any case, is to try to say, these are the people who exist today and are worthy of attention, and then to present them to the public and the profession. If the text remains at home in a drawer, how will posterity be able to reveal the classics of tomorrow? Subsidy serves to produce playwrights such as Daniel Danis (who was completely unknown in France two years ago). Danis writes plays for 200- to 300-seat theatres: to make a profit, you have to put it in a 1000-seat theatre. But in a 1000-seat theatre the play won't work. So because of artistic demands subsidy is entirely necessary.

The fact that we demand subsidy doesn't prevent lots of people emerging from non-subsidised work. Without that there is no theatre. There have never been so many little groups in the provinces and the suburbs, and more and more contemporary authors are associated with them. This sector is little subsidised but still exists. I'm not sure if the avant-garde exists today – it's a notion from the 1950s or 1960s, but these troupes, working in the shadows, take many more risks with contemporary authors.

INTERVIEW – Eric Emmanuel Schmitt, playwright

Who do you write for and how important is your audience?
I don't like going to my plays – you don't belong in the wings or the hall. On the other hand I like to see the actors, watch the public arriving. How are they going to react? When I write a play, I want it to appeal to my grandmother as well as to my intellectual friends. I don't believe in exclusive literature. If you haven't got the desire to be *populaire*, you're not really making theatre. By giving pleasure to people you are able to lead them to reflections they might not have thought of themselves. I try to incite interrogation, a theatre of questioning. I don't want to give my solutions.

At the moment I am working with the SACD [Société des auteurs et compositeurs dramatiques, see pp.191–2] for two reasons – to see that public theatres stage more contemporary writers and also that contemporary theatre addresses the public. The public theatres practise a kind of theatre which makes the public run away. It's false culture.

Is there a divide between public and private theatre in France, then?
The audience in public theatres is a cultured public, but one which doesn't have the means to go out to private theatre. The problem with private theatre is the ticket prices, which attract a bourgeois audience. A pessimistic play like my *Golden Joe* wouldn't work there either. You need optimistic, lively plays, with famous actors. An author has to know which plays are more suitable for private and public, and you have to pass from one to the other. I belong to the 'private', because my successful play *Le Visiteur* was played in the private theatre. But my plays have been performed in both. It's up to the author to create the bridge between the two. I don't want my plays to be performed

only fifteen or twenty times, then to die. *Le Visiteu*r had 450 performances in the end – if I had played the game the subsidised theatre was asking of me my play would have been performed thirty times. I started my career as a writer, not as an actor or director who writes. Now I'm accepted, but at the beginning I wasn't part of the seraglio! As soon as an author has been a success in the private theatre or abroad, it disconcerts public-theatre people. This is an élitist practice – they're out of touch with real people.

Should there be more or less subsidy in French public theatre?

I'm scandalised by the expenditure of some of the grand barons of public theatre, by the money they have to organise publicity, marketing and the like. This money could go to other theatre companies. I'm not against subsidy, but the way the money is distributed should be fairer. People have got used to giving money to directors. Directors are in charge of all the subsidised theatres. We've made a ghetto for all the young authors and the logic of the ghetto is to marginalise – with play-readings. I love theatre, so I hate readings.

Are you happy with the way in which directors handle your work?

What I really hate is when the first production of a play is a flop. Suddenly, the play becomes difficult to put on again. If a play's already been successful, has a reputation and has played all over the place, I'm not so bothered about its failure.

There are lots of directors who like to take a non-theatrical text and stage it to give voice to their own notions of theatricality. I'm sorry, I've already put theatricality in the text. This creates conflict between you, even if you're not an argumentative character. I don't want to direct my own plays. I doubt my text all the time. I need someone to believe in it. I need directors and actors. But I live in France, a place where directors have the power, so sometimes it's a bit difficult. In some ways I'm almost inclined to work with directors who perhaps have less talent at the end of the day, or a talent less revered than that of the big directors – they'll be more faithful, less likely to do a production with their stamp all over it. Saying that, *Le Visiteur* was directed in many different ways, from Barcelona to Paris, and I was extremely happy about it.

Do theatre critics have much influence in France?
A theatrical success isn't necessarily dependent on media success. Sometimes plays are full at first because of the media, then empty, and vice versa. If you have no star, then the papers are important. If you have stars, you may be able to avoid endangering the play despite a bad press. The problem is that critics are fairly good judges of direction, but when the production is based on a new text they have problems. Abroad, people ask the question. where does this fit in with the tradition, what is the playwright asking? In France they only talk of the wonderful or beautiful *performance*. Sometimes they don't seem to understand anything.

Do you write with a particular theatre space/actor/director in mind?
No. I visualise relatively little. I even try to avoid reference points which limit the imagination. I carry my plays around for many years, subconsciously. I only write when it's ripe and ready. Usually it only takes me ten days to write a play, but years to think about it.

Is it important to you that your work is published, or is it more important that it is staged?
The published script is only a back-up for performance. A theatrical text is one which offers several layers, below the spoken one involving flesh-and-blood actors, stage design and so on. My texts are always published eventually. *Le Visiteur* sold 30,000 copies, so it is read, but to have a play only published but not performed would upset me: a text is most important because it gives you another chance to be performed.

What makes a text theatrical?
I belong to a tradition in which the dramatic situation must generate the play. It must generate a dialogue, an exchange of ideas. My problem is to find the best situation for conflict. After that, things come together naturally. I believe in situation and in characters. I don't believe in theatre based purely on language, without character. In the case of a monologue, for example, it's a question of thinking of more than the words alone. Urgency must justify the words. Someone comes on stage because he or she has a need to say something.

My play *Variations énigmatiques* is really a reflection on identity

– is there really a 'me'? I wanted to address myself to the theatrical tradition, where you believe in a character, in a 'self'. I don't really believe in the ideology of modernity. I believe in a more classical ideology of apprenticeship, learning from the works of others. I dream in ancient and modern culture, but I want to fit in, not cause ruptures in order to create.

Theatricality is the opening up of space in psychological, intellectual and temporal terms, with complex relationships between people; with the exchange of different ideas; with a situation which unfurls in a certain time period and which seeks a solution. It's created by tensions and oppositions, and it's the force of these tensions which give life to a performance. There should be no immobility, no anonymity, but there should be characters, contradictions and often lies. Theatre is also frequently about words which lie and and the actor's body which tells the truth – a contradiction. Theatre should also have a beginning and an end – that's very important too. Lack of a coherent narrative bores me. I like poetry, but theatre has to be more, because theatre is the stage, a gesture and much more than a word. You have to put characters in a situation which justifies why they are talking. You have to have a dramaturgy which advances in time – you can't not move on. We belong to an age of negative metaphysics, there no order, no sense, no plan. Naturally, artistic projects copy and reproduce the chaos, but I don't hold with that philosophy. I try to uphold form. In theatre, form is an artistic illusion. Theatre permits form to triumph over chaos and sense over nonsense. Sartre said all technique was a metaphysical state – but can a metaphysical state produce authors? Beckett is an example of someone who spoke of the nonsense of the world and at the same time chose to do so in a certain form. His work is a contradiction: he's one of the rare men this century to have transformed this contradiction into an art form.

INTERVIEW – Roger Planchon, director and writer – by Gilles Costaz

You are still in Villeurbanne [at the TNP]. Have you never been tempted to move to Paris?

I have turned down the Comédie-Française and the Chaillot theatre several times. I'm a bumpkin who believes in decentralisation, who believes it to be useful to the country and indispensable to the progress of theatre. Without it, theatre would be even deader than it is today. It has to be kept moving along and authors and actors will make it progress. But it's important to distinguish between the artistic adventure, which will always be lived by the young – they re-invent theatre and will always re-invent it – and the setting up of mechanisms which will facilitate development. It wasn't the private sector which created Beckett, but in the 1950s little theatres were necessary for Beckett to be performed, just as, later, large-scale European institutions were required for Peter Stein to work in. The problem for ministers is to set up institutions which are favourable to the artistic developments of their times, to empower those who work in them.

How do you look back on 1972 when your company the Théâtre de la Cité was awarded the title Théâtre National Populaire [previously the title of Jean Vilar's theatre]?

My first reaction was that to take on that title wouldn't be easy. I had so much respect for Vilar! But the Minister of Culture, Jacques Duhamel, insisted because it gave him the chance to increase our subsidy. That was when I decided not to be sole director and brought in Patrice Chéreau, who worked here for ten years. After that, Georges Lavaudant came and stayed for ten years. I am proud of these two partnerships. I have great admiration for both men. Our mission was to offer the public the best theatre and to keep them up to date with what was happening, from Vitez to Savary and from Kantor to Wilson. That was what we did for twenty years.

You are once again sole director of the TNP – what are your plans?

For the future of the TNP there are several possible solutions. I can imagine a project built around a company where the power would be in the hands not of a director, but of a company of actors, like the Comédie-Française was in the beginning. The group could put on five plays a year and take responsibility for everything. Authors would come and read their plays to it, just as Dumas and Hugo did in the nineteenth century.

Another more interesting model would be to give it to a group of authors. That's how the future lies, I believe. I would call it a National Studio for Dramatic Creation. Its work would find outlets in live performances and also in television and film production. I think I know how to get it on the rails and I've asked the Minister to consider it. I think his decision will be positive.

If a second wind is to be given to the decentralisation movement and to creative theatre artists in France we must turn to writers. A writer cannot earn a living from the theatre. Look at England, where there has been an important development: playwrights have been able to write for television. Theatre must take its media destiny into its own hands. The great period of the director has lasted 150 years. I look forward to the epoch of the author. It will be astonishing and exciting. In France we should be trying out new things. So let's try. It's not happening yet because decrees are necessary, as are contracts with the State and with television companies. Ministerial determination is also needed.

You are also a film producer.

I am managing director on an entirely honorary basis of the Rhône-Alpes Cinema Company. It's a heavy responsibility. It's a plc and the Rhône-Alpes region has been given permission to have shares in it. It has produced around fifty films and contributes to the well-being of French cinema. With this in mind, I am also working on a new idea: a film writer's studio. The idea is for the State to get involved with helping authors.

You are counting on authors while some people say there are no more authors.

We must work out how authors may become producers and take a more central role in both theatre and media. There are authors, but they are impeded by the system of decision makers and power structures. Can an author seriously contemplate offering a new play to a theatre in the provinces? The provincial theatre has to commit itself to a certain number of performances in Paris, for which there would need to be a theatre there dedicated to decentralised companies. Today, authors look to the private theatres of Paris, or else they put on plays themselves.

You have been criticised for directing your own plays.
An author who runs a theatre should be able to put on his own plays, or else he should not be put in charge of the theatre. It's a joke. The proportion of the TNP's budget which has gone on my own plays is insignificant.

This season you are putting on two of your own plays in Paris [Le Radeau de la Méduse *and* La Tour de Nesle, *adapted from Dumas*] *and at Villeurbanne you are directing* Le Triomphe de l'amour *by Marivaux. In the first two you're dealing with the nineteenth century, and in the latter, the eighteenth century . . .*

I strive to be a director who is profoundly French. That's why I'm interested in the French repertoire and French history. Hence in Marivaux, *Le Triomphe de l'Amour* is one of the high points of the eighteenth century. The whole mechanism of libertinage was perfected by Marivaux, then Sade and Laclos took it over and changed its meaning, borrowing Marivaux's mechanisms of cynical seduction. Marivaux is the sole successor of Racine in his cruel aspect. Look at the scenes of blackmail in Marivaux and Racine – they have the same sharpness.

Until the 1950s Marivaux was misunderstood. The first person to reveal his true profundity was Jean-Louis Barrault, or rather Madeleine Renaud. Then there was Vilar who also put on *Le Triomphe de l'amour*. Around the same time I presented *La seconde surprise de l'amour*. Then came *La Dispute*, produced by Chéreau. Today Marivaux, Laclos and Sade still occupy a very large space in our imagination as it relates to love.

INTERVIEW – *Philippe Minyana, playwright*

In general terms, could you pin-point any major tendencies in contemporary French theatre?
As writers we are less isolated in our art. We're also theatre people, so things have changed in that sense. And language has imposed itself in the theatre – before, the text would be cut left, right and centre. There's a lot of interest in new texts, even within State education, which is a very recent thing. Now there are *baccalauréat* texts by contemporary writers.

Theatre is no longer the maudlin theatre of the 1960s. That's all finished. It's a way of talking about the world, it's more visionary, epic. The theatre of Camus and Sartre is out of date and old. The demand now is for a research arena which is in constant motion. Playwrights like Renaude and myself work with actors to experiment with form. Theatre is live, it's about what happens on the stage.

What makes a text theatrical?

'Theatrical' means something that is only made for the theatre. There are people who do popular theatre to entertain, and those who do *théâtre de recherche* [experimental theatre] which might have less appeal to the public and is not necessarily to please. My earlier plays, like *Fin d'Eté à Baccarat*, told more of a story and I still had characters who were called by a real name. They were quite realistic, although with stylisation. I passed on quite quickly to plays with what I would call theatrical language, a language which belongs to the theatre, not to television. and not to the street. This theatrical language quickly led me into a different kind of theatre, which deals solely with language.

What is the importance of character, story and form?

We have less and less of what you would call character in French drama – it's the current fashion At the first residence, at La Chartreuse in 1988, we stopped calling characters by names, but referred instead to 'the woman with the big dark eyes', or 'the man in black'. That's highly symbolic: we're not talking about faces any more, but about the essence of psychological character. The world is no longer a political world, it's destroying itself. It's not a question of writing a play about a homeless person, for example. I try to introduce these people, but not *per se*. It's about projection. I wouldn't call a character 'the homeless man', but 'the man in tears' or the 'silhouette'.

We have passed on to a narrative which transcends the spirit of the person. Spoken words don't just present that one character, but a panoply of characters of this type. Sub-text is a fashion, in the same way as there have been fashions for characters and plot. We're no longer into more open, generalised speech; we're into the intimate. Dialogue rarely works, I find. People don't really answer each other – they speak alone.

Plot has disappeared totally in my work. There's no more story. There's not much difference between theatrical language and that of other forms of writing like poetry. The writing of so-called poetry and of this kind of theatre is the same, using words and rhythms, like music. I detest Naturalism, everything which is 'televisual'. It's false realism. But I don't like lyrical, sophisticated, *manièriste* poetry either.

I've written a longer play which is more complex, with six movements, prologue and epilogue [*La Maison des morts*]. It's based on a theme – like music, or art – a series in midnight blue, in white, etc. I feel more like a musician, an architect or a photographer – it's all about point of view. We see what the camera takes – not what's around it. I want to paint little moments, to make characters enter this world, which is very intricate work. What do you say – what don't you say? What's going to appear in the frame, which angle, is there a red or blue character or not? I love the strangeness of the situation.

Form used to mean acts one to five in classical theatre, with a denouement in the fifth. Today there are other conceptions. For example, Noëlle Renaude's *Ma Solange* is a series of stories. It's a chronicle of provincial life, the people, their morals, the countryside. This is pushing at the boundaries of theatre. Her idea of theatricality is very open. I've asked myself a lot about theatrical form: monologues, verses, stories, public speaking, and I've noticed that at all times of political or economic crisis people write in shorter forms – like the short texts of Calaferte and Maeterlinck, for example. It's like that at the end or beginning of centuries, or in post-war periods. Instead of developing a subject, one cuts it short and creates sketches on a theme to be considered in their own right. In my play *Drames Brefs 1* the theme is mourning. At the end of the century we're in mourning for lots of things. It's the spirit of the times, a metaphor for all mourning.

Do you write with a particular type of theatre space/actor/director in mind?

I do, and although stage directions are often ignored by the time of rehearsals, they do help to 'fix' the fiction, when writing. I've always been lucky enough to work with companies and notably with the director Robert Cantarella, so I've written for specific actors and actresses. I have the actors' voices, ways of speaking and breathing in my head. I often change things in rehearsals: I love that– it's the stage that counts.

Should there be more subsidy in theatre?

The people with money aren't necessarily the most interesting. Money shouldn't always be given to the same people either. But it's not true that lack of money is a handicap. Where's the *desire* to make theatre? At the moment there's a scandal about the amount of money given to big directors – the media are creating about it. But there are some young directors who have come back to the most essential things in theatre – the actors and the text. The reign of star directors is in the process of burning itself out.

INTERVIEW – *Bernard Faivre d'Arcier director, of the Avignon Festival*

In general terms, could you pin-point any major tendencies in contemporary French theatre?

Nobody really stands out. Everyone has an individual approach. Mnouchkine and Chéreau are key reference points, but their work is completely different. As far as texts go, there are conventional-style texts, which are quite structured with dialogue, exposition, characters and progression. But there are also texts which are essentially non-theatrical, but which appeal to directors. The director is a creator himself and he uses text like a raw material, so there is a tendency for texts which look like one long monologue, but which the director transforms.

How would you describe the relationship between writers and directors in France today?

In England and the United States the director is very respectful of the author. Not so in France – that's why French authors are always complaining. Sometimes I wish directors were more respectful of authors – but they have practised on the classics and if they've done it with Molière they'll do it with contemporary authors. The problem is that there isn't enough contact between writers and directors. Authors have to be known in the theatre world and understand it too. When authors write plays, they have an imaginary director in their heads, but this clashes with the director's view, so there are two creative logics in conflict. The director isn't just a technician, there to sort out lighting and actors. He's also a creator, or considers himself to be such. He uses the text as he uses the theatre space. The author has to accept sometimes that his text is totally reworked, although the author is intrinsic – and must resist the director. It's up to authors to come to the theatre to get to know directors, who can then commission their work. In 'private theatre' [see pp.118–26] it is different: you find the kind of plays that private theatres expect. Eric Emmanuel Schmitt, for example, wrote a play for Alain Delon, and the play was staged [*Variations énigmatiques*]. In this case the writer is in pole position, so is the actor; but where is the director?

It's difficult to earn money writing for theatre and the only way to make money is through performances. There are many texts written, and very few published and performed, so it's difficult for writers. There are lots of organisations in France which try to bring the two together. The problem isn't an economic one – it exists in the heads of writers and directors. Directors don't want to read countless texts; they want to develop relationships with writers which last for years. like Lavaudant with Bailly, Françon with Edward Bond, Lavelli with Latin-American theatre. There's no point in an author sending his or her text out to everyone. An author becomes significant if his or her work is produced by different directors, however. Koltès at one time was only directed by Chéreau. Now his plays are directed by lots of people, in big and small companies. That is the sign of an author of importance.

Do you produce works by contemporary authors at the Avignon Festival?

Some years we put on more than others. In 1997 we are staging Olivier Py in the Cour d'honneur with a text especially written for it [*Le Visage d'Orphée*]. I would like to produce more contemporary authors, but we can't if directors don't want to. There's a balance between contemporary works and classics from year to year for artistic reasons, not financial ones, although we do plan more nights for classics; there are always bigger audiences for them. In a large venue like the Cour d'honneur which holds 2000 people, we need plays which will carry in the space, which won't get lost. Experimental theatre is done usually in smaller theatres, Nevertheless, you need to take risks, otherwise you'd be dead in fifty years. You need to do different, new things which divide the press, professionals – and the public.

What are the aims of the Avignon Festival today'?

The goal is the same as in Vilar's time – to attract the largest and most varied public possible, while presenting current tendencies in theatrical creation. The atmosphere has changed since Vilar's day because the world has changed and the Festival is bigger. But there's been a great continuity, with only four directors of the Festival in fifty years.

Who is the 'public' at the Festival?

Avignon is a place where audience members are 'trained' – they see a few plays, discuss them, visit the bookshops and so on. There are those who know the Festival, came in the 1960s and have stayed faithful to it. Now their children and grandchildren come too, so there are three generations of festival-goers. The public is very varied by age, comes from all over France, is rather well educated and reads a lot: teachers, students, professionals, managers. But they are not really rich. Our public is not diverse in comparison with the French public as a whole. There aren't really many agricultural workers, for example – they're working at the time of the Festival, anyway.

How do you choose productions?

Through meetings with directors. We call each other, discuss how a project will work, the actors, the text (if it exists), the physical and financial restraints. We are obliged to do co-productions, which means getting together in advance with the director of a Scène National, sponsors and so on. We try to put on the première at Avignon, then a tour that will include Paris.

How many productions do you stage?

In 1996 we staged fifty productions, for the fiftieth anniversary. In 1997 we're doing half that. It's not just about doing the largest number possible; the objective isn't purely quantitative.

The idea is to reduce the number of productions but to improve the ambiance, so people can see and hear properly. Twenty-five is still a lot – and 60 per cent of them are first-time productions.

What is the relationship between the official festival and the Avignon Public 'Off' [the fringe festival]?

We're neighbours – but we couldn't really collaborate. There's the official festival and around that the rest, the 'Off', installs itself. There's no real competition between the two festivals, even if there has been in the past. The 'Off' is free territory with no selection (unlike the 'In'). The 'Off' takes place in small venues, which are good for discovering actors and authors, but you can't do a brilliant *mise en scène* in a small venue. It's only in the 'In' that directors can really express themselves, in the larger venues.

Is there enough subsidy for theatre festivals in France?

The term festival is a blanket term, covering very different artistic and economic realities. The Ministry of Finance only finances a dozen festivals directly. Otherwise it's the towns – for touristic, economic and local reasons – who finance them. There are only a dozen real theatre festivals in France, of which the Festival d'Automne and Avignon are the most important. Both require co-producers to take the initiative; we want directors to come up with projects, rather than to wait to receive them. That's always been my hope. It used to be that way, but now our budgets have been cut: the finance from the Ministry of Culture is the same, but the town of Avignon is giving less money and our subsidy is going from 7 to 5 million francs. But the festival is financially important for Avignon. If they reduce the subsidy we reduce the number of productions, perhaps the duration of the Festival, and at the end of the day that's not good economically for the town.

Should there be more theatre festivals?

There's room for more theatre festivals in France, but not at the same time and in the same region, which means elsewhere apart from the South and at other times of year from the summer, like May, June and September. The South-West is noticeably lacking in festivals, despite the fact there are some big cities like Toulouse and Bordeaux. They could have some interesting autumn festivals.

INTERVIEW – Michel Azama, playwright

In general terms, could you pin-point any major tendencies in contemporary French theatre?
Directors are becoming concerned about contemporary writing and want to try what they've never tried before. When Patrice Chéreau put on Koltès no one wanted to do his plays, but today everyone puts on Koltès. It takes time, but when an author is really good everyone's interested. We are all looking for a solution, for something new. New vitality comes from authors, as it does in England. In theatre in the last ten years, no director has equalled the importance of Koltès. The past and its traditions had a harmful effect on playwrights. Vitez's *Catherine* [an adaptation of Aragon's *Les Cloches de Bâle*, see p.38] was good, but the consequence of this kind of work was to eliminate the playwright. Now there are bursaries, commissions, residences, the Aide à la création [see pp.78–9], reviews, all of which mean the author has came back to the centre of the theatrical debate. Some can even make a living from their writing.
Is it important to you that your work is published, or is it more important that it is staged?
Both. The stage reveals the power of the text, but the book is the trace, the memory, and offers the text a chance to be performed again. There's written and oral literature. Both are very important. I like my texts to be written and read. But first they should be performed. To be staged is confirmation that you're not writing for yourself alone.

The reason we still value Racine or Marivaux is that they used an extraordinary French which you never hear spoken, which belongs to them alone and was invented by them. That's what makes a text endure – an original poetic language. It's a question of moving away from language for communication (*everyday* language) and towards this poetic language.
What makes a text theatrical?
The author looks after the language, the director takes care of the illustrative action of what's being said. But it's the unexpected which is really theatrical, when you add the linguistic input of the author and the imagination and action from the director you have a production.

How important are character, story and form?
The most important thing to me is that there's a crisis experienced by the character, then metamorphosis. During crisis something is transformed and turned on its head. Crisis is the key word of theatre. I like a story to be told, but there are instances where a narrative tale becomes a burden and isn't useful dramatically. In the play I have just written [*Dissonance*] there's no plot, because it involves a contemporary chorus, with many stories, not one story. The chorus is like a Greek chorus, with different voices.

Form depends on who's speaking and who is addressed. A theme lends itself to either monologue or dialogue. In this century of false communication, of communication by machine, the monologue is also a false form of communication. It's difficult not to make a monologue turn into a *récit*: if the words just flow from beginning to end it's not theatrical.

Do you write with a particular theatre space/actor/director in mind?
I think of the stage – it's my actor's training. I like empty space, with no scenery. It's difficult to play in an empty space, but it's much more powerful. I write things if someone commissions me, but also things which I 'commission' from myself. I'll do it if it leads me somewhere new. I welcome commissions like relatives – from time to time, but not all the time. Sometimes I do workshops with actors around the subject I'm writing about and then go away and work on the text, but the actor's powers of invention isn't really in the language, it's in the action. I like watching rehearsals sometimes and discussing things with the director afterwards, but I prefer generally to let them get on with it.

Should there be more or less subsidy in French public theatre today?
I believe we should get rid of subsidy. Only then would we see who still survives and wants to do theatre.

What is the role of the theatre critics?
They have an anticipatory role, to alert us to the next major up-and-coming authors and directors. But I don't think there are any who do that well nowadays. They've lost touch with their guiding role. Critics at the time criticised Koltès for being dull and insignificant. Now they think he's great. Critics are always

ten to fifteen years behind general opinion. None of them reads the texts and they have nothing to say about playwrights. They aren't capable of initiating the public, or orientating them towards discoveries.

INFORMATION SECTION

(NB: All addresses and numbers are correct at time of publication but are subject to change.)

Theatre Associations in France

There are many organisations in France whose primary role it is to disseminate and promote contemporary French theatre. All work to their own independent remit, whether that be promotion abroad, translation, or the promotion of new writing, although it is true that their spheres of interest often overlap. It is for this reason that many of them come together for regular informal meetings of the CRAC, or the Collectif de réflection sur les auteurs contemporains. The following can be useful contacts for information, advice on texts and productions.

AFAA (Association Française d'Action Artistique)
Ministère des Affaires Etrangères
244 bd Saint-Germain
BP 103
75237 Paris Cedex 07
Tel: 01.43.17.83.00
Fax: 01.43.17.82.82
This organisation was founded in 1992, operating independently within the department of Foreign Affairs to promote international cultural exchange, including the dissemination of French theatre, dance and music abroad. Its goal is to develop contacts, ties and events between theatre practitioners, organisations and theatres internationally to promote France's artistic role on an international level. AFAA has funds to support French companies performing abroad, especially as part of joint

projects with foreign companies or theatres, and in collaboration with the French cultural network via embassies and cultural centres and organisations. Its educational projects aim to spread the news about French theatre (and all other performing and visual arts) abroad. They include visits by French teachers to theatres, companies and training establishments world-wide and the welcoming of foreign scholarship holders in France; exchange programmes between theatre and other performing-arts schools in France (including the Paris Conservatoire and Strasbourg theatre school) with their equivalents abroad, sharing teachers, producers and courses; and creative and artistic exchange programmes involving research trips abroad for theatre professionals. It supplies information and advice, and publishes a series called *Chroniques* (in French) with specific information on a particular area of the performing and visual arts. For more details on its non-theatre operations, contact AFAA direct.

Beaumarchais (SACD)
11 bis rue Ballu
75009 Paris
Tel: 01.40.23.44.44
Fax: 01.45.26.74.28
The Beaumarchais Association, which is funded by the SACD's 'Action Culturelle' (see below, p.192), aims to promote contemporary writing, providing support on a yearly basis for some sixty authors within the various fields represented by the SACD (see below, p.191). It awards writing grants which may be combined with production, publishing or translation subsidies.

Centre National du Livre
53 rue Verneuil
75007 Paris
Tel: 01.49.54.68.68
Fax: 01.45.49.10.21
Part of the Ministère de la Culture, the Centre National du Livre awards bursaries to writers in all disciplines, including playwriting.

Centre National du Théâtre
6 rue de Braque
75003 Paris
Tel: 01.44.61.84.85
Fax: 01.44.61.84.86
An essential source of information on French contemporary theatre, this resource centre (funded by the Ministry of Culture) can help with a range of enquiries, from documentation to information and advice. It has a library of over 5000 volumes, including contemporary texts, reference books, reviews, guides and directories, with a reading room available on Monday, Wednesday (2–6 p.m.) and Friday afternoons (2–5 p.m.) and a vidéothèque opening in autumn 1997. It is responsible also for helping theatre professionals with legal or tax problems, regulations or the bureaucracy of putting on a production or setting up a company (professional or amateur), and provides advice for young people on training in theatre disciplines. The CNT also organises readings and meetings for industry professionals.

La Chartreuse – Centre National des Ecritures du Spectacle
BP 30
30404 Villeneuve Avignon Cedex
Tel: 04.90.15.24.24
Fax: 04.90.25.76.21
La Chartreuse, situated in a historic fourteenth-century monastery in Villeneuve-lez-Avignon, is subsidised by the Ministry of Culture, the CNMHS (French Heritage Association) and local and county authorities. In 1991, it became the National Centre for Playwriting, a place of research, first public performances and residencies for playwrights. It has missions that involve the participation of all performing arts professionals with the aim of promoting living French writers. The CNES organises workshops on specific subjects, such as writing for specific genres (radio, cinema, children's theatre, etc.). As well as its *Première Impression* collection of plays, the CNES also publishes a theatre journal for and about playwrights, *Les Cahiers de Prospero*. In 1997, it will publish a catalogue of French contemporary playwrights. In July, the Centre is a partner in the

Avignon Festival with Les Rencontres d'été, which places playwrights in the spotlight, with several readings daily throughout
the Festival and first performances from the contemporary
repertoire shown or worked on during residency.

Directions Régionales des Affaires Culturelles (DRACs)

These organisations are each responsible for the promotion of
the arts, including theatre, within their specific region of France.
For a complete list of DRAC addresses, please contact the
Centre National du Théâtre (see p.189).

Entr'Actes–SACD

11 bis rue Ballu
75009 Paris
Tel: 01.40.23.45.14
Fax: 01.40.23.46.23

One of the most important points of contact for theatres, companies and translators outside France who are looking for French
texts to produce or information on contemporary writers,
Entr'Actes–SACD is an independently run organisation within
the 'Action Culturelle' of the Société des Auteurs et
Compositeurs Dramatiques (see below, p.191), founded in
1991. It helps with the promotion and dissemination abroad of
French and francophone plays by living contemporary playwrights and acts as a consultant for the playwrights it represents.
Entr'Actes–SACD publishes a review of the French theatre
scene, entitled *Actes du Théâtre* (bilingual English–French), as
well as other publications including *Contemporary French Theatre
1960–92* (see p.195 for details). The association is able to forward
information to authors within the SACD, should you wish to
contact specific writers such as those listed on pp.218–53.

Maison Antoine Vitez

Centre International de Traduction Théâtrale
Domaine de Grammont
34000 Montpellier
Tel: 04.67.22.43.05
Fax: 04.67.22.48.34

Founded in 1990, the Maison Antoine Vitez is responsible for
translating a large number of foreign texts into French: forgot-

ten classical, modern and a few contemporary unpublished works, to broaden the repertoire in France. It aims to bring translators together with publishers, directors and actors. It distributes its catalogue of translated works throughout France, and France Culture regularly broadcasts its public play-readings. To enlarge its repertoire and promote new forms of theatre the Maison Antoine Vitez also publishes a series called *Cahiers* (in conjunction with Editions Climats), each number being devoted to playwriting in a particular country or period, or one particular author.

Office National de Diffusion Artistique (ONDA)
13 bis rue Henry Monnier
75009 Paris
Tel: 01.42.80.28.22
Fax: 01.48.74.16.03
Since its foundation in 1975, ONDA's role within French theatre has been to promote the growth and diffusion of French and international theatre, dance and music throughout France, with a particular mission to promote contemporary work. As well as circulating information, it is also able to provide financial and other support for visiting companies and public theatres who are willing to welcome them. It especially seeks to promote young companies and new productions, including those from abroad (currently 18 per cent of total budget goes to foreign productions). It collaborates with the DRACs (see below) and works to increase the role of the GRACs (Groupes Régionaux d'Associations Culturelles) in providing a network for cultural communication and exchange of ideas, and also collaborates with AFAA in developing international relations.

SACD (Société des auteurs et compositeurs dramatiques)
11 bis rue Ballu
75009 Paris
Tel: 01.40.23.44.44
Fax: 01.45.26.74.28
The SACD is a non-profit-making association which was formed in 1777 by Beaumarchais to protect authors' rights. It collects and distributes royalties on behalf of all French-language

authors of fictional works in the performing arts, film, television and radio, including playwrights. All enquiries about performance and translation rights of works by French playwrights should be addressed to the SACD. The SACD supports cultural projects through its 'Action Culturelle' programme since 1985, which includes the Beaumarchais and Entr'Actes Associations (see above, pp.188 and 190). 'Action Culturelle' is funded from monies collected through a tax on blank video and audio cassettes in France. Today the SACD has a membership of 28,000 authors, with 1500 new members and some 3000 new works in the performing arts alone registered every year. Its members rely on the SACD for legal advice, and it also participates in the drafting of legislation and regulations affecting authors, and advises its members on negotiating individual performance or production contracts. It even manages social security and retirement funds on behalf of authors. The SACD works with trade organisations at home and abroad to try to improve the standing (financial and moral) of authors. It gives two sets of awards every June in each of the fields it represents, one for an established author, one for a newcomer, and another special prize for a lifetime's work. Other awards include the Beaumarchais prize and the French-language prize. The SACD publishes a monthly newsletter and its quarterly *Actes du théâtre* (see p.201). It holds regular debates, workshops and meetings for its members, and opened its Maison des Auteurs with this in mind in autumn 1997. The SACD manages a library of some 18,000 works dating from the eighteenth century to the present day (access open to show-business professionals, researchers and specialists).

Théâtrales/l'association
4 rue Trousseau
75011 Paris
Tel: 01.43.38.04.09
Fax: 01 49.23.06.63
Run alongside, but separate from the publishing house Editions Théâtrales, this association is funded jointly by the Ministry of Culture, the Ministry of Youth and Sport and the City of Paris to promote contemporary writing. Its reading committee selects

some fifty texts a year to promote from among 1000 French and foreign works. Théâtrales/l'association provides a reference library, which includes the 500 titles available in the Association's repertoire catalogue of published and unpublished plays from home and abroad; works from various publishers; manuscripts translated by the Maison Antoine Vitez (see p.190) and plays resulting from Ministry of Culture grants (Aide à la Création) or produced by Radio France International. It also supplies information on playwrights, publications, including press packs, reviews and books. The reading room is open Monday to Friday, 2 p.m.–6.30 p.m. Théâtrales/l'association also supplies a catalogue of Théâtrales plays to other sites in France, Belgium, Switzerland and Quebec, and runs training courses and workshops for theatre professionals (including writers), as well as regular debates and readings.

Théâtre Ouvert
Jardin d'Hiver
4 bis cité Véron
75018 Paris
Tel: 01.42.55.74.40
Fax: 01.42.52.67.76
Founded at the Avignon Festival in 1971, Théâtre Ouvert moved to its permanent base at the Jardin d'Hiver, Paris, in 1981, and in 1987 was made the first Centre Dramatique National de Création (National Drama Centre) devoted to research, promotion and dissemination of texts by contemporary French playwrights. Co-directors Lucien and Micheline Attoun and their team read hundreds of manuscripts a year sent in by hopeful young writers from France and other francophone countries. Five of these a year are published as *tapuscrits* (printed play texts) for distribution to directors and other influential theatre professionals. Others are read in the 'Cartes Blanches' series of readings, or workshopped within the 'Mises en espace' programme or '*Chantiers*', actors and directors, or occasionally staged at the Jardin d'Hiver theatre space. Like Entr'Actes–SACD and Théâtrales/l'association, Théâtre Ouvert should be one of the first points of contact when looking for contemporary French scripts.

Practical Information for Theatre Professionals

Bringing a play to France

If you are interested in bringing a production/tour to France, make contact with ONDA (see p.191), as well as your country's cultural attaché or council (e.g. The British Council, 11 rue Constantine, 75007 Paris, Tel: 01.49.55.73.00). Such bodies work closely in conjunction with French organisations to help bring interesting work from abroad into France.

While you can try approaching individual theatres all over France with a production in English, certain theatres which stage English work on a more regular basis are a good starting point. Venues such as the Odéon or Bobigny do stage English plays (providing a venue for famous companies such as the Royal Shakespeare Company, as well as for smaller productions) from time to time, while theatres such as the Théâtre de Nesle (8 rue de Nesle, 75006 Paris, Tel: 01.46.34.61.04) and the Théâtre de Ménilmontant (15 rue du Retrait, 75020 Paris, Tel: 01.46.36.03.43) make a feature of their English-language productions.

It could be worth approaching individual festivals directly, although ONDA is also a possible contact point. Avignon, for example, attracts a number of foreign-language productions each year, the official festival offering appearances at its invitation and the 'Off' fringe festival open to anyone prepared to put on a show. Other festivals which feature productions from outside France include those at Saint-Etienne, Grenoble, Maubeuge, Strasbourg, Dijon, Nancy and Douai, as well as Paris's Festival d'Automne. For a complete list of festivals, contact the Centre National du Théâtre (see p.189), or see our list of the main events on pp.203–6.

Financial aid for translation and publishing

Contact the Cultural Affairs department at the French Embassy in your country for details of existing programmes (ask for the Attaché du livre).

Performing/translation rights (French works)
All queries should be addressed to the Société des Auteurs et Compositeurs Dramatiques (see above, p.191).

European Theatre Convention
For a directory of plays recommended by member countries' reading committees, entitled *The European Theatre Today, The Plays*, or details on membership, contact:

Comédie de Saint-Etienne
7 ave Emile Loubet
42001 Saint-Etienne
Tel: 04.77.25.01.24
Fax: 04.77.41.96.34
(The current (1997–8) president of the European Theatre Convention is its director, Daniel Benoin.)

Lists of plays/authors
- *Contemporary French Theatre 1960–92*, by Nurit Yaari (a selection of authors from the 1960s to the 1980s published by and available from Entr'Actes – SACD).
- *241 pièces contemporaines de langue française* (catalogue of authors and details of their plays compiled by Claude Confortès, at the Centre de Création Contemporaine, 15 rue des Beaux Arts, 75006, Paris).
- Théâtre Ouvert repertoire catalogue (available from Théâtre Ouvert).
- Théâtrales catalogue (available from Théâtrales/l'association – note: this includes Editions Théâtrales publications, but also many play texts from other publishers).
- La Chartreuse (CNES) will publish a catalogue of contemporary French playwrights in 1997.
- CD-ROM *Mascarille* – a list of over 18,000 French-language works, available for PC/Mac (Centre ressources théâtres, MJC Ste Foy 112 ave Ml Foch, 69110 Ste Foy lès Lyon. Tel: 04.78.59.66.71. Fax: 04.78.59.30.08. Email: mjc.stefoy @wanadoo.fr).

Government offices

Ministére de la Culture
3 rue de Valois
75001 Paris
Tel: 01.40.15.80.00
Fax: 01.40.15.81.72

Direction du Théâtre et des Spectacles
53 rue Saint-Dominique
75007 Paris
Tel: 01.40.15.88.84
Fax: 01.40.15.89.93

Libraries and resource centres

Bibliothèque Nationale de France – Département des arts du spectacle
Quai François Mauriac
75706 Paris Cedex 13
Tel: 01.53.79.53.79

Bibliothèque de la SACD
11 bis rue Ballu
75442 Paris Cedex 09
Tel: 01.40.23.44.20
Fax: 01.40.23.46.69

Centre de documentation Centre National des Arts du Cirque
1 rue du Cirque
51000 Chalon-sur-Marne
Tel: 03.26.21.12.43

Centre National du Théâtre
6 rue de Braque
75003 Paris
Tel: 01.44.61.84.85
Fax: 01.44.61.84.86

Département des études et de la prospective – Ministère de la Culture (DEP)
2 rue Jean-Lantier
75001 Paris
Tel: 01.40.15.73.00

Goliath – Hors les Murs Centre de ressources sur les arts de la rue et les arts de la piste
74 ave Pablo Picasso
92000 Nanterre
Tel: 01.46.69.96.96
Fax: 01.46.69.96.98

Institut Mémoires de l'Edition contemporaine (IMEC)
Archives et Documentation
25 rue de Lille
75007 Paris
Tel: 01.42.61.29.29
Fax: 01.49.27.03.15

Maison Jean Vilar
Bibliothèque Nationale
Département des arts du
spectacle
8 rue de Mons
84000 Avignon
Tel: 04.90.86.59.64

**Lieux Publics – Centre
National de Création des
arts de la rue**
16 rue Condorcet
13016 Marseille
Tel: 04.91.03.81.28
Fax: 04.91.03.82.24

Bookshops

As well as ordering direct from the following bookshops in
France, it may also be possible to obtain certain texts through
selected specialist bookshops in the UK and other countries.

Le Coupe-Papier
19 rue de l'Odéon
75006 Paris
Tel: 01.43.54.65.95

**Librairie des Arts du
Spectacle**
31 rue Bonaparte
75006 Paris
Tel: 01.43.26.97.56
Fax: 01.43.29.44.65

Librairie Coup de Théâtre
7 rue des Moulins
75001 Paris
Tel: 01.47.03.40.12

**Librairie du spectacle
Garnier-Arnoul**
5 rue Montfaucon
75006 Paris
Tel: 01.43.54.80.05
Fax: 01.43.54.82.92

Librairie des Femmes
74 rue de Seine
75006 Paris
Tel: 43.29.50.75

Librairie Théâtrale
3 rue Marivaux
75002 Paris
Tel: 42.96.89.42

Librairie la Vouivre
11 rue Saint-Martin
75004 Paris
Tel: 01.42.71.32.39
Fax: 01.42.72.02.83

Theatrical publishers

Actes Sud
Le Méjan
Place Nina Berberova
13200 Arles
Tel: 04.90.49.86.91
Fax: 04.90.96.95.25
and
18 rue Séguier
75006 Paris
Tel: 01.55.42.63.00
Fax: 01.55.42.63.01

Actes Sud-Papiers
18 rue Séguier
75006 Paris
Tel: 01.55.42.63.16
Fax: 01.55.42.63.01

Albin Michel
22 rue Huyghens
75014 Paris
Tel: 01.42.79.10.00
Fax: 01.43.27.21.58

L'Arbalète
8 rue Paul Bert
69150 Decines
Tel: 04.72.93.34.34
Fax: 04.72.93.34.00

L'Arche Editeur
86 rue Bonaparte
75006 Paris
Tel: 01.43 26.60.72
Fax: 01.46.33.56.40

L'Avant-Scène Théâtre
6 rue Gît-le-Coeur
75006 Paris
Tel: 01.46.34.28.20
Fax: 01.43.54.50.14

Les Cahiers de l'Egaré
BP 9
83200 Le Revesd les Eaux
Te: 04.94.98.99.03
Fax: 04.94.98.91.51

Michel Chomarat
160 rue Vendôme
69003 Lyon
Tel: 04.78.62.88.59

Dramaturgie Editions
11 rue Gît-le-Coeur
75006 Paris
Tel: 01.43.26.42.36
Fax: 01.43.29.67.42

L'Ecole des Loisirs
11 rue de Sèvres
75006 Paris
Tel: 01.42.22.94.10
Fax: 01.45.48.04.99

Editions Christian Bourgois
116 rue du Bac
75007 Paris
Tel: 01.45.44.09.13
Fax: 01.45.44.87.86

Editions Cicéro
6 rue de la Sorbonne
75005 Paris
Tel: 01.40.88.37.09
Fax: 01.46.37.41.88

Editions Comp'Act
157 Carré Curial
73000 Chambéry
Tel: 04.79.85.27.85
Fax: 04.79.85.29.34

Editions Corps Puce
5 rue des Provinciales
80090 Amiens
Tel: 03.22.46.76.32
Fax: 03.22.49.63.51

Editions Crater
7 place Charles Dullin
75018 Paris
Tel/fax: 01.43.57.04.55

Editions Circé
67420 Saulxures
Tel: 03.88.47.24.78
Fax: 03.88.47.21.60

Editions de l'Aube
Le Moulin du Château
84240 La Tour-d'Aigues
Tel: 04.90.07.46.60
Fax: 04.90.07.53.02

Editions de l'Elan
6 rue de Rotterdam
4000 Liège
Belgium

Editions de l'Harmattan
16 rue des Ecoles
75005 Paris
Tel: 01.43.54.79.10
Fax: 01.43.29.86.20

Editions de Minuit
7 rue Bernard Palissy
75006 Paris
Tel: 01.44.39.39.20
Fax: 01.45.44.82.36

Editions des Quatre-Vents
6 rue Gît-le-Coeur
75006 Paris
Tel: 01.46.34.28.20
Fax: 01.43.54.50.14

Editions du Laquet
rue droite près l'église
46600 Martel
Tel: 05.65.37.43.54
Fax: 05.65.37.43.55

Editions Dumerchez
BP 329
60312 Creil Cedex
Tel/fax: 03.44.74.04.67

Editions Gallimard
5 rue Sébastien Bottin
75328 Paris Cedex 07
Tel: 01.49.54.42.00
Fax: 01.45.44.94.00

Editions Julliard
24 ave Marceau
75008 Paris
Tel: 01.53.67.14.00
Fax: 01.53.67.14.14

Editions Lansman
63 rue Royale
B–7141 Carnières
Morlanwelz
Belgium
Tel: 64.44.75.11
Fax: 64.44.31.02

Editions Lattès (Jean-Claude)
17 rue Jacob
75006 Paris
Tel: 01.44.41.74.00
Fax: 01.43.25.30.47

Editions le livre à la carte
14 rue Soleillet
75020 Paris

Editions Les Solitaires Intempestifs
14 rue de la République
25000 Besançon
Tel: 03.81.83.30.03
Fax: 03.81.83.32.15

Editions POL
33 rue Saint-André des Arts
75006 Paris
Tel: 01.43.54.21.20
Fax: 01.43.54.11.31

Editions Point hors ligne
c/o Editions Eres
19 rue Gustave Courbet
31400 Toulouse
Tel: 05.61.75.15.76
Fax: 05.61.73.52.89

Editions du Seuil
27 rue Jacob
75261 Paris Cedex 06
Tel: 01.40.46.50.50
Fax: 01.43.29.08.29

Editions Solin
18 rue Séguier
75006 Paris
Tel: 01.55.42.63.00
Fax: 01.55.42.63.01

Editions Stock–Théâtre Ouvert
(see below, Théâtre Ouvert)

Editions Théâtre de la Croix Rousse
Place Joannes Ambre
69004 Lyon
Tel: 04.78.39 52.53
Fax: 04.78.39.05.24

Editions Théâtrales
4 rue Trousseau
75011 Paris
Tel: 01.43.38.44.20
Fax: 01.49.23.04.62

Editions Verdier
234 rue du fbg Saint-Antoine
75012 Paris
Tel: 01.43.79.20.45
Fax: 01.43.79.84.20

Flammarion
26 rue Racine
75006 Paris
Tel: 01.40.51.31.00
Fax: 01.43.29.21.48

La Fontaine (Editions)
44 rue de la Clef
59800 Lille
Tel: 03.20.55.76.11
Fax: 03.20.55.76.12

**Laboratoire de Recherches
sur les Arts du Spectacle**
CNRS
27 rue Paul Bert
94200 Ivry
Tel: 01.49.60.41.29
Fax: 01.46.71.84.98

Le Bruit des Autres
5 rue du Pont
87110 Solignac
Tel: 05.55.00.46.06
Fax: 05.55.00.58.36

Librairie des Femmes
6 rue de Mézières
75006 Paris
Tel: 01.42.22.60.74
Fax: 01.42.22.62.73

Médianes Editions
72 rue d'Amiens
76000 Rouen
Tel: 02.35.88.85.71
Fax: 02.35.15.28.44

Première Impression
La Chartreuse
BP 30
30404 Villeneuve
Avignon Cedex
Tel: 04.90.15.24.24
Fax: 04.90.25.76.21

**Théâtre Ouvert – Tapuscrits
(see organisations)**
4 bis Cité Véron
75018 Paris
Tel: 01.42.55.74.40
Fax: 01.42.52.67.76

Très Tôt Théâtre
Editions Le Mot de Passe
4 rue Trousseau
75011 Paris
Tel: 01.48.06.47.48
Fax: 01.49.23.04.62

REVIEWS AND JOURNALS

Actes du Théâtre
Entr'Actes–SACD
11 bis rue Ballu
75009 Paris
Tel: 01.40.23.45.14
Fax: 01.40.23.46.23

Action Théâtre
Centre Français du Théâtre
10 rue de la Chaussée
d'Antin
75009 Paris
Tel: 01.47.70.39.84
Fax: 01.42.46.42.19

Actualité de la Scénographie
58 rue Servan
75011 Paris
Tel: 01.47.00.19.52
Fax: 01.43.55.81.94

Alternatives Théâtrales
Rue des Poissonniers 13
1000 Brussels
Belgium
Tel: 25.11.78.58
Fax: 25.02.70.25

Arts de la Piste/Hors les Murs
74 ave Pablo Picasso
92000 Nanterre
Tel: 01.46.69.96.96
Fax: 01.46.69.96.98

Bouffonneries
BP 43
32700 Lectoure
Tel: 05.62.68.88.57

Cahiers de la Comédie-Française
Place Colette
75001 Paris
Tel: 01.44.58.14.08
Fax: 01.44.58.13.46

Cassandre: Le Théâtre en Courants
4 rue de la Michodière
75002 Paris
Tel: 01.42.65.11.55
Fax: 01.42.65.00.21

Coups de Théâtre
17 rue de la Procession
75015 Paris
Tel/Fax: 01.45.67.82.72

Du Théâtre (La Revue)
18 rue de Savoie
75006 Paris
Tel: 01.43.25.35.36
Fax: 01.43.54.24.10

Etudes Théâtrales
Ferme de Blocry
Place de l'Hocaille
B–1348 Louvain-La-Neuve
Belgium
Tel: 10.47.22.72
Fax: 10.47.22.37

Jeu–Cahiers de Théâtre
c/o Lansman Editeur
63 rue Royale
B–7141 Carnières
Morlanwelz
Belgium
Tel: 64.44.75.11
Fax: 64.44.31.02

Le Journal du Théâtre
176 rue du Temple
75003 Paris
Tel: 01.40.29.10.50
Fax: 01.40.29.46.56

Les Cahiers
Maison Antoine Vitez
Centre International de la
Traduction Théâtrale
Domaine de Grammont
34000 Montpellier
Tel: 04.67.22.43.05
Fax: 04.67.22.48.34

Les Cahiers de Prospero
Centre National des
Ecritures du Spectacle
BP 30
30404 Villeneuve
Avignon Cedex
Tel: 04.90.15.24.24
Fax: 04.90.25.76.21

Mû–l'autre continent du théâtre
18 rue Gergovie
75014 Paris
Tel: 01.43.95.01.13
Fax: 01.45.45.76.63

Plateaux
21 bis rue Victor Massé
75009 Paris
Tel: 01.42.85.88.11
Fax: 01.45.26.47.21

Puck
Institut International de la
Marionnette
7 place Winston Churchill
08000 Charleville-Mézières
Tel: 03.24.33.72.50
Fax: 03.24.33.54.28

Spectacles Info
Le Magazine des
Professionels du Spectacle
97 rue de Réamur
75002 Paris
Tel: 01.40.41.04.54
Fax: 01.40.26.54.78

Théâtre/Public
Théâtre de Gennevilliers
41 ave des Grésillons
92230 Gennevilliers
Tel: 01.41.32.26.10
Fax: 01.40.86.17.44

Theatre Festivals

For a complete list of festivals in France, contact the Centre National du Théâtre (see p.189). This is a selection of some of the theatre festivals, listed chronologically:

JANUARY
Festival Mondial
Cirque de Demain
10 rue des Filles du Calvaire
75003 Paris
Tel: 01.44.61.06.00
Fax: 01.44.61.06.01

MARCH
**Festival International
d'Humour du Mont Blanc**
MJC Saint-Gervais
111 ave de Miage
74170 Saint-Gervais
Tel: 04.50.47.73.40
Fax: 04.50.78.32.61

**Maubeuge International
Theatre**
Le Manège
Rue de la Croix
59600 Maubeuge
Tel: 03.27.65.15.00
Fax: 03.27.64.45.11

APRIL
Festival Exit
Maison des Arts
Place Salvator Allende
94000 Créteil
Tel: 01.45.13.19.19
Fax: 01.43.99.48.08

**Passages – Théâtre de l'Est
de l'Europe à Nancy et en
Lorraine**
Théâtre de la Manufacture
10 rue Louis Baron
54000 Nancy
Tel: 03.83.37.12.99
Fax: 03.83.37.18.02

APRIL–MAY
Festival Mettre en Scène
Théâtre National de Bretagne
1 rue Saint-Hélier
35000 Rennes
Tel: 02.99.30.88.88
Fax: 02.99.67.66.19

MAY
Aventures
La Ferme du Buisson
Allée de la Ferme
77437 Noisiel
Tel: 01.64.62.77.00
Fax: 01.64.62.77.99

Enfantillages
Théâtre Gérard Philipe
59 bd Jules Guesde
93207 Saint-Denis Cedex 01
Tel: 01.48.13.70.10
Fax: 01.42.43.03.37

Théâtre en Mai
Théâtre National de Dijon-
Bourgogne
BP 1230
21029 Dijon Cedex
Tel: 03.80.68.47.47
Fax: 03.80.68.47.48

JUNE
Turbulences
Le Maillon
13 place André Maurois
67200 Strasbourg
Te: 03.88.27.61.71
Fax: 03.88.27.61.82

**Qu'on Te Le Dise – Festival
du Conte de Bordeaux
Saint-Michel**
Gustave Productions
60 rue Saint-Fort
33000 Bordeaux
Tel: 05.56.51.16.09
Fax: 05.56.51.14.52

JUNE–JULY
Printemps des Comédiens
Parc Euromédecine
34097 Montpellier Cedex 5
Tel: 04.67.61.06.30
Fax: 04.67.04.21.50

JULY
Festival d'Avignon
6 rue de Braque
75003 Paris
Tel: 01.44.61.84.84
Fax: 01.44.61.84.83
and
8 bis rue de Mons
(administration)
84000 Avignon
Tel: 04.90.27.66.50
Fax: 04.90.27.66.83

Avignon Public-Off
BP 5
75521 Paris Cedex 11
Tel: 01.48.05.20.97
Fax: 01.48.05.40.67

**Chalon dans la Rue –
Festival National des
Artistes de la Rue**
5 place de l'Obélisque
71100 Chalon-sur-Saône
Tel: 03.85.48.05.22
Fax: 03.85.93.68.62

Festival d'Eté de Nantes
Porte Saint-Pierre
Rue de l'Evêché
44000 Nantes
Te: 02.40.08.01.00
Fax: 02.40.48.12.64

**Festival de Théâtre
Européen de Grenoble**
8 rue Pierre Duclot
38000 Grenoble
Tel: 04.76.44.60.92
Fax: 04.76.51.74.27

**Rencontres Théâtrales
d'Hérisson**
Les Fédérés–Montluçon
Rue des Faucheroux
03100 Montluçon
Tel: 04.70.03.86.18
Fax: 04.70.05.88.57

JULY–AUGUST
Paris Quartier d'Eté
22 rue Chauchat
75009 Paris
Tel: 01.44.83.64.40
Fax: 01.44.83.64.43

AUGUST
**Mimos – Festival
International du Mime**
Centre Culture de la
Visitation
Rue Littré
24000 Périgueux
Tel: 05.53.53.55.17
Fax: 05.53.04.30.84

SEPTEMBER–OCTOBER
**Festival International des
Francophonies en Limousin**
11 ave du Général de Gaulle
87000 Limoges
Tel: 05.55.10.90.10
Fax: 05.55.77.04.72

Festival Mondial des Théâtres de Marionnettes
BP 249
08103 Charleville Mézières
Tel: 03.24.59.94.94
Fax: 03.24.56.05.10

SEPTEMBER–DECEMBER
Festival d'Automne à Paris
156 rue de Rivoli
75001 Paris
Tel: 01.53.45.17.00
Fax: 01.53.45.17.01

OCTOBER
Tendances Nord – Festival International de Danse et de Musique Vivante
L'Hippodrome
BP 79
59502 Douai Cedex
Tel: 03.27.87.07.78
Fax: 03.27.87.29.59

Festival Acteurs-Acteurs
Autruche Théâtre
15 rue Fernand Léger
37000 Tours
Tel: 02.47.38.29.29
Fax: 02.47.37.41.51

Festival de Lille
64 ave du Président Kennedy
59000 Lille
Tel: 03.20.52.74.23
Fax: 03.20.85.91.75

DECEMBER
Festival International de la Marionnette à Mirepoix
10 rue Astronome Vidal
09500 Mirepoix
Fax: 05.61.68.71.39

Theatres

National Theatres

There are five national theatres in France, given that the Vieux-Colombier and the Studio are spaces operating under the auspices of the Comédie-Française.

Comédie-Française – Salle Richelieu
Place Colette
BP 2141
75021 Paris Cedex 01
Tel: 01.44.58.14.00
Fax: 01.44.58.15.50

Comédie-Française – Théâtre du Vieux-Colombier
21 rue du Vieux-Colombier
75006 Paris
Tel: 01.44.39.87.10
Fax: 01.44.39.87.19

Comédie-Française – Studio Théâtre
Carrousel du Louvre
Place de la Pyramide
inversée
99 rue de Rivoli Boite no.16
75039 Paris Cedex 01
Tel: 01.44.58.98.58
Fax: 01.42.60.35.65

Odéon–Théâtre de l'Europe
1 place Paul Claudel
75006 Paris
Tel: 01.44.41.36.00
Fax: 01.44.41.36.01

Théâtre National de Chaillot
1 place du Trocadéro
75016 Paris
Tel: 01.53.65.31.00
Fax: 01.53.65.10.31

Théâtre National de la Colline
15 rue Malte Brun
75980 Paris Cedex 20
Tel: 01.44.62.52.00
Fax: 01.44.62.52.90

Théâtre National de Strasbourg
13 rue de Phalsbourg
BP 184R5
67005 Strasbourg Cedex
Tel: 03.88.35.63.60
Fax: 03.88.37.37.71

Major public theatres (centres dramatiques nationaux)

Ile de France (ie, Paris region)
Théâtre de la Commune
2 rue Edouard Poisson
BP 157
93304 Aubervilliers Cedex
Tel: 01.48.33.16.16
Fax: 01.48.34.35.55

Théâtre de Gennevilliers
41 ave des Grésillons
92230 Gennevilliers
Tel: 01.41.32.26.10
Fax: 01.40.86.17.44

Théâtre Nanterre-Amandiers
7 ave Pablo Picasso
92022 Nanterre Cedex
Tel: 01.46.14.70.70
Fax: 01.47.25.17.75

Théâtre Ouvert
(see structures for promotion of new writing, p.193)

MC93 Bobigny
1 bd Lénine BP 71
93002 Bobigny Cedex
Tel: 01.41.60.72.60
Fax: 01.41.60.72.61
*(This international producing
theatre is part of the Scènes
Nationales network – see p.211)*

Théâtre Gérard Philipe
Centre Dramatique National
de Saint-Denis
59 bd Jules Guesde
93207 St-Denis Cedex
Tel: 01.48.13.70.10
Fax: 01.42.43.03.37

*Regions (listed alphabetically by
town)*
Nouveau Théâtre d'Angers
CDN et Association Maison
de la Culture
12 place Louis Imbach
BP 2107
49021 Angers Cedex 02
Tel: 02.41.88.90.08
Fax: 02.41.88.37.80

**Centre Dramatique
National de Savoie
Bonlieu**
1 rue Jean Jaurès
74000 Annecy
Tel: 04.50.52.76.74
Fax: 04.50.51.04.24

**Nouveau Théâtre de
Besançon**
Centre Dramatique National
de Franche-Comté
Parc du Casino
ave Edouard Droz
25000 Besançon
Tel: 03.81.88.55.11
Fax: 03.81.50.09.08

**Centre Dramatique
National Région Nord-Pas-
de-Calais**
La Comédie de Béthune
Studio–Théâtre
Place Foch
BP 631
62412 Béthune Cedex
Tel: 03.21.63.29.00
Fax: 03.21.63.29.13

Théâtre du Port de la Lune
Centre Dramatique National
Bordeaux–Aquitaine
Square Jean Vauthier BP7
33031 Bordeaux Cedex
Tel: 05.56.91.01.81
Fax: 05.56.92.81.50

**Théâtre National
Dijon Bourgogne**
BP 1230
21029 Dijon Cedex
Tel: 03.80.68.47.47
Fax: 03.80.68.47.48

**Centre Dramatique
National des Alpes**
4 rue Paul Claudel
BP 2448
38034 Grenoble Cedex 2
Tel: 04.76.25.05.45
Fax: 04.76.62.98.69

Comédie de Caen
Centre Dramatique National
de Normandie
1 square du Théâtre
BP 94
14203 Hérouville-St-Clair
Tel: 02.31.46.27.27
Fax: 02.31.46.27.28

La Métaphore
Théâtre National de la
Région Nord–Pas-de-Calais
4 place du Général de Gaulle
BP 302
59026 Lille Cedex
Tel: 03.20.14.24.00
Fax: 03.20.14.24.14

Théâtre de l'Union
Centre Dramatique du
Limousin
20 rue des Coopérateurs
BP 206
87006 Limoges Cedex
Tel: 05.55.79.74.79
Fax: 05.55.77.37.37

**La Criée – Théâtre National
de Marseille**
30 quai de Rive Neuve
13007 Marseille
Tel: 04.91.54.74.54
Fax: 04.91.54.28.18

Les Fédérés
Centre Dramatique National
Région d'Auvergne
Théâtre des Ilets
Espace Boris Vian
03100 Montluçon
Tel: 04.70.03.86.18
Fax: 04.70.05.88.57

Théâtre des Treize Vents
Centre Dramatique National
du Languedoc-Roussillon
BP 9622
34054 Montpellier Cedex 01
Tel: 04.67.64.14.42
Fax: 04.67.15.09.77

Théâtre de la Manufacture
Centre Dramatique National
de Nancy-Lorraine
10 rue Baron Louis
BP 3349
54014 Nancy Cedex
Tel: 03.83.37.12.99
Fax: 03.83.37.18.02

Théâtre de Nice
Centre Dramatique National
Nice Côte d'Azur
Promenade des Arts
06300 Nice
Tel: 04.93.13.90.90
Fax: 04.93.62.19.46

**Cado – Centre National de
Création**
Carré Saint-Vincent
45000 Orléans
Tel: 02.38.54.29.29
Fax: 02.38.81.77.64

Centre Dramatique National Orléans-Loiret-Centre
Carré Saint-Vincent
45000 Orléans
Tel: 02.38.62.15.55
Fax: 02.38.62.20.98

La Comédie de Reims
3 chaussée Bocquaine
51100 Reims
Tel: 03.26.48.49.10
Fax: 03.26.88.76.95

Théâtre National de Bretagne
1 rue Saint-Hélier
BP 675
35008 Rennes Cedex
Tel: 02.99.31.55.33
Fax: 02.99.67.66.19

Comédie de Saint-Etienne
Centre Dramatique National
7 ave Emile Loubet
42001 Saint-Etienne
Tel: 04.77.25.01.24
Fax: 04.77.41.96.34

Le Sorano
Théâtre National de
Toulouse Midi-Pyrénées
35 allée Jules Guesde
BP 449
31009 Toulouse Cedex
Tel: 05.61.52.95.50
Fax: 05.61.55.39.93

Théâtre National Populaire
8 place Lazare Goujon
69627 Villeurbanne Cedex
Tel: 04.78.03.30.30
Fax: 04.78.84.03.20

Other public theatres

As well as the Centres Dramatiques Nationaux, there are also seven Centres Dramatiques Régionaux in France, whose mission is specifically local and regional.

Théâtre Régional des Pays-de-la-Loire
112 rue de Frémur
BP612
49006 Angers Cedex 01
Tel: 02.41.44.17.50
Fax: 02.41.68.42.88

Atelier du Rhin – La Manufacture
Centre Dramatique
Régional d'Alsace
6 route d'Ingersheim
BP 593
68008 Colmar Cedex
Tel: 03.89.41.71.92
Fax: 03.89.41.33.26

Centre Dramatique de Bretagne
Théâtre de Lorient
11 rue Claire Droneau
BP 726
56107 Lorient Cedex
Tel: 02.97.83.51.51
Fax: 02.97.83.59.17

Centre Dramatique Poitou-Charentes
16 rue Scheurer Kestner
BP 504
86012 Poitiers
Tel: 05.49.41.43.90
Fax: 05.49.41.03.73

Théâtre des Deux Rives
Centre de Création
Dramatique de Haute-Normandie
48 rue Louis Ricard
76000 Rouen
Tel: 02.35.89.63.41
Fax: 02.35.70.59.83

Théâtre Populaire de Lorraine
BP 146
57103 Thionville Cedex
Tel: 03.82.53.33.95
Fax: 03.82.53.40.55

Centre Dramatique Régional de Tours
Compagnie Gilles Bouillon
3 rue Léonard de Vinci
37000 Tours
Tel: 02.47.64.48.64
Fax: 02.47.20.17.26

There is also a network of fifty-nine State-funded theatres (excluding overseas *departements*) known as Scènes Nationales, formerly Maisons de la Culture, Centres d'action culturelle or Centres du développement culturel. These are responsible for creating new productions, as well as welcoming visiting companies and productions. For details of these, contact the Centre National du Théâtre (see p.189).

Privately and independently run theatres
There are many theatres which are independently run, but receive partial funding from the Direction du Théâtre or the City of Paris, as well as from other sources. This funding is paid

either direct to the theatre or to the company running the theatre. These, along with the private theatres of Paris (and one in Lyon) which operate under a very different system from State-funded theatres (see p.118), are listed together. Municipal theatres, which are run by the City of Paris, are listed separately. For details of municipal theatres outside Paris, contact the Centre National du Théâtre. Theatres are listed by keyword – e.g., Théâtre du Soleil is listed under 's' for Soleil.

Théâtre Antoine – Simone Berriau
14 bd de Strasbourg
75010 Paris
Tel: 01.42.08.46.28
Fax: 01.42.08.38.40

Théâtre de l'Aquarium
Cartoucherie
Route du Champ de
Manoeuvre
75012 Paris
Tel: 01.43.74.72.74
Fax: 01.43.28.13.60

Théâtre de l'Atelier
1 place Charles Dullin
75018 Paris
Tel: 01.46.06.19.89
Fax: 01.42.64.55.80

L'Athénée – Théâtre Louis Jouvet
24 rue Caumartin
75009 Paris
Tel: 01.47.42.67.81
Fax: 01.47.42.18.78

Théâtre de la Bastille
76 rue de la Roquette
75011 Paris
Tel: 01.43.57.42.14
Fax: 01.47.00.97.87

Les Bouffes du Nord
(Centre International de
Créations Théâtrales)
37 bis bd de la Chapelle
75010 Paris
Tel: 01.46.07.33.00
Fax: 01.42.05.54.33

Les Bouffes Parisiens
4 rue Monsigny
75002 Paris
Tel: 01.42.96.97.03
Fax: 01.42.86.88.73

Comédie et Studio des Champs-Elysées
15 ave Montaigne
75008 Paris
Tel: 01.47.20.07.79
Fax: 01.49.52.06.89

Théâtre du Chaudron
Cartoucherie
Route du Champ de
Manoeuvre
75012 Paris
Tel: 01.43.28.97.04
Fax: 01.43.28.40.15

**Théâtre de la Cité
Internationale**
21 bd Jourdan
75014 Paris
Tel: 01.45.88.81.54
Fax: 01.45.80.91.90

Dix-Huit Théâtre
Compagnie Macqueron-
Djaoui
16 rue Georgette Agutte
75018 Paris
Tel: 01.42.26.47.47
Fax: 01.42.26.63.98

Théâtre de l'Epée de Bois
Cartoucherie
Route du Champ de
Manoeuvre
75012 Paris
Tel: 01.48.08.39.74
Fax: 01.43.28.56.53

Théâtre Essaïon de Paris
6 rue Pierre au Lard
75004 Paris
Tel: 01.42.78.46.42
Fax: 01.42.74.04.54

**Théâtre de la Gaîté
Montparnasse**
26 rue de la Gaîté
75014 Paris
Tel: 01.43.20.60.56
Fax: 01.43.22.56.51

Théâtre Hébertot
78 bis bd des Batignolles
75017 Paris
Tel: 01.43.87.24.24
Fax: 01.42.93.95.61

Théâtre de la Huchette
23 rue de la Huchette
75005 Paris
Tel: 01.43.26.51.62
Fax: 01.40.51.75.34

Théâtre La Bruyère
5 rue la Bruyère
75009 Paris
Tel: 01.48.74.88.21
Fax: 01.40.23.94.51

Théâtre du Marais
Compagnie Jacques Mauclair
37 rue Volta
75003 Paris
Tel: 01.42.78.03.53
Fax: 01.40.29.92.52

Théâtre de la Madeleine
19 rue de Surène
75008 Paris
Tel: 01.42.65.06.28
Fax: 01.42.66.27.80

Théâtre de la Main d'Or
15 passage de la Main d'Or
75011 Paris
Tel: 01.48.05.67.89
Fax: 01.49.23.93.19

Théâtre Marigny
Carré Marigny
75008 Paris
Tel: 01.43.59.70.00
Fax: 01.43.59.01.80

Théâtre des Mathurins
36 rue des Mathurins
75008 Paris
Tel: 01.42.65.90.01
Fax: 01.49.24.91.69

Théâtre Mogador
25 rue de Mogador
75009 Paris
Tel: 01.53.32.32.20

Théâtre Montparnasse/Petit Montparnasse
31 rue de la Gaîté
75014 Paris
Tel: 01.43.22.77.30
Fax: 01.43.20.08.83

Théâtre de Paris
15 rue Blanche
75009 Paris
Tel: 01.48.74.10.75
Fax: 01.48.74.28.09

Théâtre Poche Montparnasse
75 bd du Montparnasse
75006 Paris
Tel: 01.45.44.50.21
Fax: 01.42.84.12.91

Théâtre des Quartiers d'Ivry
La Balance
7 place Marcel Cachin
94200 Ivry sur Seine
Tel: 01.46.72.37.43
Fax: 01.46.71.27.75

Théâtre du Rond-Point
Compagnie Marcel Maréchal
2 bis ave Franklin D. Roosevelt
75008 Paris
Tel: 01.44.95.98.00
Fax: 01.40.75.04.48

Théâtre du Soleil
Cartoucherie
Route du Champ de Manoeuvre
75012 Paris
Tel: 01.43.74.87.63
Fax: 01.43.28.33.61

Théâtre de la Tempête
Cartoucherie
Route du Champ de Manoeuvre
75012 Paris
Tel: 01.43.74.94.07
Fax: 01.43.74.14.51

Théâtre de la Tête d'Or
24 rue Dunoir
69003 Lyon
Tel: 04.78.95.46.69
Fax: 04.78.71.77.08

Théâtre des Variétés
7 bd Montmartre
75002 Paris
Tel: 01.42.33.11.41
Fax: 01.42.33.83.62

Municipal Theatres (Paris)
Théâtre Musical de Paris Châtelet
2 rue Edouard Colonne
75001 Paris
Tel: 01.40.28.28.28
Fax: 01.42.36.89.75

Théâtre de la Ville
16 quai de Gesvres
75180 Paris Cedex 04
Tel: 01.48.87.54.42
Fax: 01.48.87.81.15

Théâtre Paris-Villette
211 ave Jean Jaurès
75019 Paris
Tel: 01.42.03.02.55
Fax: 01.42.02.02.68

Théâtre 13
24 rue Daviel
75013 Paris
Tel: 01.45.88.16.30
Fax: 01.45.89.42.41

Théâtre 14 – Jean-Marie Serreau
20 ave Marc Sangnier
75014 Paris
Tel: 01.45.45.49.77
Fax 01.40.44.52.01

Nouveau Théâtre Mouffetard
73 rue Mouffetard
75005 Paris
Tel: 01.43.36.87.88
Fax: 01.43.31.53.70

Théâtre Silvia Monfort
Compagnie Sans Domicile Fixe
106 rue Brancion
75015 Paris
Tel: 01.45.33.66.70
Fax: 01.45.31.15.71

Théâtre Molière
Maison de la Poésie
161 bis rue Saint-Martin
75003 Paris
Tel: 01.44.54.53.10
Fax: 01.42.71.11.02

Theatre Schools

The following list includes a selection of the top public and private establishments in France, listed under discipline (acting, stage design, etc.). Fuller lists of public (including national conservatoires and national schools) and privately run establishments are available from the Centre National du Théâtre (see p.189), as are lists of university courses and training for various theatre disciplines. For details of French-language requirements, contact the school direct.

Acting courses (State-funded establishments)

Conservatoire National de Région de Bordeaux
Centre André Malraux
22 quai Sainte-Croix
33800 Bordeaux
Tel: 05.56.92.96.96
Fax: 05.56.92.22.30

Conservatoire National de Région de Montpellier
14 rue Eugène Lisbonne
34000 Montpellier
Tel: 04.67.60.79.33
Fax: 04.67.66.06.99

Conservatoire National Supérieur d'Art Dramatique
2 bis rue du Conservatoire
75009 Paris
Tel: 01.42.46.12.91
Fax: 01.48.24.11.72

Ecole de Théâtre du Théâtre National de Bretagne
1 rue Saint Hélier
BP 675
35008 Rennes Cedex
Tel: 02.99.31.55.33
Fax: 02.99.67.66.19

Ecole du Centre Dramatique National de St-Etienne
7 ave Emile Loubet
42000 St-Etienne
Tel: 04.77.25.01.24
Fax: 04.77.41.96.34

Ecole Régionale d'Acteurs de Cannes
68 ave du Petit Juas
06400 Cannes
Tel: 04.93.38.73.30
Fax: 04.93.68.35.03

Ecole Supérieure d'Art Dramatique du Théâtre National de Strasbourg
13 rue de Phalsbourg
BP 184R5
67005 Strasbourg Cedex
Tel: 03.88.35.63.60
Fax: 03.88.37.37.71

ENSATT (Ecole Supérieure des Arts et Techniques du Théâtre) (Contact CNT for addresses relocating in autumn 1997)

Private acting schools (including international programmes)
The following are recognised as the principal private acting academies. There are many more schools than we are able to list here. For full information, contact the Centre National du Théâtre.

Ecole de l'Acteur
35 quai d'Anjou
75004 Paris
Tel: 01.43.29.60.22
Fax: 01.40.36.06.65

Ecole Internationale de Théâtre Jacques Lecoq
57 rue du Faubourg Saint-Denis
75010 Paris
Tel: 01.47.70.44.78

Ecole du Théâtre National de Chaillot
1 place du Trocadéro
BP 1007–16
75016 Paris
Tel: 01.53.65.31.00
Fax: 01.53.65.10.31

Atelier International du Théâtre
14 rue Crespin du Gast
75011 Paris
Tel: 01.43.55.69.61

Cours Franco-Américain
65 rue de Reuilly
75012 Paris
Tel: 01.43.44.76.98

Stage design
Ecole Nationale Supérieure des Arts Decoratifs
31 rue d'Ulm
75005 Paris
Tel: 01.42.34.97.00
Fax: 01.42.34.97.85
(See also Strasbourg and ENSATT schools above)

Lighting and Sound (technical theatre)
Centre de Formation Professionelle des Techniciens du Spectacle
92 ave Galliéni
93170 Bagnolet
Tel: 01.48.97.25.16
Fax: 01.48.97.19.19

Institut Grenoblois des Techniques du Spectacle
Chateau de Rochepleine
1 rue du Rif Tronchard
38120 Saint Egreve
Tel: 04.76.75.32.82
Fax: 04.76.75.01.59

Institut Supérieur des Techniques du Spectacle
Cloître Saint-Louis
20 rue du Portail Boquier
84000 Avignon
Tel: 04.90.14.14.17
Fax: 04.90.14.14.16
(See also Strasbourg and ENSATT schools above)

Costume design
See ENSATT above

Theatrical make-up
Atelier International de Maquillage – Hélène Quille
34–6 rue de la Folie Régnault
75011 Paris
Tel: 01.43.48.47.46
Fax: 01.43.48.86.56

Circus arts

More detailed lists are available from the Centre National Théâtre (see p.189).

Ecole Supérieure des Arts du Cirque
1 rue du Cirque
51000 Chalon-sur-Marne
Tel: 03.26.21.12.43
Fax: 03.26.64.60.13

Ecole Nationale du Cirque de Rosny-sous-Bois
Stade Pierre Letessier
Rue Jules Guesde
93110 Rosny-sous-Bois
Tel: 01.48.55.44.65
Fax: 01 .48.55.21.29

Ecole Nationale du Cirque Annie Fratellini
Parc de la Villette
2 rue de la Cloture
75019 Paris
Tel: 01.48.45.58.11
Fax: 01.48.40.20.66

Puppetry

Ecole Supérieure Nationale des Arts de la Marionnette
7 place Winston Churchill
08000 Charleville Mézières
Tel: 03.24.33.72.50
Fax: 03.24.33.54.28

Mime

Centre International d'Action Culturelle de Mimodrame de Paris Marcel Marceau
17 rue René Boulanger
75010 Paris
Tel: 01.42.02.32.82
Fax: 01.40.18.95.62

Contemporary French Dramatists

The following is a representative list of playwrights (some well known, others less so) who have been prominent in French theatre during the 1980s and 1990s. Unless otherwise stated, all were born in France. For further information, particularly on lesser-known works or unpublished writers, contact one of the associations listed on pp.187–94. For publishers in French, see pp.198–201 (note – occasionally works may be out of print, but have been included here for library reference purposes).

Nourrédine Aba
b. 1921, Algeria; d. 1996
First a journalist, then a poet and playwright since the 1950s, Aba is known for his militant support of the downtrodden, which provided the focus for his playwriting. He won many awards, including the Franco-Arab friendship prize for *Telle el Zaâtar s'est tu à la tombée du soir* in 1985 and an award for his collected works from the Fondation de France in the same year. He was appointed a member of the Haut Conseil de la Francophonie by François Mitterrand in 1992. His more recent works, some broadcast on radio by France Culture, include *La Récréation des clowns* (1982), *Le Dernier Jour d'un nazi* (1986) and *A l'aube sans couronne* (1990). Published by Ed. Lansman; Ed. de l'Harmattan; Ed. Stock; Ed. Quatre Vents.

Catherine Anne
b. 1960
A graduate of the Rue Blanche school, Catherine Anne is a popular contemporary playwright, actress and director who often stages her own works and began writing in the 1980s. Her many plays include *Une année sans été* (1987), *Tita Lou* (1991), *Agnès* (1994) and *Surprise* (1996). Anne's works have been performed in many major theatres, including the Théâtre de la Bastille, Théâtre Nanterre-Amandiers and at the Avignon Festival. Published by Actes Sud-Papiers and L'Ecole des Loisirs.

Fernando Arrabal
b. 1932, Spanish Morocco
Arrabal is a major international writer of unconventional ritualistic, and tumultuous dramas, mostly resulting from his family's experiences of the Spanish Civil War and his own resultant tragedy, as illustrated by plays such as *Pique-nique en campagne* (1959) and *Le Cimetière des Voitures* (1957). His *L'Architecte et l'empereur d'Assyrie* was first directed in France by Lavelli in 1967 and his *Le Labyrinthe* by Savary in the same year. All Arrabal's plays continue to be widely performed as part of the French repertoire today. Plays since 1980 include *La Traversée de l'Empire* (1987), *Une pucelle pour une gorille* (1987), *The red Madonna* (1987) and *La Nuit est aussi un soleil*, followed

by *Roue d'lnfortune* (1990). Published by Christian Bourgois and Actes Sud-Papiers.

Jean Audureau
b. 1932

Audureau is a writer of densely poetic plays, whose main output was during the 1960s and 1970s. In 1983, *Félicité*, a play dealing with a servant–employer relationship between two women, was performed at the Comédie-Française. In 1994 four of his plays were staged in a season at Aubervilliers: *Katherine Barker, Le Jeune Homme, Félicité* and *La Lève*. Published by Ed. Gallimard and Actes Sud-Papiers.

Michel Azama
b. 1947

An ex-actor, Azama is now primarily a playwright, having written numerous theatre plays including *Vie et Mort de Pier Paolo Pasolini* (first staged in 1984), *Le Sas* (1986) and *Croisades* (1988), both first staged in 1989 and performed abroad as well as in France. His latest play is *Zoo de nuit* (1995). A notable characteristic of his work is its dreamlike quality, mixing differing realities and time spans. From 1989 to 1992 he was dramaturge at the CDN in Dijon, then from 1994 to 1996 editor in chief of *Les Cahiers de Prospero* (see p.203), the journal published by La Chartreuse (see p.189), for and about practising writers in France today. Published by Ed. Théâtrales, L'Avant-Scène and Actes Sud-Papiers.

Alain Badiou
b. 1937, Morocco

Alongside playwriting, Badiou has enjoyed a successful academic career teaching at Paris VIII University since 1969 and has written numerous articles and books on the theatre. His career as a playwright began in 1979, with the opera *L'Echarpe Rouge*, directed by Antoine Vitez, followed by the plays *Ahmed le Subtil ou Scapin 84*, staged at the Comédie de Reims and the Avignon Festival in 1994, and *L'Incident d'Antioche* (both written in 1984). *Ahmed Philosophe* and *Ahmed se fâche* were both staged for the first time in Reims in 1995, followed by *Les Citrouilles* in

1996, which was also directed by Christian Schiaretti at the Théâtre des Quartiers d'Ivry in 1997. Published by Actes Sud-Papiers.

Jean-Christophe Bailly
b. 1949

As well as writing novels, poetry, art books and essays, Bailly has written several plays for the theatre, including *Le Régent* (1987), *Pandora*, which was created at the Théâtre National Populaire in Villeurbanne in 1992, and *Les Céphéides*, directed in the Cour d'honneur at the 1983 Avignon Festival. Georges Lavaudant has directed much of his work. Published by Christian Bourgois.

Bauer, Jean-Louis
b. 1952

A graduate in ethnology and from the Rue Blanche school, Bauer has worked in theatre in education and university teaching, as well as writing plays, some of which have been broadcast by France Culture. In autumn 1996, his play *Page 27* was staged at the Théâtre Tristan-Bernard. Other works include *L'homme assis* (1990), *Pourquoi aujourd'hui* (1993), *Le millième soir* (1996) and the melodramatic musical *Le Ugui* (1993), both in collaboration with Piotr Moss. Published by L'Avant-Scène; Actes Sud-Papiers; Albin Michel; L'Arche; Ed. Très Tôt Théâtre (see Ed. Théâtrales) and Le livre à la carte.

Bruno Bayen
b. 1950

Bruno Bayen's plays over the last two decades include *Schliemann, épisodes ignorés* which was first staged in 1982 at the Théâtre National de Chaillot in Paris, employing some thirty actors, plus musicians, audiovisual material and puppetry and with Vitez in the main role. His other plays include *Weimarland*, and *L'Enfant Bâtard*; both were staged for the first time in 1992. He directed the first performance of Genet's *Elle* with Maria Casarès in 1991 at the Théâtre de Gennevilliers. Published by Ed. Gallimard, L'Avant-Scène and L'Arche.

Samuel Beckett
b. 1906, Ireland; d. 1989

Although Beckett is primarily famous for earlier works (see p.10), he continued to produce plays for the theatre throughout the 1980s, experimenting in the reduction of theatrical form to a minimum with various '*dramaticules*' – published in a group of six, with the earlier work *Cette Fois* (1974) by Ed. Minuit in 1992. These were *Solo* (1980), *L'Impromptu d'Ohio* and *Berceuse* (both 1981), *Catastrophe* (1982) and *Quoi où* (1985). During the same decade his interest in the televisual medium grew and he produced several television plays, including *Nacht und Traüme* and *Quad* in 1982, and a television version of *Quoi où* (see above) in 1985. Published in French by Ed. Minuit and L'Avant-Scène.

Arnaud Bédouet
b. 1958, Africa

Bédouet studied at the Rue Blanche in Paris, and led a varied career as actor, director, translator (of Julian Mitchell and Terence Rattigan) and adapter, before writing his first play, *Kinkali*, set in Africa. This was staged at the Théâtre de la Colline in January 1997, directed by Philippe Adrien (see p.254) and won him the 1997 Molière award for best writer. Published by Actes Sud-Papiers.

Loleh Bellon
b. 1925

After reaching the top of the theatrical and cinematic acting profession and winning acclaim for her classical roles at the Renaud–Barrault company in the 1960s, Bellon moved on to writing plays which are regarded as 'feminist' by some critics. Sensitively written, many have won awards, including *Les Dames du Jeudi*, her first play (1976), *Le Coeur sur la Main* (1980) and *Une absence* (1988), for which she won the Molière award for best writer. Published by L'Avant-Scène; Actes Sud-Papiers; Ed. Gallimard.

Slimane Benaïssa

b. 1943, Algeria

Benaïssa has seen his plays widely performed in Algeria and France since 1975, and has also followed a career as an actor and director. Since 1981 he has been under threat of death from Algerian extremists and in 1993 decided to take refuge in France, where he has been awarded various writer's residencies. His plays include *Conseil de discipline* (1992) and the acclaimed *Les Fils de l'amertume*, created at the 1996 Avignon Festival. Published by Ed. Lansman and Actes Sud-Papiers.

André Benedetto

b. 1934

Benedetto is a colourful figure known for his lively, often controversial support of causes and political standpoints. He was founder of La Nouvelle Companie d'Avignon in 1963 (see p.135) and still works from the Théâtre des Carmes in Avignon. His work during the 1960s included *Napalm* (1967), *Zone Rouge* (1968) and *Le Petit Train de M. Kamodé* (1969). He took up the regional Occitan cause with works such as *Geronimo* in 1974 (performed for four years) which drew parallels between Apache and Provençal history; the Mediterranean identity continues to be a preoccupation in his creations. In 1991 *L'acteur loup* marked the first in a series of shows based on improvisations, followed by others such as *Nous les Eureupéens* [sic], which was also staged in Saarbrücken and St Petersburg. Plays published by P. J. Oswald (Honfleur), Ed. de l'Harmattan, Actes Sud-Papiers and Ed. du théâtre des Carmes.

Daniel Besnehard

b. 1954

Besnehard was dramaturge at the Comédie de Caen from 1978 to 1985, and has been general secretary and dramaturge at the Nouveau Théâtre d'Angers since 1986. Based on recent history and diverse themes, his plays include *L'Etang gris* (1982), *Passagères* (1984), *Arromanches* (1986), *Mala Strana* (1988), *L'Ourse blanche* staged by Claude Yersin at the Nouveau Théâtre d'Angers in 1990, and *Clair de Terre* (1989). *L'Enfant d'Obock* was directed by Yersin in 1994 at the Scène National d'Aubusson and the Nouveau Théâtre d'Angers. Published by Ed. Théâtrales; L'Avant-Scène; Actes Sud-Papiers and Théâtre Ouvert.

Jean–Marie Besset
b. 1959
Besset is the author of many popular plays performed mainly in private but also in public theatres, dealing with middle-class themes and situations, such as political corruption in *Un coeur français* (1996), and the pressure at top business schools in *Grande Ecole* (1995). Other plays include *La Fonction* (1988), *Villa Luco* (1989) and the extremely successful *Ce qui arrive et ce qu'on attend* (1990), staged by Patrice Kerbrat at the Gaîté Montparnasse in 1993. Having spent much time in New York, his work is relatively Anglo-American in its approach to style and form. Patrice Kerbrat (see p.263) directs much of it in France. Besset has also translated plays, by authors including Alan Bennett, Michael Frayn and Tom Stoppard. Published by Actes Sud-Papiers.

François Billetdoux
b. 1927; d. 1991
Billetdoux's long career as a playwright spanned five decades, from his début in the Parisian art theatres in the 1950s with plays such as *Tchin-Tchin* (1959) to his last work, *Réveille-toi Philadelphie*, completed in 1988. His plays are noted for their crisp, acute dialogue and unconventional viewpoint. He was also a novelist and television screenwriter. Published by Actes Sud-Papiers, L'Avant-Scène and Ed. Seuil.

Denise Bonal
b. 1921, Algeria
An actress in radio and theatre, who has performed all over France, Bonal turned her hand to writing plays in 1968. Often dealing with family issues in colloquial language, they include *Légère en août* (1974), *Portrait de Famille* (1983), *Passions et Prairie* (1987), *Turbulences et Petits Détails* (1993) and *Féroce comme le coeur* (1994). Published by Ed. Théâtrales and Actes Sud-Papiers.

Michel-Marc Bouchard
b. 1958, Canada

Bouchard is a Québecois playwright, whose play *Les Muses orphelines* (1988), a family tale of three sisters and a brother, has been adapted for the French stage by Noëlle Renaude. Bouchard has written several other plays, including *Histoire de l'oie* (1986) and *Les grandes chaleurs* (1993). Published by Ed. Théâtrales.

Gildas Bourdet
b. 1947

After a spell involved with création collective in the 1970s, Bourdet went on to write several plays in the 1980s, known for their irony and linguistic sharpness, which he has also directed and designed. These include *Derniers Details* (1981), *Le Saperleau* (1982), *Une station service* (1985) and *Les Crachats de la lune* (1986). He has also written for television. He has been director of La Criée in Marseille since 1995 (for more details of his directing work, see p.256) Published by L'Avant-Scène, Actes Sud-Papiers and Ed. Solin.

Jean-Louis Bourdon
b. 1955

Bourdon, who first attracted notice as a playwright in the late 1980s, has written novels and several radio plays, as well as for the stage. His plays include *Jock*, staged by Marcel Maréchal at La Criée, Marseilles, in 1988; *Visite d'un père à son fils* (1989), *Fin de programme* (1991), *L'Hôtel du silence* (1991), *Derrière les collines* (1992), directed by the author at the 1992 Avignon Festival, and *Scènes de la misère ordinaire*, staged in 1997 at the Théâtre 18, Paris. Published by Ed. Julliard, Actes Sud-Papiers and Flammarion.

Philippe Braz
b. 1959

Primarily a novelist, Braz has written several theatre plays: *Dialogue sur Minetti* (1988), *La Nuit des baleines* (1989), *Dernière Station avant le paradis* (1991), *Transits* (1993) and *Rencontres* (1995). Set in everyday life situations, his plays mostly focus on characters who are idealistic drifters and dreamers.

Jean-Claude Brisville

b. 1922

Brisville was literary editor of Editions Julliard (1959–70) and a television writer (1964–71), before going on to direct the drama department of the Office de Radio et de Télévision Française (ORTF), then the literary department of Livre de Poche between 1974 and 1981. As well as *récits*, essays and children's stories, in the 1980s and 1990s he has written several theatre plays which have premièred at mainstream Parisian theatres. These include *Le Fauteuil à bascule* (staged in 1982 at the Petit Odéon by Jean-Pierre Miquel); *L'Entretien de M. Descartes avec M. Pascal le jeune* (also at the Petit Odéon, 1985), *Le Souper* (staged at the Théâtre Montparnasse, 1989, and made into a film), *L'Antichambre* (at the Atelier, 1991), *Contre-jour* (at the Studio des Champs-Elysées, 1993) and *La Dernière Salve* (at the Théâtre Montparnasse, 1995). He has also adapted Christopher Hampton's stage version of *Les Liaisons Dangereuses* for the French stage (1988). Published by Actes Sud-Papiers and L'Avant-Scène.

Jean-François Caron

b, 1961, Canada

After theatre school in Montreal, Caron has gone on to write a handful of plays staged in Canada; his play *Saganash* premièred in France at the Théâtre de Châtillon in 1995. He received a bursary from the Centre National des Lettres in 1992 and completed a period as author in residence at Limoges, as part of the Festival International des Francophonies. His other plays include *Le Scalpel du Diable* (1990) and *Aux hommes de bonne volonté* (1991). Published by Actes Sud-Papiers.

Jean-Claude Carrière

b.1931

Carrière is well known as a novelist, essayist and screenplay writer for notable directors such as Louis Malle, Tati and Luis Buñuel. In the theatre he is renowned as a dramaturge and adapter, especially for his work for Peter Brook, whose *Mahabharata* he worked on in 1985. As well as Shakespeare adaptations such as *Timon of Athens* (1974) and *Measure for*

Measure (1978), Carrière has also written stage plays, including L'*Aide-Mémoire* (1968, and revived in 1994); *La Conférence des oiseaux* (1979) and *La Terrasse* (1997). He is vice-president of the SACD and has been president of the national cinema and television school, FEMIS. Published by Actes Sud-Papiers; L'Avant-Scène; Ed. du Laquet and CICT (Peter Brook's research centre in Paris).

Denise Chalem
b. 1952, Egypt

As well as a successful stage, television and film-acting career, working with big-name directors at major theatres, Chalem has also written many plays and television screenplays, inspired and encouraged by her teacher at the Paris Conservatoire, Antoine Vitez. Stage plays include *A cinquante ans, elle découvrait la mer* (staged at the Petit Odéon, 1980); *Selon toute Ressemblance* (directed by the author in 1986 at the Gaîté Montparnasse) and *Couki et Louki sont sur un bateau* (1987). Published by Actes Sud-Papiers and L'Avant-Scène.

Pierre Charras
b. 1945

Alongside many novels since his writing career began in 1982, Charras has worked as an actor with many well-known directors, including Guy Rétoré, Stephan Meldegg, Michel Fagadau and Jacques Mauclair, and has translated several novels. His works for the theatre are *Francis Bacon, le Ring de la Douleur,* which was given a public reading at the 1996 Avignon Festival, and *Dimanche Prochain*, which premièred at the Théâtre de l'Œuvre in January 1997.

Bernard Chartreux
b. 1942

An author, dramaturge and translator, Chartreux worked with Jean-Pierre Vincent at the Théâtre National de Strasbourg (1974–83), and at the Comédie-Française until 1986, when he moved to the Théâtre Nanterre-Amandiers, where he has been co-director since 1990. Known for adapting foreign and classical works into contemporary form and social documentary style, he also co-wrote with Jean Jourdheuil in the 1970s. His later stage plays include *Violences à Vichy* (1980) (*Violences à Vichy II* was created in 1995 at Nanterre-Amandiers), *Dernières Nouvelles de la peste* (1983) and *Cité des oiseaux* (1989). Published by Ed. Théâtrales; Ed. Stock-Théâtre Ouvert; L'Avant-Scène and Ed. Solin.

Hélène Cixous
b. 1935, Algeria
Cixous is a writer, novelist, essayist and academic, well known for her collaboration with Ariane Mnouchkine at the Théâtre du Soleil during the 1980s and 1990s, although she has been writing for the theatre since the early 1970s, and with other directors including Simone Benmussa and Viviane Théophilides. Her 'epic' works for Mnouchkine in the 1980s were *L'Histoire terrible mais inachevée de Norodom Sihanouk, roi du Cambodge* (1985) and *L'Indiade, ou l'Inde de leurs rêves* (1987). After translating the *Eumenides* for Mnouchkine's cycle *Les Atrides* (see p.97), she went on to write the contemporary tragic epic *La Ville parjure ou le réveil des Erinyes* based around the theme of haemophiliacs given blood contaminated with AIDS. This was first staged in 1994, as was *L'Histoire (qu'on ne connaîtra jamais)*, a work based around the Nibelungen and directed by Daniel Mesguich at the Théâtre de la Ville. Published by Ed. Théâtrales; Librairie des Femmes; L'Avant-Scène; Ed. Seuil and the Théâtre du Soleil.

Hubert Colas
b. 1957
Colas has been writing plays since the 1980s, as well as directing and designing for the theatre company Dipthong Cie, based in Marseilles. He has been the recipient of various prizes and bursaries. His plays include *Temporairement epuisé* (1988), *Terre ou l'Epopée sauvage de Guénolé et Matteo* (1991), *La Brûlure* (1993), *Visages* (1993, staged at the Théâtre de la Cité Internationale in 1995), *La Croix des oiseaux* (staged at the 1996 Avignon Festival) and *Traces ou Semence(s) au père* (1997). Published by Actes Sud-Papiers.

Copi

b. 1939, Argentina; d. 1987

Copi was a popular cartoonist, writer, humorist and actor of his own short plays, which were intended to surprise and shock, e.g. *L'Homosexuel ou la difficulté de s'exprimer* in 1971, and *Une Visite inopportune*, under direction from Lavelli, about his own death (from AIDS) in 1987. His last play, *Cachafaz*, was staged by Lavelli and Arias at La Colline in 1993. Published by Christian Bourgois; L'Avant-Scène and Actes Sud-Papiers.

Enzo Cormann

b. 1954

After studying philosophy, Cormann has devoted himself to writing, acting and directing in the theatre since 1980. His work is noted for his experimentation with style and form, often using non-narrative structure and metaphorical language, and for his preference for big social issues in terms of subject matter. His plays include *Noises* (1981), *Cabale* (1983), *Corps perdus* (1985), *Sang et eau* (1986), *Takiya! Tokaya!* (1992) *Âmes Soeurs* (1992) and *Diktat* (1995), staged at the Avignon Festival in 1995. He also works on musical productions such as the mini-opera *Diverses Blessures*, staged at the Théâtre de la Tempête, Paris, in 1996. Published by Ed. Minuit; L'Avant-Scène; Ed. Théâtrales, Actes Sud-Papiers and Théâtre Ouvert.

Gilles Costaz

b. 1943

Costaz has been a theatre journalist and critic since 1967, currently associated with *Politis* and *Le Journal du théâtre* which he edits. He has written three plays: *Le Crayon*, staged in 1991 at the Rond-Point; *Retour à Petersbourg* at the Théâtre Poche-Montparnasse in 1994; and *Tour de France*, part of the *Eloge du cycle* series at the Artistic-Athévains in 1997.

Bernard Da Costa

b. 1939

One of the founders of the café-theatre movement in Paris during the 1960s, Da Costa has written some thirty plays for the stage, the best known of which are *Les Adieux de la Grande*

Duchesse (1970), *Messe pour un sacre viennois* (written for radio in 1972, and staged at the Petit Odéon in 1982), *L'Elève de Brecht* (1984), *Frederick et Voltaire* (staged at the Petit-Montparnasse in 1986), *Pat et Sarah* (1988) and *Nous, Charles XII,* directed by Pierre Santini in 1991. He has also written novels, radio plays and a history of café-theatre. Published by Actes Sud-Papiers; Ed. Quatre Vents; Ed. Crater and L'Avant-Scène.

Daniel Danis
b, 1962, Canada
Danis is a Québecois playwright who has produced four plays to date and is enjoying current acclaim in France with works such as the prizewinning *Celle-là* (1992) and *Cendres de cailloux* (1992). His other plays are *Le Pont de pierres* (1996) and *Les Nuages de Terre* (1994). Published by Actes Sud-Papiers, Théâtre Ouvert and Ed. L'Ecole des loisirs.

Philippe Delaigue
b. 1961
An ex-student of the Lyon Conservatoire and the national theatre school in Strasbourg, Delaigue became an actor and director (see p.258), founding the Travaux 12 company in 1982, before beginning to write and direct his own plays in 1990. His works include *La Retraite d'Eugène* (1990), *L'Exil de Jacob* (1991) and *Haro!* (1993). Published by Editions Travaux 12 (Delaigue's company at La Fabrique Théâtre, 78 ave Maurice Faure, 26000 Valence) and Comp'Act.

Richard Demarcy
b. 1942
Demarcy was founder of the Naïf Théâtre Atelier for contemporary creation in 1972, and writes plays linking myths, social comment and history. *Quatre Soldats et un accordéon* (staged at the 1976 Festival d'Automne), for example, deals with the Portuguese civil war and *La Nuit du père* (1991) with social decay. His play *L'Etranger dans la maison* (staged at Théâtre de la Tempête in 1982) is published in English (*New French Plays*, Methuen, 1989). Demarcy's adaptations include Lewis Carroll's *Hunting of the Snark* (*Disparitions*, 1979) and Pessoa's *Ode*

Maritime; he also translates Portuguese plays into French and is a professor at Paris III University. Published by Actes Sud-Papiers, L'Avant-Scène, Ed. des Quatre Vents, Christian Bourgois and Ed. Théâtrales. His published thesis (1973) is entitled *Eléments d'une sociologie du spectacle* (Paris: Union Générale d'éditions).

Michel Deutsch
b. 1948

A playwright, poet and essayist, whose earlier dramatic work is part of the Théâtre du Quotidien of the 1970s (see p.59), Deutsch has been a member of the dramaturgy collective at the Théâtre National de Strasbourg and has written numerous plays, some philosophical, dealing with social issues. These include *Dimanche* (1974), *Convoi* (1980), *Feroé, La Nuit* (1989), *La Négresse Bonheur* (1995), *John Lear* (1995), and collaboration with Lavaudant, Bailly and Duroure on *Lumières I* and *II* (1995). His series of *Imprécations*, three plays about destructive influences in contemporary times, have been played together since 1991; these were followed by *Imprécations IV* at Théâtre de la Bastille in 1996. Published by Christian Bourgois; Théâtre Ouvert; Ed. Stock–Théâtre Ouvert; L'Avant-Scène and L'Arche.

Alain Didier-Weill
b. 1939

A trained psychiatrist, Didier-Weill's articles exploring the relationship between theatre and psychoanalysis led him to start writing plays. The first, *Pol*, was staged by Jacques Seiler as part of the Festival d'Automne in 1975. Other plays include *Trois Cases blanches* written in 1982 and *L'Heure du thé chez les Pendlebury* in 1992. Published by J. C. Lattès and Actes Sud-Papiers.

Louise Doutreligne
b. 1948

Doutreligne has written for theatre, radio and film, as well as working as a professional actress. In 1975 she founded the Théâtre du Quotidien company with Jean-Paul Wenzel. She went on to found another with Jean-Luc Paliès (Compagnie Fiévet-Paliès), who has directed many of her plays. Theatre writings, several produced as a result of writing bursaries, include *Femme à la Porte Cochère* (1987), *Les Jardins de France* (1990) and *L'Esclave du Démon* (1996). Published by Ed. Théâtrales; Actes Sud-Papiers; Ed. Stock–Théâtre Ouvert; Tapuscrits Théâtre Ouvert; Ed. Quatre Vents.

Roland Dubillard
b. 1923

A poet, short-story writer, actor, screenwriter and adapter, the multi-talented Dubillard is nevertheless best known for his plays, some of which he has acted in himself and many of which are still performed today. His earlier works included the well-known *Naïves Hirondelles* (1961), *La Maison d'os* (1962), *Le Jardin aux betteraves* (staged in 1969 by Roger Blin), *Les Crabes* (1971, more recently staged at the Théâtre de la Bastille in 1995), *Où boivent les vaches* (staged by the Compagnie Renaud–Barrault in 1972), *Les Diablogues et Les Nouveaux Diablogues* (1975, based on his 1950s radio characters *Grégoire et Amédée*). *Les Chiens de conserve* (1995), first written as a radio play, was staged at the Théâtre 13, Le Sorano and the Théâtre du Maillon, Strasbourg, in 1996. Published by Ed. Gallimard; L'Avant-Scène, and L'Arbalète.

Marguerite Duras
b. 1914, Indo-China; d. 1996

Most famous as a novelist and screenwriter, Duras also wrote plays for the theatre, many of which she directed. Known for her stream-of-consciousness style of prose and imagery-packed language, she has made a marked impression on theatrical writing in France over the last four decades, with works such as *L'Amante anglaise* (1967), *Yes, peut-être* (1968), *India Song* (commissioned by Peter Hall at the National Theatre, London, in 1972) and *Eden Cinema* (1977). From 1980 she produced a number of texts, including *Savannah Bay* (1983) and *La Musica deuxième* – a revised version of her earlier work, expanded to include developments twenty years on (1985). Published by Actes Sud-Papiers; Ed. Minuit and Ed. Gallimard.

Eugène Durif
b. 1950

Durif writes arts and literary reviews and poems, as well as adaptations and plays. *Conversation sur la Montagne* (1986), *Tonkin Alger* (1988), *Le petit bois* (1991), *Les petites heures* (1992) and, most recently, *Via Negativa* and *Nefs et naufrages* (both 1996) are some of his many works. He has also adapted many plays, including Québecois Jean-Paul Dalpé's *Le Chien*. Published by Actes Sud-Papiers; Comp'Act; Michel Chomarat and Théâtre Ouvert.

Xavier Durringer
b. 1963

Durringer is a popular contemporary writer, whose plays focus primarily on issues facing young people, using contemporary, colloquial language. Plays include *Bal Trap* (1989), *Une envie de tuer sur le bout de la langue* (1990), *La Quille* (1993) and most recently *Chroniques des jours entiers, des nuits entières* (1995) and *Polaroïd* (1996). As well as winning several playwriting bursaries, Durringer has continued to act and direct (including his own texts) through La Lézarde theatre company (Paris) which he founded in 1988. He also writes and directs for the cinema. Published by Ed. Théâtrales.

Olivier Dutaillis
b. 1958

A vet, sporadic traveller and writer, Dutaillis has published two novels, as well as winning the grand prix du jeune théâtre de l'Académie française in 1995 for his first set of plays. His first theatre play was *Les Grandes Personnes* in 1990. In 1994, he also wrote *L'Inventeur mirobolant*, a play for children, the monologue *Une femme du terrain*. *On s'entendait si bien* (1991) is one of his best-known works. Published by Actes Sud-Papiers and Première Impression–La Chartreuse (see p.189).

Paul Emond
b. Belgium

Emond has written several plays for the theatre, as well as some four novels: his theatre works include *Les Pupilles du tigre* (created in Brussels for the first time in 1986, and made into a film the following year), *Inaccessible amours* (1992), staged in France for the first time at the Théâtre du Gymnase, Marseille, and Théâtre Ouvert in 1995, and M*alaga* (1993), staged at the Théâtre du Rond-Point in 1997. Published by Ed. Lansman and Théâtre Ouvert.

Jean-Pol Fargeau
b. 1950
Fargeau founded the 'Dépense' group, for which he wrote a series of unpublished plays between 1974 and 1980. Since the 1980s his plays include the trilogy *Daniel et le monde*, the first part of which (*Hôtel de l'homme sauvage*) was staged at Chaillot by Stuart Seide in 1985 and the second (*Voyager*) at the Théâtre des Saints-Anges, Marseille by Alain Fournier in the same year. Other works include *Brûle, rivière brûle* the Maison de la Culture in La Rochelle and the 1989 Avignon Festival. Published by Ed. Théâtrales and Ed. Solin.

Philippe Faure
b. 1952
An actor and director as well as a playwright, Faure has directed the Théâtre de la Croix Rousse in Lyon since 1994. His many theatre plays include *Le Petit Silence d'Elisabeth* (1988), *La Caresse* (1991), *La Nuit de Michel-Ange* (1991), *Je ne suis pas Frankenstein* (1993) and *Moi, Paul Verlaine, père et mère* (1995). He has also adapted numerous texts for the theatre, including Zola's *Thérèse Raquin* and Molière's *Le Bourgeois Gentilhomme*. Published by Actes Sud-Papiers; L'Avant-Scène and Dumerchez.

Jean-Noël Fenwick
b. 1950
Fenwick has written several plays for café-theatre, including *Ma vie est un navet* (1981), *C'était ça ou le chômage* (1984) and *Huis Glauque* (1986), staged at the Comédie Italienne, as well as his award-winning theatre play *Les Palmes de M. Schutz* (1989), staged at the Théâtre des Mathurins in 1990–1, which won four Molière awards, including that of best author and the best private-theatre show, and went on to be made into a film. It has

since been adapted for performance in nineteen countries. Fenwick has also co-written a screenplay with Gérard Oury, entitled *Les Géants de la Terre*, filmed in 1991. Published by L'Avant-Scène.

Roland Fichet
b. 1950

Fichet was involved with the foundation of the Laboratory of Theatrical Studies at the University of Haute Bretagne and created the company Théâtre de Folle Pensée in 1978, which he also directs. He has written a number of works during the 1980s and 1990s, including *De la paille pour mémoire* (1985), *Terres promises* (1987), *Plage de la libération* (1988), *La Chute de l'ange rebelle* (1989), *Suzanne* (1990) and *Naître* (1993). Published by Ed. Théâtrales and Actes Sud-Papiers.

Didier-Georges Gabily
b. 1955; d. 1996

A novelist, screenwriter and theatre director, Gabily also wrote a large number of plays, often directing his own work, as well as running his own theatre company, T'Chang'G! His plays include the two-part *Violences* (1991), *Gibiers du Temps: un triptyque* (staged at Gennevilliers in 1995), *Voix* (staged at Les Fédérés, Montluçon, 1995) and *Théâtre du Mépris 3* (1993), based partly on the Italian novel *Il Disprezzo* by Moravia and partly on the film *Le Mépris* by Jean-Luc Godard, first staged by Gabily in 1996 at Gennevilliers. Published by Actes Sud-Papiers and Théâtre Ouvert.

Fatima Gallaire
b. 1944, Algeria

Gallaire is a novelist as well as a playwright. Her theatrical works deal with subjects ranging from religious extremism in *Ah! Vous êtes venus . . . là ou il y a quelques tombes!* (1986) to the break-up of an old couple in *Témoignage contre un homme stérile* (1987) or the relationships between women in Muslim society in her best-known play *Princesses* (staged at Nanterre-Amandiers by Jean-Pierre Vincent in 1991). Published by L'Avant-Scène; Ed. Théâtrales and Ed. Quatre Vents.

Armand Gatti
b. 1924, Monaco

Gatti's belief in the power of poetry, theatre and self- expression all stem from his experiences as a survivor of the Nazi concentration camps. A journalist in the 1950s, prolific dramatist in the 1960s, he has concentrated in the past three decades on plays and projects based in working-class communities all over France (as well as in Northern Ireland), using video and film as well as dramatic performance. His recent work includes a play devised with prisoners at Fleury-Mérogis in 1989 for the bicentenary of the French Revolution and *Adam quoi?*, staged in Marseille in 1993, about the concentration camp experience (see p.35). Published by L'Arche; Ed Seuil; Actes Sud-Papiers; Comp'Act; Ed. Verdier and L'Avant-Scène.

Alain Gautré
b. 1951

Teacher at the Lecoq school in Paris, actor, director and co-founder of the Théâtre du Chapeau Rouge company, he wrote a number of theatre plays for this company, including *Place de Breteuil* (1978) and *Gevrey-Chambertin* (1981). More recent works include *Genèse* (1990), *Chef-lieu* (staged at the Théâtre Gérard Philipe in 1992), *Hôtel du grand-large* (1995) and *La Chapelle en Brie* (1996). He has also written a novel and collaborated on the textbook *Théâtre du Geste* (Bordas, 1980). Plays published by Actes Sud-Papiers and Ed. Théâtrales.

Jean-Claude Grumberg
b. 1939

Grumberg has written and adapted works for the theatre since 1965, his best-known plays being *L'Atelier* (1979), *Dreyfus* (1974) and *Zone libre* (in which he played the title role in Vincent's 1990 staging at Théâtre National de la Colline). His play *Linge Sale* (1988) was staged at the 1994 Avignon Festival and *Adam et Eve* was directed by Gildas Bourdet at La Criée, Marseille and the Théâtre National de Chaillot in 1997. He has also written television scripts and a screenplay, *Les Années Sandwichs* (1988). His work employs differing formats and subjects, using humour to make social observation (see pp.116–7). Published by Actes Sud-Papiers.

Denis Guénoun
b. 1946, Algeria

As well as being director of the theatre company L'Attroupe-ment and author of various theatre essays, Guénoun has also written several plays, including *Le Pas* (1991) with a mammoth cast of thirty-seven (playable by fifteen actors). Others include *Le Printemps* (1985), *L'Eneide, d'après Virgile* (1983), *X, ou Le Petit Mystère de la Passion* (1990) and *Lettre au directeur du théâtre* (1997). Published by Ed. l'Aube and Actes Sud-Papiers.

Victor Haïm
b. 1935

Haïm is a journalist, writer and playwright, whose first play was performed in 1963. One of his best-known plays, *Abraham et Samuel*, was staged at the Petit Odéon in 1973. He began writing on a more full-time basis for radio, television and the theatre in 1977, although he also acts and teaches drama. He has enjoyed international success with his works, which have played in some twenty countries and have been translated into fifteen different languages. During the 1980s and 1990s, his plays have included *La Valse du hasard* (1986) and *Le Rire de David* (first staged at the Petit Odéon in 1989). Published by L'Avant-Scène; Actes Sud-Papiers; Ed. Crater; Ed. Stock-Théâtre Ouvert and Ed. Quatre Vents.

Adel Hakim
b. 1953, Egypt

As well as achieving a doctorate and graduating from top business school Hautes Etudes Commerciales, Hakim has also forged a successful career as an actor, playwright, director and theatre director. Having trained with Mnouchkine and Strasberg, Hakim went on to found the Théâtre de la Balance with Elisabeth Chailloux in 1984 and since 1992 they have co-directed the Théâtre des Quartiers d'Ivry. His plays include the monologue *Exécuteur 14* (1990), *Made in Europa* (1992) and *Corps* (1995). His adaptations for theatre include Joseph Delteil's *François d'Assise* (1994). He teaches at various theatre schools, including the Théâtre National de Strasbourg and ENSATT. Published jointly by Théâtre des Quartiers d'Ivry-La

Balance/Lecture-Média/CRDC Nantes/CNL and Ed. Quatre Vents.

Jaoui, Agnès and Bacri, Jean-Pierre
b. 1964 and 1951
Jaoui and Bacri are co-writers of the successful play *Un air de famille* (1994), which won two Molière awards in 1995 and the earlier *Cuisine et dépendances* (1991), which won four Molières in 1993, including that for best author. Both are actors (Jaoui studied with Patrice Chéreau) and have also won a César (the French equivalent of an Oscar) for their screenplay *Smoking et No Smoking* by Alain Resnais in 1994, adapted from Alan Ayckbourn's *Intimate Exchanges*. Bacri has also written several other plays, including the prizewinning *Le grain de Sable* (1981) and *Le Doux Visage de l'amour*. Published by L'Avant-Scène.

Jean-Luc Jeener
b. 1949
As well as writing poetry, directing the Compagnie de l'Elan which he co-founded in 1976, and reviewing theatre for 'Figaroscope' (the weekly leisure supplement in *Le Figaro*), Jeener is a prolific playwright, with over fifty works to his name. A few are published, and around twenty have been staged; they include *L'An mil* featuring fifty different characters (1980), *Le Noël du loup* (1983), *La Lettre* (1993), *Le divan des divas* (1996) and *Procès de Jeanne* (1995). Published by Collections de l'Elan.

Joël Jouanneau
b.1946
A journalist, theatre director and author, Jouanneau began his writing career in the 1980s, after ten years managing the Centre Culturel in St-Denis. In the early 1980s he spent several years as a Middle Eastern correspondent, an experience which has influenced his writings. On his return he joined Bruno Bayen's theatre company and since 1989 has been a member of the artists' collective at Sartrouville. In the 1990s he has become known for his directing, as well as plays such as *Nuit d'orage sur Gaza* (1985), *Kiki l'Indien* (1989) and *Allegria opus 147* (1994), staged to acclaim at the Théâtre de la Colline in 1996. Published by Actes Sud-Papiers.

Jean Jourdheuil

b. 1944

Jourdheuil began to collaborate with Jean-Pierre Vincent in 1968 and together they formed a company which, for five years, was noted for its reinterpretation of the Marxist classics, especially Brecht and Vishnevski. Jourdheuil was one of the first to translate the plays of Heiner Müller, several of whose works he directed with Jean-François Peyret when they formed a joint company in the 1980s. As well as this, they adapted non-dramatic works by authors as various as Rousseau, Montaigne and Lucretius for stage performance. A theoretician as well as a practitioner, Jourdheuil has written books analysing contemporary arts policy and has a teaching post at the University of Paris X, Nanterre. Published by L'Avant-Scène.

Stéphane Keller

b. 1958

After training as an actor, Keller founded and toured with two theatre companies. He directed his own first play, *Actor's Studio*, in 1986, followed by *Quoi de neuf à Paris?* in 1988 and *Au jour le jour* in 1989. The latter won him the First Student Theatre Prize for a subsequent production at the Théâtre de la Main d'Or in 1993. Since then he has written several plays set in the suburbs: his best known is *Route 33* (1994). He also writes for television.

Bernard-Marie Koltès

b. 1948; d. 1989.

Koltès continues to be one of the most regularly performed contemporary playwrights in French theatre since his death (from AIDS) in 1989. His works, which deal with contemporary issues, from homelessness to inter-family relationships, use a variety of settings and well-orchestrated structure and language, in general preferring to link personal life to a series of social and political gestures rather than make direct political comment. Relationships centre on the idea of the deal, epitomised in his play *Dans la solitude des champs de coton*, the tension in buyer–seller negotiations symbolising individual and ideological, and class and cultural struggle.

After a period travelling in the States (his beloved New York was to provide the setting for his later work, *Quai Ouest*), he attracted the attention of Hubert Gignoux at the Strasbourg national drama school when performing a play with friends and was offered a place at the school while continuing to write: it was during this period that Lucien Attoun began to broadcast his early plays on France Culture. After completing his first novel during the 1970s, Koltès returned to theatre with *Sallinger* and his dramatic monologue, *La Nuit juste avant les forêts*, both performed in 1977. Travels in South America and Africa then led to his writing *Combat de nègre et de chiens* (1979), staged by Patrice Chéreau at the Théâtre des Amandiers, Nanterre, in 1983, followed by *Quai Ouest*, 1986. Koltès worked on celebrated Chéreau productions at Nanterre during the 1980s, including Genet's *Les Paravents* (1983) and his translation of *A Winter's Tale* (1988), and wrote *Le Retour au désert*, given its première by Chéreau at the Rond-Point theatre in 1988. In the last year of his life Koltès also wrote *Roberto Zucco*, first produced by Peter Stein at the Berlin Schaubühne in 1990. Published by Ed. Minuit and Ed. Stock.

Serge Kribus
b. 1962, Belgium
After studying theatre at the Brussels Conservatoire, Kribus acted on stage and in cinema, as well as writing several plays. *Arloc ou Le Grand Voyage* (1993) was staged at the Théâtre de la Colline in 1996. Others include *Le Grand Retour de Boris Spielman* (1992), *Cagoul* (1993) and *Max et Gilberte* (1994). Published by Actes Sud-Papiers.

Jean-Luc Lagarce
b. 1957; d. 1995
Author, director and director of the Compagnie La Roulotte until his death, Lagarce wrote numerous plays for the theatre since his début in 1980, many of which have been broadcast on radio by France Culture. Lagarce worked closely with the Théâtre Ouvert, which was responsible for distributing many of his works, and provided the space for their performance or public reading. Lagarce's plays include *Le Voyage de Madame Knipper vers la Prusse Orientale* (1980) and most recently *J'étais*

dans ma maison et j'attendais que la pluie vienne (1995), staged at the Théâtre Ouvert in March 1997 and *Le Pays lointain* (1995), scheduled for the 1997 Avignon Festival (both directed by Stanislas Nordey). Published by Théâtre Ouvert; L'Avant-Scène and Les Solitaires Intempestifs (the publishing company founded by Lagarce).

Yves Lebeau
b. 1945
After studying at the Rue Blanche and the Paris Conservatoire, Lebeau has followed a career as an actor and director, as well writing numerous plays. Many have been staged at top theatres including the Odéon and the Théâtre Gérard Philipe (Saint-Denis), or have been broadcast on radio by France Culture. They include *Fraternité* (1986), *Le chant de la baleine abandonnée* (1991) and *Dessin d'une aube à l'encre noire* (1995). He has won several awards for his writing, including prizes from the SACD. Published by Actes Sud-Papiers, Ed. Théâtrales, and Théâtre Ouvert.

Daniel Lemahieu
b. 1946
As well as writing and translating plays, Lemahieu is also closely involved with new writing workshops for professionals and students at the Institut d'Etudes Théâtrales at the University of Paris III. He worked with Vitez (see pp.37–9) in the 1980s and was secretary general of the Théâtre National de Chaillot from 1985 to 1988. He is also a member of the company Le Théâtre d'Essai. His plays include *Entre chien et loup* (1992), *L'Etalon-or* and *Djebels* (1988). Published by Théâtre Ouvert; Ed. Quatre Vents; Théâtrales/Edilig; Actes Sud-Papiers and L'Avant-Scène.

Lorraine Lévy
b. 1959
Lévy founded the Compagnie de l'Entracte which performed her first play, *Finie la comédie* (1987). Her second play, *Le Partage*, was read at la Chartreuse by the Avignon Festival in 1990 and staged at the Petit Odéon in 1992, the Avignon Festival in 1994

and broadcast by France Culture in 1993. Her third play is entitled *Zelda* (1992). While writing for the theatre, she also works as an editor in art publishing. Plays published by Point hors ligne and Librairie Théâtrale (see bookshops, p.197).

Armando Llamas
b. 1950, Spain
After studying in Argentina and writing for the Spanish theatre, Llamas came to France in 1973, working as a writer and journalist for publications including *Libération* and *Théâtre Public* (see p.203). He began writing and translating plays in 1976. His more recent works include *Lisbeth est complètement pétée* (1992), *Quatorze pièces piégées* (1991) and *Sextuor, banquet* (1991). His translation and adaptation of Ramon Del Valle Inclàn's work *Comédies barbares* was staged in 1989 by Jorge Lavelli at Théâtre de la Colline. Published by Michel Chomarat; Comp'Act; Actes Sud-Papiers and Théâtre Ouvert.

Jean-Daniel Magnin
b. 1957, Switzerland
Magnin is noted for creating productions in the early 1980s designed for performance 'outside' the theatre, as well as plays performed at the Avignon Festival and theatres such as the Théâtre de la Bastille, which were taken on international tour. These include *La Tranche ou le Retour de l'enfant prodigue* (1991), directed at the 1993 Avignon Festival by Philippe Adrien, *Le Blé Cornu* (1992) and *Opéra Savon*, given a public reading at the Rond-Point in 1996. Magnin also directs plays and writes for the cinema. Published by Actes Sud-Papiers, Théâtre Ouvert and Ed. Lansman.

Eduardo Manet
b. 1927, Cuba
Manet was director of Cuban theatres and cinemas until his play *Les Nonnes*, directed by Blin in France in 1969, sparked off a prolific French writing career. Plays written since 1980 include *Mendoza en Argentine* (1983), *Ma'déa* (1986) and *Monsieur Lovestar et son voisin de palier* (1995). His earlier play *Un balcon sur les Andes*, written in 1978, is also regularly performed today.

Published by Ed. Gallimard; Actes Sud-Papiers and L'Avant-Scène.

Fanny Mentré
b. 1968

Mentré is an actress, director and author, whose works have been staged at the Avignon Festival, Théâtre Ouvert, and broadcast on radio by France Culture. She has also been a writer in residence at La Chartreuse (writing *Lisa 1 et 2* in 1995). Other works include *Un paysage sur la tombe* (1994) and *Chabada (Bada)*, created at Le Volcan theatre in Le Havre in 1996. Published by Actes Sud-Papiers.

Jean-Pierre Milovanoff
b. 1940

A noted novelist, playwright and writer for radio, Milovanoff has been writing for theatre since the 1980s. He has written a number of plays, including *Squatt* (1984), *Side-car* (1994), *Cinquante mille nuits d'amour* (1993) and *L'Ange des Peupliers*, created at La Chartreuse in July 1996. Published by Ed. Comp'Act, Ed. Théâtrales and Ed. Julliard.

Philippe Minyana
b. 1946

Minyana left literature and drama teaching to write and act in 1980. The style and form of his early, more realist works such as *Fin d'été à Baccarat* (1985) differs greatly from more recent texts such as *Drames Brefs 1* (staged at Le Sorano, Toulouse, in 1996) and *La Maison des Morts* (1996), as he explains in the interview on p.178. Other notable works include *Chambres* (1986); *Inventaires* (1987); *Les Guerriers* (1987) and *Où vas-tu, Jérémie?*, staged at the 1993 Avignon Festival. He often collaborates with the composer Georges Aperghis and the director Robert Cantarella (see p.257), who has staged many of his works. Published by Actes Sud-Papiers; L'Avant-Scène; Théâtre Ouvert and Ed. Théâtrales.

Jean-Gabriel Nordmann
b. 1947

A stage and television actor, working with directors such as

Barsacq and Brook, Nordmann is also a director, adapter, writer and translator of plays and television scripts. Theatre plays, many broadcast on radio by France Culture, include *Simple Suicide* (1985), *La Mer est trop loin* (1987), *Les Petits Mondes* (1996) and *A la porte* (1996). In 1980 he created Le Grand Nord theatre company. He teaches at theatre schools including the Comédie de St Etienne and the Théâtre National de Strasbourg. Published by L'Avant Scène; Actes Sud-Papiers; Ed. Crater and Ed. Théâtrales.

Valère Novarina
b. 1942, Switzerland
Novarina came to prominence as a playwright in France during the 1980s and is known for his use of poetic language, which is rich, dense and complex. Some of his staged works are, in fact, adaptations of his poetry, such as *La Chair de l'homme*, which he directed at the Théâtre du Rond-Point in 1995. Other works include *Le Drame de la vie* (1984, created at the 1986 Avignon Festival); *Vous qui habitez le temps* (1989 Avignon Festival), *Je suis* (1991 Avignon Festival) and *Le Jardin de Reconnaissance*, which Novarina directed at the Théâtre de l'Athénée in 1997. *Le Repas*, which was staged by Claude Buchvald at the Centre Pompidou as part of the 1996 Festival d'Automne, is an adaptation for the stage of the first pages of *La Chair de l'homme*. Published by POL; Christian Bourgois and L'Avant-Scène.

Jean-Yves Picq
b. 1947
An author, director and actor, Picq worked at the TNP with Roger Planchon until 1979. He has received various grants and residencies over his two decades of writing, including La Chartreuse residencies in 1991 and 1993. His plays include *Falaises* (1990), *Doberman* (broadcast on radio by France Culture in 1993), *Partition* (1995), *Le Cas Gaspard Meyer* (1994) and *De la démolition comme art et comme projet* (1995). Published by Les Cahiers de l'égaré; Première Impression-La Chartreuse (see p.189); Théâtre en vie (Université Lyon II) and Color Gang.

Roger Planchon
b. 1931

Planchon is one of France's greatest post-war theatre directors, one of the most successful proponents of the new blend of social historical theatre to emerge in France during the years of decentralisation in the 1950s and 1960s (see pp.41–44). He has written and staged his own work at Villeurbanne (and elsewhere) since the 1960s. His more recent plays include *Alice par d'obscurs chemins* (1983), *Fragile Forêt* and *Le Vieil Hiver* (1991), and *Le Radeau de la Méduse* (1995), staged by Planchon in Paris in 1997 at the Théâtre de la Colline. For details of his directing career see pp.271–2. Published by Ed. Gallimard.

Joël Pommerat
b. 1963

Pommerat's writing career began with the monologue *Le Chemin du Dakar* in 1985. Four years later he founded the Compagnie Louis Brouillard, with whom he has directed the first productions of his plays *Le Théâtre* (1991), *Vingt-cinq années de littérature de Léon Talkoi* (1993) and *Les Evénements* (1994), *Pôles* (1995) and *Treize Etroites Têtes* at the Théâtre Paris-Villette in 1997.

Natacha de Pontcharra
b. 1960

Since her theatre-writing début in 1991, de Pontcharra has seen six of her plays staged, and broadcast in the case of her monologue, *Mickey la Torche* (1993). Most of her works are directed by her close collaborator Lotfi Achour. They include *Œil de cyclone* (1991) and more recently *La Trempe*, staged in residence at La Chartreuse in 1997. Published by Ed. Comp'Act and Théâtre de la Croix-Rousse, Lyon.

Olivier Py
b. 1965

After training at ENSATT and the Paris Conservatoire, Py has gone on to become a top young writer, director and actor of the 1990s. His plays include the twenty-four-hour-long cycle of five plays, *La Servante*, staged non-stop at the Avignon Festival in 1995, as well as *Des oranges et des ongles* (1988), the children's play *La Jeune Fille, le Diable et le moulin* (1993) and *La Chèvre* (1992), another series of plays, incorporating *La Chèvre de M. Seguin, Le Manège enchanté* and *Le Lit lumineux*. He directed his own play *Le Visage d'Orphée* in the Cour d'Honneur at the 1997 Avignon Festival. Published by Actes Sud-Papiers; Ed. Les Ecoles des loisirs and Les Solitaires Intempestifs.

Pascal Rambert
b. 1962
Rambert has been directing and writing for the theatre since the beginning of the 1980s. He staged his own first play, *Météorologies*, in 1985, which like many of his works was based on collaboration with actors. Other works include *Les Parisiens* in 1989, and the prizewinning *John et Mary* and *Les Dialogues*, published together in 1992. His work has been performed at many major French theatres and festivals. Rambert also teaches dramatic writing at the Ecole Régionale d'Acteurs de Cannes and wrote and directed *Long Island*, based on student workshops at the Ménagerie de Verre, Paris, in 1996. Published by Actes Sud-Papiers.

Jacques Rampal
b. 1944, Algeria
Rampal is a cartoonist, who began writing plays at the age of forty. His first play was *Célimène et le cardinal* (staged at the Théâtre de la Porte Saint-Martin in 1992), followed by *Alma Malher, la fiancée du vent* (1992) and *La Fille à la trompette* staged at the Théâtre de la Michodière in 1994. Published by Ed. Librairie Théâtrale.

Noëlle Renaude
b. 1949
Renaude is one of the new generation of playwrights to experiment with language and form in the 1990s (see p.110). She has been awarded various bursaries and prizes for her works, which include *Rose, la nuit australienne* (1988), *Le Renard du Nord* (1989), *Blanche, Aurore, Céleste* (1991), *Petits Rôles* (1992) and the stream–of–consciousness *roman-théâtral Ma Solange, comment*

t'écrire mon désastre Alex Roux (1994) which lasts twenty-seven hours and features around 800 characters in a monologue to be played by one actor. Robert Cantarella, Florence Giorgetti and François Rancillac have directed her plays. Published by Ed. Théâtrales and Théâtre Ouvert.

Yves Reynaud
b.1947

After training as an actor at the Théâtre National de Strasbourg school, Reynaud has acted with many established directors, as well as writing plays. The first, *Souvenir d'Alsace*, was written in collaboration with Bayen and staged at Théâtre Ouvert in 1975. During the 1980s he continued to write, and often directed or co-directed his plays, which included *Regarde les femmes passer* (1981), *Baptême* (1985), *La Tentation d'Antoine* (1988) and *Monologues de Paul* (published in 1997 with *Regarde les femmes passer*). Published by Ed. Théâtrales and Théâtre Ouvert.

Yasmina Reza
b. 1959

Most famous for being the author of the successful *'Art'*, which has enjoyed international performance and acclaim since its first staging in Paris in 1994 by Kerbrat at the Comédie des Champs-Elysées. After training as an actress at Jacques Lecoq's school, Reza went on to write numerous film scripts, adaptations and plays which have been performed in both public and private theatres in France. She also translated Steven Berkoff's adaptation of Kafka's *Metamorphosis* for Roman Polanski. Stage works include *Conversations après un enterrement* (1986), *La Traversée de l'hiver* (1989) and *L'Homme du hasard* (1995). Patrice Kerbrat directs much of her work in France (see p.263). Published by Actes Sud-Papiers.

Serge Rezvani
b. 1928

Rezvani's Persian and Russian background has influenced much of his work as a painter, novelist, song writer and playwright. His prolific theatre writings include *Capitaine Schelle, capitaine*

Eçço (1970) and *Le Camp du drap d'or* (1970). While producing little for the theatre for most of the 1980s, Rezvani turned back to writing for the stage with *Na* (1989), followed by *Glycine* (1993), now in the Comédie-Française repertoire, and *Décor Néant* (1993), his latest play. Published by Actes Sud-Papiers and Ed. Stock–Théâtre Ouvert.

Jean-Michel Ribes
b. 1946
A director and playwright since the 1960s, Ribes has directed many of his own works in both private and public sectors. His plays include *L'Odyssé pour une tasse de thé* at the Théâtre de la Ville in 1974; the prizewinning *Omphalos Hotel*, staged at the Théâtre de Chaillot in 1975 and *Tout contre un petit bois* at the Théâtre Récamier in 1976. Among his more recent works are *Palace* (1989) and *La Cuisse du steward* (1990). He has also written many works for television, radio and cinema during the 1970s and 1980s. Published by Actes Sud-Papiers and L'Avant-Scène.

Jean-Loup Rivière
b. 1948
Rivière's career includes, as well as playwriting, spells as the drama critic for *Libération* (1981–2); secretary general (1983–6) and literary–artistic adviser (since 1986) to the Comédie-Française; academic and university teacher; producer at France Culture and editor of various theatre journals, including the Comédie-Française's *Cahiers*. His play *La Pièce de Scirocco* was performed at the Théâtre National de Chaillot and the Avignon Festival in 1983, and *Jours plissés* was broadcast on France Culture in 1991 and given a public reading at the Rond-Point in 1995. Published by L'Avant-Scène.

Mohamed Rouabhi
b. 1965
Born in Paris, Rouabhi studied at ENSATT, going on to work with directors such as Wenzel and Braunschweig, and, in so doing, working on contemporary texts by authors including Durif, Jouanneau and Bailly, which encouraged him to write.

His plays, written in the 1990s, include *Les Acharnés* (1994), *Fragments de Kaposi* (1994) and *Les Hommes de fer et de sang* (1995). Published by Actes Sud-Papiers.

Nathalie Sarraute
b. 1900, Russia

Sarraute is best known as a novelist, but has also written for the theatre, thanks to encouragement from Jean-Louis Barrault in the late 1960s. She describes her view of theatre, and consequently her play texts, as dialogue- and language-driven, rather than visually conceived (for discussion of her work in more detail, see pp.54–7), which has made them eminently suitable for radio broadcast as well as frequent performance in theatres in France and abroad. They include *Le Silence* (1967), *C'est beau* (1975), *Elle est là* (980), *Pour un oui pour un non* (1982), *La Promenade autour de Nathalie Sarraute* (1993). Published by Ed. Gallimard.

Jean-Pierre Sarrazac
b. 1946

University professor at Paris III University, Sarrazac has written several plays since the 1990s, including *Le Mariage des morts* (1985), *L'Enfant roi* (1984), *Harriet* (1991) and *La Fugitive* (1996). He has also written many influential articles on the theatre, including the collection *L'Avenir du drame* (L'Aire: Lausanne, 1981). Published by Ed. Théâtrales; Médianes; L'Avant-Scène; P. J. Oswald and Circé Théâtre.

Eric Emmanuel Schmitt
b. 1960

Schmitt gained a doctorate in philosophy from the Ecole Normale Supérieure, before turning to writing for the theatre, television and cinema full-time. Influenced by his philosophical background, his plays are discursive and traditional in structure and form, enjoying success in both public and private theatre in France, as well as abroad. His first play was *La Nuit de Valognes* (1991), followed by *Le Visiteur* in 1993. His big 1996 success was *Variations enigmatiques*, starring Alain Delon and Francis Huster at Paris's Théâtre Marigny, closely followed by the popular *Le*

Libertin (based on Diderot's life) in 1997 at the Théâtre Montparnasse. Schmitt has won several Molière awards for his plays and has also written a prizewinning novel. Published by Actes Sud-Papiers and Albin-Michel.

Gilles Ségal
b. 1929

An actor, novelist and director of pantomimes (working in the Compagnies Maréchal and Renaud–Barrault), Ségal has also written several plays, including *Monsieur Schpill et Monsieur Tippeton*, which won the 1996 Molière awards for best author and play. Other plays include *Le marionettiste de Lödz* (1984) and *Le Temps des muets* (1992). Published by Actes Sud-Papiers; L'Avant-Scène and Ed. Lansman.

Coline Serreau
b. 1957

Serreau is an actress, playwright and film producer–writer, who has written several successful stage plays, including the popular *Trois hommes et un couffin* (1984) later made into a film, *Lapin, lapin* (1986), most recently staged at the Théâtre de la Porte Saint-Martin in 1996, *Le Théâtre de verdure* (1987) and *Quisaitout et Grobeta* (1993). Published by Actes Sud-Papiers.

Louis-Charles Sirjacq
b. 1949

As well as adaptations and poetry, Sirjacq has written some twenty works during the 1980s and 1990s, in particular a seven-play cycle around the character of Léo Katz, including *Œil pour œil* (1982), *La Nuit, L'Hiver Chapitre 1* (1989), *Album de famille* (1990) and *Des Fakirs, des momies et maman* (1994). His play *L'Argent du beurre* (1987) has enjoyed a lengthy run at the Théâtre Poche-Montparnasse since May 1996. He has also written screenplays and a novel. Published by Ed. Quatre Vents; L'Arche; L'Avant-Scène and Ed. Théâtrales.

Daniel Soulier
b. 1950

As an actor during the 1970s, Soulier worked notably with Vitez at the Théâtre des Quartiers d'Ivry, then the Théâtre National de Chaillot; he has also worked as a director, puppeteer and teacher, as well as writing for the stage. His plays include *Après l'amour* (1991), *Bernard est mort* (1992) and *Les Chutes du Zambèze* (1995), staged at the Théâtre National de Chaillot in 1995 starring Annie Girardot. Published by Le Bruit des Autres and Ed. de l'Espérance.

Anne Théron
b. 1959

Anne Théron is a novelist, screenwriter and director, as well as a playwright. Her theatre works include *Faire-part*, broadcast by France Culture in 1993, and the unstaged *Notre être de misère* and *Villa Nova de Milfontes*. Published by Ed. Comp'Act.

Tilly
b. 1946

After ten years as a television and theatre actor in Paris, Tilly turned to writing and directing for the stage and cinema in 1978. His plays include *Charcuterie fine* (1980), restaged in 1994 at Théâtre de la Colline, *Spaghetti Bolognese* (1981), *Les Trompettes de la mort* (1985), restaged most recently at La Colline in 1996, and *Y'a bon Bamboula* (1986). He has directed them all, apart from *Spaghetti Bolognese*. He also wrote the film *Loin du Brésil* in 1992. Published by L'Avant-Scène and Actes Sud-Papiers.

Serge Valletti
b. 1951

An actor (working with Mesguich, Lavaudant and Wenzel, among others), playwright and television writer, Valletti has been writing, directing and performing his own works since the late 1960s. In the last two decades they have included *Le Jour se lève, Léopold!* (1988), *Saint Elvis* (1990), *Au rêve de gosse* from 1995. He has also written a comic musical play, *Tentative d'Opérette en Dingo-Chine*, with extracts from Lehar's *Le Pays du Sourire*, staged at the Théâtre 71 Malakoff in 1997. Published by Christian Bourgois; Comp'Act and Théâtre Ouvert.

Didier Van Cauwelaert

b. 1960

A prize-winning novelist primarily, Van Cauwelaert also writes and acts in the theatre. His plays for the theatre include *L'Astronome*, his first play in 1985, *Le Nègre* (1986) and *Noces de Sable*, which was staged at the Comédie des Champs-Elysées in 1995. Published by Actes Sud-Papiers and Albin Michel.

Jean-Jacques Varoujean

d.o.b. unknown

Varoujean's career has included periods as ex-assistant director at the Théâtre de la Michodière (1952–8), as a journalist on *Le Parisien* (1962–75) and as literary adviser to Editions Gallimard (until 1985). He is the writer of some twenty play texts since the 1950s. His most recent plays include *Le Roi des Balcons* (1980), *Apsoss* staged at the 1985 Avignon Festival, *Les Baigneuses de Californie* staged at the Petit Odéon in 1986, *L'Ankou* at the Théâtre de l'Est Parisien in 1989 and *Chacun pleure son Garabed* (directed by Guy Rétoré at the Comédie de St Etienne in 1991). Published by Ed. Gallimard, L'Avant-Scène, Actes Sud-Papiers and Ed. Quatre Vents.

Michel Vinaver

b. 1927

One of the most frequently performed contemporary playwrights in France today, Michel Vinaver's career as a writer spans fifty years, during which time he was equally successful as the managing director of the French division of a multinational company until the 1980s, when he began concentrating on writing for the theatre full time. Like authors from the Théâtre du Quotidien (see pp.59–72) in terms of language and subject matter, his work is especially noted for its experimentation with structure, time and form.

His early plays from the 1950s include *Aujourd'hui ou les Coréens* (1956) and *Iphigénie Hôtel* (1959). During the 1960s he concentrated on commercial interests, returning to playwriting in the late 1960s with *Par dessus-bord* (1967–9), marking the beginning of a steady flow of plays during the 1970s and 1980s. These included *La Demande d'emploi* (1971), *Nina, c'est autre chose* (1976), *Dissident, il va sans dire* (1976), *Les Travaux et les Jours* (1977) and *A la renverse* (1980). *L'Ordinaire* was written in 1981, *Portrait d'une femme* in 1984, *L'Emission de Télévision*, with the theme of television's destructive effects, in 1988 and *Le dernier sursaut* in 1990. His *Les Voisins* (1984) won the Ibsen prize, when it was staged by Alain Françon at Théâtre Ouvert in 1986.

Vinaver has also been a critic and campaigner on behalf of the playwright. In 1987 he published a report commissioned by the Ministry of Culture entitled *Le Compte Rendu d'Avignon* (Actes Sud, Paris 1987), highlighting the need for more theatrical texts to be published and explaining the problems facing the French playwright. Published by Actes Sud-Papiers and L'Aire.

Romain Weingarten
b. 1926
A playwright (for theatre and radio) and poet since the 1940s, Weingarten is still performed today, although his last new play to date was *La Mort d'Auguste* in 1982. *L'Eté*, originally staged in 1966, was restaged in 1991 by Gildas Bourdet (see p.256) at the Théâtre de la Colline, to huge acclaim. Published by Christian Bourgois; Ed. Gallimard; Flammarion; L'Avant-Scène and Actes Sud-Papiers.

Jean-Paul Wenzel
b. 1947
After studying at the Théâtre National de Strasbourg's school, Wenzel became a writer, following work as an actor with directors such as Peter Brook, and helped to create the company Théâtre du Quotidien in 1975. His plays include *Loin d'Hagondange* (1975), *Vater Land, le pays de nos pères* (1983), *Boucherie de nuit* (1985), *Mado* (1985) and *La Fin des monstres* (1994). Wenzel directs the Centre Dramatique National at Montluçon, Les Fédérés (see also directors, p.278). Published by Ed. Stock, Albin Michel, Théâtre Ouvert and L'Avant-Scene.

Directors in Contemporary French Theatre

The following list, by no means exhaustive, gives details of some of the most important directors working in France during the 1980s and 1990s. Some are attached to a public theatre or company, others work independently.

Philippe Adrien
b. 1939

A director, author and screenplay writer for over thirty years, Adrien has been director of the Atelier de Recherche et de Réalisation (Research and Production Workshop) at the Cartoucherie, Vincennes, since 1985, where he also took over the role of director of the Théâtre de la Tempête in 1994. He directs here and elsewhere: recent productions include Grumberg's *Maman revient, pauvre orphelin* at the Vieux-Colombier (1994), Copi's *L'Homosexuel ou la difficulté de s'exprimer* at the Tempête (1997), Genet's *Les Bonnes* at the Vieux-Colombier (1995) and Arnaud Bédouet's *Kinkali* at the Théâtre de la Colline (1997), which won the 1997 Molière award for best first production. He also teaches at the Paris Conservatoire.

Maurice Bénichou
d.o.b. unknown

Bénichou began his theatrical career as an actor in 1965 in Lyon with Marcel Maréchal, going on to act with well-known directors in Paris, including Patrice Chéreau and Jean-Pierre Vincent, before joining Peter Brook's company in 1974 as an actor (subsequently playing in many of Brook's famous productions) and assisting in the direction of *La Cerisaie* and *La Tragédie de Carmen*. As a director, he notably co-directed Jean-Claude Grumberg's *L'Atelier* at the Odéon with Jacques Rosner and the author in 1979; he directed *Dom Juan* in 1985 at the Bouffes du Nord and Grumberg's *La Nuit les chats* at Théâtre Ouvert in 1989.

Simone Benmussa
b. 1932, Tunisia

Benmussa is a writer and director, best known for her feminist standpoint and her adaptations and stagings of all kinds of texts (dramatic or otherwise), including her own, and those of Hélène Cixous, Nathalie Sarraute, Henry James and Edna O'Brien. She directed her first production in 1976 at the Petit-Orsay, Paris (Hélène Cixous's *Portrait de Dora*). Benmussa was literary manager at the Renaud–Barrault company in the 1960s and 1970s, and was editor of its *Cahiers* until 1989.

Daniel Benoin
b. 1947
Pro-European director and actor with a particular interest in German theatre. His work at the Daniel-Sorano theatre in Vincennes during 1973–4 attracted much attention and he was made co-director of the Comédie de St Etienne the following year, where he also directs the theatre school. His productions have included *Woyzeck* (1975) and *Faust* (1987), as well as plays by writers such as Botho Strauss and Sacha Guitry. He has also written for the theatre. He is currently president of the European Theatre Convention (see p.195).

Didier Bezace
b. 1946
Bezace co-founded the Théâtre de l'Aquarium at the Cartoucherie in 1970, where he remains co-director with Jean-Louis Benoit. Since the company's creation he has taken part in all its productions as author, actor or director, as well as conducting a career in cinema, television and theatre elsewhere. As an adapter and director, his productions at the Aquarium have been Arthur Schnitzler's *La Débutante* (1983), *Les Heures Blanches* (1984, 1987 and 1991) adapted from Ferdinando Camon's *La Maladie Humaine*, *Héloïse et Abélard* (staged at the Théâtre National de Strasbourg in 1986), *L'Augmentation* by Georges Perec (1988), *Le Piège* by Emmanuel Bove (1990), *Marguerite et le président* (1992) adapted from text by Marguerite Duras, and *La Femme changée en renard* by David Garnett (1994).

Luc Bondy
b. 1948, Switzerland
A freelance theatre and opera director working mainly in Germany, Belgium and France, Bondy has divided his time

evenly between austere productions of the classics and inventive stagings of contemporary dramatists, especially Peter Handke and Botho Strauss. In the 1980s he worked both at the Berlin Schaubühne and the Théâtre des Amandiers, Nanterre. In this way he was responsible for channelling some of the Schaubühne's ideas and practice into the French theatre. He directed Koltès's adaptation of Shakespeare's *Winter's Tale* at Nanterre in 1988. Recent Parisian productions include Strindberg's *Playing with Fire*, starring Emmanuelle Béart and Pascal Greggory, at the Bouffes du Nord in autumn 1996.

Gildas Bourdet

b. 1947

Director of La Criée – Théâtre National de Marseille since 1995, Bourdet's theatrical career nevertheless began in the north of France, in Le Havre, where he founded his theatre collective La Salamandre in 1969 and developed a very physical style of comic performance. In 1974 Bourdet took over from Jacques Rosner as director of the CDN, and in 1982 La Salamandre was promoted to Théâtre National de la Région Nord–Pas-de-Calais. In 1989, it set up in the Roger Salengro theatre, Lille, where notable Bourdet productions were *Le Saperleau* (1982), a mock medieval farce, and *Une station service* (1985), both devised by Bourdet with his company in order to concentrate on contemporary civilisation from the point of view of the underprivileged. In 1991 he left Lille to become a freelance director, returning to the classic repertoire and directing in various theatres, including the Comédie-Française, until moving to Marseille in 1995.

Stéphane Braunschweig

b. 1964

Braunschweig is a young star director, who, since 1993, has been director of the CDN, Orléans-Loiret-Centre. After studying with Vitez, he founded his own company, Théâtre-Machine, and began directing opera and theatre. He has staged productions at Gennevilliers, the Odéon and Théâtre du Châtelet (opera), recent successes including Wedekind's

Franziska (1996) at the Odéon and Ibsen's *Peer Gynt* in Orléans (1995) and at the 1996 Festival d'Automne. In 1997 he worked with the Edinburgh Festival and Nottingham Playhouse on a production of *Measure for Measure* with English actors.

Peter Brook
b. 1925, UK
One of the best-known international directors to have made Paris his base, Peter Brook is famed for his experimental methods and his questioning approach to theatre (see pp.45–7). Founding the CIRT, or Centre International de Recherches Théâtrales (International Theatre Research Centre) in 1970, Brook moved with his team into the Théâtre des Bouffes du Nord in 1974, and changed the name of his company to Centre International de Création Théâtrale. At the Bouffes he staged many notable productions in the 1970s and 1980s, including *Timon of Athens* (1974), *Ubu aux Bouffes* (1974) and *La Conférence des Oiseaux* (1979), as well as his famous *Mahabharata* (1985). Since then, Brook has continued to explore international theatrical traditions, for example, in *The Tempest* (1990) and the *'cycle du cerveau'* ('brain cycle') of plays in 1992, which included *L'Homme Qui* based on an Oliver Sacks's book, *The Man Who Mistook his Wife for a Hat*. *Qui est là?* in 1995 examined different directorial and theatrical approaches through Shakespeare's *Hamlet*. In autumn 1996 he directed his first Beckett production, *Oh les beaux jours!*, starring Natasha Parry, also featured in the programme of the 1997 French theatre season in London.

Robert Cantarella
b. 1985
Director of the Compagnie des Ours, and associate director at the Sorano–Théâtre National de Toulouse Midi-Pyrénées from 1995 until 1997, Cantarella has most notably collaborated over the last two decades with playwright Philippe Minyana, as well as with many other contemporary writers including Noëlle Renaude, Roland Fichet and Jean-Luc Lagarce. Now based in Marseille, he is involved also with training actors, as well as directing. Most recently he has directed *Hamlet* at the Sorano in September 1997.

Patrice Chéreau
b. 1944

Chéreau is one of the most influential and dynamic theatre directors and actors in France today, as well as a well-respected film director (films include the 1994 *La Reine Margot*). He is particularly recognised for championing and producing the work of playwright Bernard-Marie Koltès during the 1980s (see pp.85–92 above), and his revival of *Dans la solitude des champs de coton*, in which he acted with Pascal Greggory at the Manufacture des Œillets, Ivry, in November 1995, was a sell-out success. He began his directorial career in 1969 at Sartrouville and also worked for a short time at the Piccolo Teatro in Milan, until becoming co-director with Planchon at the Théâtre National Populaire in Villeurbanne in 1972, bringing with him from Italy the stage designer Richard Peduzzi (with whom he still works today). His 1973 *La Dispute* by Marivaux is among the most acclaimed productions from this period of his career. In 1982 he became director of the Théâtre des Amandiers-Nanterre, where he set up a film and theatre school, and began promoting new writing, particularly that of Koltès. Between 1982 and 1988 Chéreau mounted four Koltès works, as well as important productions of Genet's *Les Paravents*, Heiner Müller's *Quartet* and Chekhov's *Platonov*. Following the death, in 1989, of Koltès, whom Chéreau had come to regard as the greatest playwright of his era, he left Nanterre in 1990 to work independently, pursuing a career in cinema and theatre.

Philippe Delaigue
b. 1961

Delaigue's Travaux 12 company, which he founded in Lyon in 1982 to promote contemporary writing, moved to Valence in 1992, to develop a Centre de Création Théâtrale (Centre for Theatrical Creation). He became director of the Comédie de Valence in January 1997. He has directed productions at several Lyon theatres as well as the Comédie de Saint-Etienne and the Théâtre National Populaire de Villeurbanne, in 1989 staging *Passé cinq heures* by Jean-François Abert and in 1991 assisting Planchon with *Le Vieil Hiver* and *Fragile forêt*. Delaigue has written three plays for the theatre since 1990: *La Retraite d'Eugène*, *L'Exil de Jacob* and *Haro!*

Anne Delbée
b. 1946

Actress, author and director since the early 1970s, when she founded her own company, Delbée came to note during the 1970s for productions such as Claudel's *L'Echange* in 1975 at the Théâtre de la Ville. From 1981 to 1985 she worked in Angers, staging more Claudel, Racine (she is a passionate director of both) and opera, and in 1986 became head of the Centre Dramatique National in Nancy, where she recommended acting in her own productions. Leaving there in 1991, she has since staged productions in various Parisian theatres, including a Racine cycle at the Théâtre 14 and Racine's *Phèdre* at the Comédie-Française (1996).

Jérôme Deschamps
b. 1947

Deschamps is an ex-pensionnaire at the Comédie-Française, who directed his first creation at the behest of Vitez in 1974: *Baboulifiche et Papavoine*. However, his career really took off with his collaboration with Macha Makeieff, *La Famille Deschiens*, in 1977, which began a series of productions combining minute observations of everyday life with burlesque clowning. These include *En avant!* (1981) *C'est Dimanche* (1985), *Les Pieds dans l'eau* (1992), *C'est magnifique* (1994) and *Le Défilé* for the 1996 Festival d'Automne.

Michel Dubois
b. 1937, Switzerland

Dubois is an actor and translator as well as a director known for his 'théâtre populaire' stance and support of decentralised theatre. His career began after leaving the Strasbourg national theatre school in 1961 to assist Dasté at the Comédie de St Etienne, where he worked with his own company, les Tréteaux de St Etienne. He became director of the Comédie de Caen in 1973, where he worked on many contemporary creations with a collection of artists, actors and other theatre professionals, including Daniel Besnehard as dramaturge. He has directed the works of a handful of contemporary authors, including Edward Bond's *Summer* (1985) and Lemahieu's *L'Etalon-or* (1988), although he has also tackled the more established repertoire, including Kleist, Pirandello and Shakespeare. Under his guidance, the new Théâtre de Hérouville Saint-Clair was inaugurated in 1987.

Jean-Claude Fall
b. 1947, Tunisia

Fall began directing with Philippe Adrien in the 1970s, co-directing several productions during the 1970s, including Brecht's *Fear and Misery in the Third Reich* (1975) and Karl Sternheim's *Schippel* (1976) at Aubervilliers. A supporter of contemporary writers, Fall has also directed at Théâtre Ouvert (1978) and staged Lagarce's *Le Voyage de Madame Knipper* in 1982. From 1982 to 1988 he directed the Théâtre de la Bastille, where he welcomed young companies, and featured contemporary creations incorporating a mixture of performing arts disciplines. In 1989 he took over the direction of the Théâtre Gérard Philipe in St-Denis, where he mounted (among others) four Chekhov plays in the 1990 season, the Alain Gautré play *Chef-lieu* in 1992, and has worked with Catherine Anne, Stanislas Nordey and Adel Hakim. In 1997 he became director of the Théâtre des Treize Vents, the CDN in Montpellier.

Pierre Franck
b. 1922

Franck was well known in the 1960s and 1970s as a director of productions by authors such as Paul Claudel and Paul Valéry at top Paris theatres including the Comédie-Française, the Odéon, and the Théâtre de l'Atelier, where he is currently director. Taking a break from direction between 1978 and 1988, Franck returned to the theatre that year, with *L'Avare* at the Atelier. Productions since include an adaptation of de Staël's *Les Passions* (1993) and *La Panne* by Dürrenmatt (1996).

Alain Françon
b. 1945

Françon has been director of the Théâtre National de la Colline since November 1996; his productions there so far include Eugène Durif's *Les petites heures* in September 1997 and Edward Bond's *In the Company of Men* in 1994 and again in October 1997. He was director of CDNs at the Lyon-Théâtre du Huitième (1989–92) and Annecy (1992–6). Following various collective creation projects in the 1970s, his career included several notable productions of Vinaver's work in the 1980s, such as *L'Ordinaire* at the Théâtre National de Chaillot in 1983 and *Les Voisins* at the Jardin d'Hiver, Paris, in 1986. He is also a great interpreter of Edward Bond, whose *In the Company of Men* (see above) and *War Plays* he staged together at the 1994 Avignon Festival. At the 1996 Festival, he directed Marlowe's *Edward II* in the Cour d'honneur.

Gabriel Garran
b. 1927

One of the directors who, in the 1960s, established theatres in the 'red belt' of communist workers' suburbs around Paris, Garran was the first director of the Théâtre de la Commune d'Aubervilliers in 1965, which became a CDN in 1971. Garran's policy was to favour the production of new and unpublished plays (a function taken over by Lavelli at La Colline in the 1990s). In 1985 he left to found the Théâtre International de Langue Française, a theatre dedicated to producing work from francophone countries overseas, especially the work of African playwrights.

Philippe Genty
b. 1938

Working from his own eponymous Paris-based company founded in 1968 with Mary Underwood, Genty combines non-text-based theatre with other performing arts including dance and pantomine, using techniques learned from puppet theatre, where his career began. He has staged ambitious theatrical productions throughout the 1980s and 1990s, including *Rond comme un cube* (1980), *Ne m'oublie pas* (1992) and *Le Voyageur immobile* (1995), all created at the Théâtre de la Ville and enjoying international tours.

Jean-Christian Grinevald
b. 1945

As director of the Théâtre de la Main d'Or Belle de Mai in Paris, since 1989, Grinevald has staged a number of productions of contemporary authors such as Philippe Minyana, Denise Bonal, Jean-Claude Grumberg and Fatima Gallaire. At La Main d'Or he won the Fauteuil d'Or award for his programming in 1992 and has directed plays including *Après l'amour* by Daniel Soulier (1991), *Au coeur la brûlure* by Fatima Gallaire (1992) and *L'Aberration des Etoiles Fixes* by Manlio Santanelli (1993).

Jean-Louis Hourdin
b. 1944

Trained at the Strasbourg national theatre school, Hourdin founded his company, the GRAT (Groupe Régional d'Action Théâtrale), in 1976. This company, which has been associated with Wenzel and Perrier, and helped to found the Hérisson Festival (see p.205), has never settled for long in one place. Its shows always have an anarchic, joyously anti-establishment edge, beginning with collectively devised shows in the 1970s. Hourdin then moved on to sketches by Karl Valentin and Dario Fo, and produced a memorable Büchner cycle in 1980–3. He recently adapted the plays of Albert Cohen, and has also directed works by contemporary playwrights including Michel Deutsch and Eugène Durif.

Brigitte Jaques
b. 1946, Switzerland

After studying with Vitez, Jaques began directing in 1974, founding the Compagnie Pandora with François Regnault (her co-director at Aubervilliers) two years later. In 1981 she began teaching at ENSATT. Influenced by Vitez in her style of direction, Jaques has staged many contemporary writers, including Sallenave and Kushner, as well as repertoire classics, from Marivaux to Claudel. From 1991 to 1997 she directed the Théâtre de la Commune d'Aubervilliers, while continuing to teach, act and adapt. She has worked in many major theatres (public and private), including the Odéon, Chaillot, and the Comédie-Française, where she staged Tennessee Williams's *Night of the Iguana* in 1991. Her recent productions have included Kushner's *Angels in America* (1996) and Corneille's *Sertorius* (1997) at Aubervilliers. On leaving Aubervilliers in 1997, she re-founded the Compagnie Pandora, with plans to work in collaboration with other theatres such as the Comédie de Genève.

Patrice Kerbrat
b. 1948

Actor at the Comédie-Française (1973–83) and with Vitez at Chaillot, Kerbrat has since become best known for directing, mainly works of contemporary authors including Jean-Marie Besset's *Ce qui arrive et ce qu'on attend* at the Gaîté Montparnasse (1993); Yasmina Reza's Molière-award-winning *'Art'* at the Comédie des Champs-Elysées (1994); Jean-Marie Besset's *Grande Ecole* the Théâtre 14 (1995) and his *Un coeur français* at the Hébertot (1996). He has also staged Koltès's *La Nuit juste avant les forêts* at La Criée in Marseille; Strindberg's *The Father* at the Comédie-Française (both in 1991) and Loleh Bellon's *L'Une et l'Autre* at the Comédie des Champs-Elysées in 1992.

Jacques Kraemer
b. 1938

Director of the Théâtre de Chartres since 1993, Kraemer is also a playwright, actor and lecturer at the University of Strasbourg II. Founder of the Théâtre Populaire de Lorraine, in Metz in the 1960s (moving to Thionville in 1977 and becoming a Centre Dramatique National in 1989), he produced a varied classic and contemporary repertoire, as well as famous collective creations in the 1970s, including *Splendeur et misère de Minette la bonne Lorraine*. He has written a handful of plays, including *Les Histoires de l'oncle Jakob*, which he staged in 1977. In the 1980s he continued to work at the TPL, and throughout France and Germany, and also taught at ENSATT (1987–93).

Jacques Lassalle
b. 1936

Founder of the Studio-Théâtre in Vitry-sur-Seine in 1967 and a teacher at the Paris III University between 1969 and 1971, Lassalle directed several productions at the Comédie-Française and the Odéon, before being appointed director of the Théâtre National de Strasbourg, where he worked between 1983 and 1991. Here he promoted many new and rediscovered and writers, including Vinaver, Sarrazac and Besset, and collaborated with set designer Kokkos. Lassalle was director of the Comédie-Française between 1991 and 1993, where, alongside Racine, Marivaux and Goldoni, he staged Vinaver's *L'Emission de télévision* in 1990 at the Odéon, Nathalie Sarraute's *Elle est là* and *Le Silence* in 1993 at the Vieux-Colombier. He has since directed in many major theatres in France and abroad. In 1997, Paris productions included Pirandello's *All for the best* at the Hébertot and *Who's Afraid of Virginia Woolf?* at the Gaîté Montparnasse. Lassalle has been professor at the Conservatoire National d'Art Dramatique since 1994.

Georges Lavaudant
b. 1947

Currently director of the Odéon (since 1996), Lavaudant made his name working with stage designer Vergier during the 1970s. He became co-director of the CDN des Alpes in 1976, where he remained for ten years; during this period he also staged productions such as *Richard III* (1984) for the Avignon Festival; Genet's *Le Balcon* at the Comédie-Française (1985) and Gounod's opera *Roméo et Juliette* at the Opéra de Paris (1982). In 1986 he became co-director of the Théâtre National Populaire in Villeurbanne. There he went on to mount, among others, several notable Brecht productions and two of his own plays: *Vera Cruz* (1988) and *Terra Incognita* (1992). His contemporary productions have included Jean-Christophe Bailly's *Lumières I Près des ruines* and *Lumières II Sous les arbres*, created in 1995 by a collective including Michel Deutsch, Jean-François Duroure and Bailly. On taking over at the Odéon he directed *An Italian Straw Hat* by Labiche, Le Clézio's *Pawana* and his own play *La Dernière Nuit* in the Petit Odéon (all in 1997).

Jorge Lavelli

b. 1932, Argentina

Most prominent of Latin-American writers and directors who have been active in French theatre since the 1960s, Lavelli was director of the Théâtre National de la Colline from its inauguration in 1988 until autumn 1996. He made La Colline into a centre for new writing, including new work in translation. Recent productions by Lavelli have included plays by Serge Kribus, Tony Kushner, George Tabori, Steven Berkoff, Edward Bond and Brian Friel. But his major strength was in giving theatrical life to the work of Hispanic dramatists such as Arrabal and Copi: the play with which he chose to open his first season at La Colline was Lorca's *The Public.*

Anne–Marie Lazarini

b. 1945

Lazarini began her career in the early 1970s at the Théâtre des Deux-Portes in Paris, going on to direct the Artistic-Athévains in 1979, where she has staged little-known Russian productions by authors such as Tirso and Gorky, as well as contemporary texts by playwrights such as Jacques Guimet. She favours plays which feature unusual or strong female roles, such as *L'Etrange Histoire de Peter Schlemihl*, staged in 1994. She also trains and conducts theatrical research projects alongside directing.

Marcel Maréchal

b. 1937

A flamboyant actor and director of the Compagnie Marcel Maréchal at Paris's Théâtre du Rond-Point, Maréchal is noted for productions of works by authors including Vauthier and Audiberti. After moving from Lyon to Marseille in the 1970s, his eponymous company became the first occupants of La Criée, the theatre built in the former fish-market, which received regional dramatic centre status in 1981. He moved to Paris in 1995. Recently, Maréchal's productions at the Rond-Point have included Claudel's *Les Coufontaine* in 1995 and Prévert's *Les Enfants du Paradis* in 1997.

Jean-Louis Martinelli
b. 1951
Director of the Théâtre National de Strasbourg since 1994, Martinelli founded his first theatre company in 1977, the Théâtre du Réfectoire in Lyon, where his repertoire ranged from Chekhov and von Horváth to contemporary writers including Eugène Durif during the 1980s. In 1987 he took over at the Théâtre de Lyon, where he staged Heiner Müller's *Quartett* (1988), a theatre version of Jean Eustache's film *La Maman et la Putain* in 1990 and *Les Marchands de gloire* by Marcel Pagnol in 1993. In 1995 his *Roberto Zucco* by Koltès appeared in Strasbourg and at the Théâtre Nanterre-Amandiers, and he directed Fassbinder's *L'Année des treize lunes* at the 1995 Avignon Festival.

Stephan Meldegg
b. 1937, Hungary
Meldegg is director of the private Théâtre La Bruyère in Paris, as well as an actor for theatre, cinema and television. His career in France began in 1962, and he has worked with Jean Vilar, Guy Rétoré and François Périer, among others. His successful early productions include Vaclav Havel's *Audience et Vernissage* (1979) (subsequently broadcast on television by TF1) and Ronald Harwood's *The Dresser* (1980). Since taking over direction of La Bruyère in 1982, Meldegg's many productions include the Molière-award-winning *Cuisine et dépendances* by Agnès Jaoui and Jean-Pierre Bacri in 1993.

Daniel Mesguich
b. 1952, Algeria
An ex-pupil of Vitez, Mesguich first came to note with controversial productions of Kafka's *Castle* and Marivaux's *Le Prince Travesti* in 1973. The following year he founded the Théâtre du Miroir company, which produced *King Lear* for the Avignon Festival in 1981. In 1986 Mesguich became director of the CDN at the Théâtre Gérard Philipe, St-Denis, where he remained until 1989. Since 1991 he has directed the Théâtre National de la Région Nord–Pas-de-Calais at Lille, which he renamed La Métaphore, where he stages a varied repertoire,

including Hélène Cixous. He continued to conduct a television and film-acting career throughout the 1970s and 1980s, and now teaches at the Paris Conservatoire and Lille III University. In spring 1997 he staged the Comédie-Française's first production of the operetta *La Vie parisienne* by Offenbach.

Jean-Pierre Miquel
b. 1937
Miquel has been artistic director of the Comédie-Française since 1993. His career began in the 1960s with the Groupe de Théâtre Antique de la Sorbonne, after which he went on to direct plays by new authors such as Grumberg and Haïm. After a period as artistic director of the Odéon he taught at and then ran (1983–92) the Paris Conservatoire, while continuing to direct plays by authors such as Brisville, Molnar and Billetdoux. In 1995 he staged Marivaux's *La Double Inconstance* at the Vieux-Colombier, and in 1996–7 *Les Fausses Confidences* by the same author at the Comédie-Française. This production was invited to visit at the 1997 French theatre season in London.

Ariane Mnouchkine
b. 1939
As head of the Théâtre du Soleil company, Ariane Mnouchkine is perhaps the most influential director in France today, noted for her experimental and pioneering approach, as well as for her explorations of international theatre traditions. In 1963 she founded the Théâtre du Soleil, which since 1971 has been based at the Cartoucherie, Vincennes. In the 1970s the company were the leading exponents of création collective such as the renowned *1789* (see pp.21–6). In 1975–6 Mnouchkine turned to the cinema, making a film about Molière with a cast from the Théâtre du Soleil. She went on to adapt Thomas Mann's *Mephisto* for the theatre, before returning to text-based productions inspired by her knowledge of Eastern theatre traditions, including her renowned Shakespeare cycle and subsequently, between 1990 and 1992, *Les Atrides*, a cycle of Greek tragedies. In the last decade she has collaborated actively with Hélène Cixous, who has written epic plays for the Soleil (sometimes nine hours long), including *L'Histoire terrible mais inachevée de Norodom Sihanouk roi du*

Cambodge in 1985, *L'Indiade* in 1987 and *La Ville parjure* in 1994. In 1995 Mnouchkine staged her memorable production of *Tartuffe*, set in an Algeria torn apart by war and fundamentalism.

Chantal Morel
b. 1955
Morel became an actor after studying at the Grenoble Conservatoire and directed her first production in 1980, when she founded the Alerte Theatre Company, which staged productions including Euripides and Racine, as well as more contemporary works such as Robert Pinget's *Lettre morte* (at the Avignon Festival and the Maison de la Culture, Grenoble, 1987). In 1988 she became director of the CDN des Alpes in Grenoble, where she directed Serge Valletti's *Le Jour se lève, Léopold!*, which she took on tour for three years, along with Valletti's *Solos*. In 1989 she left to set up independently, founding L'Equipe de Création Théâtrale, whose productions have included *Roman avec cocaïne*, an adaptation of an Aguéev novel (1990) and *King Lear* (1993).

Bernard Murat
b. 1941, Algeria
Murat has directed mainly in the private theatre sector, with a mixed repertoire ranging from Feydeau to Neil Simon, Harold Pinter and Marguerite Duras. His productions, often featuring big-name stars, are staged in theatres such as the Atelier, Marigny, Montparnasse and Bouffes Parisiens. Most recently he is best known for Eric Emmanuel Schmitt's *Variations enigmatiques*, starring Alain Delon and Francis Huster at the Théâtre Marigny in autumn 1996, and *Le Libertin* at the Théâtre Montparnasse in spring 1997.

Arlette Namiand
b. 1951
Director, playwright, and collaborator–dramaturge with Jean-Paul Wenzel at the CDN Les Fédérés, at Montluçon, Namiand also writes for the theatre. Her own plays include *Surtout quand la nuit tombe* and *Sang Blanc*, and among her adaptations are works by Maupassant and Koestler.

Jacques Nichet
b. 1942
Nichet was a leading figure in the Théâtre de l'Aquarium's création collective experiments in the 1970s (see p.31) and founder of the Maison Antoine Vitez international theatre translation centre in 1990. He was director of the CDN du Languedoc-Roussillon Montpellier between 1986 and 1997, concentrating on a contemporary and regionally (hence Mediterranean) orientated repertoire, including contemporary comedy. Recent productions include a successful revival of Koltès's *Le Retour au désert* in 1995 and of Césaire's *La Tragédie du Roi Christophe* at the Avignon Festival in 1996. In 1997 Nichet became director of Le Sorano, the CDN in Toulouse.

Stanislas Nordey
b. 1966
A popular young director who founded the Compagnie Nordey in 1988, Nordey attracted success early in his career, becoming director in residence at the Théâtre Gérard Philipe for two seasons (1992–4) with productions including *Tabataba* by Koltès, his own *La Légende de Siegfried* (1992) and two plays by Pasolini: *Calderon* (1993) and *Pylade* (1994). He has directed for festivals from Avignon to Saint-Herblain and from 1995 to 1997 worked as associate director with Vincent at the Théâtre Nanterre-Amandiers. Productions there included *Splendid's* by Genet and *La Noce* by Stansislas Wyspianski (1996). In 1997, he also directed two operas at the Théâtre du Châtelet and Jean-Luc Lagarce's *J'étais dans ma maison et j'attendais que la pluie vienne* at Théâtre Ouvert. In 1997 he also took over from Jean-Claude Fall as the director of the Théâtre Gérard Philipe, Saint-Denis.

Lluis Pasqual
b. 1951, Catalonia
A theatre and opera director, Pasqual was appointed to run the Odéon-Théâtre de l'Europe as a full-time European theatre centre in 1990. Prior to that he had worked in Spain and Italy (regularly at the Piccolo Teatro in Milan), and with numerous directors internationally, including Grotowski and Brook. In

1976 he founded the Teatro Lluire (Free Theatre) school, the first theatre school in Spain, which led to his appointment as head of the national drama centre in Madrid (1983–9), where his première of Lorca's *El Público* brought him international acclaim. At the Odéon from 1990 to 1996 he succeeded in bringing new work from all over Europe to the French public, including a production (in Russian) with actors from Lev Dodin's St Petersburg company of Koltès's *Roberto Zucco* (1994).

Laurent Pelly
b. 1962

Laurent Pelly has been director of the CDN des Alpes since July 1997. He was assistant director at the CDN Nord–Pas-de-Calais (1986–9), becoming co-director of the Compagnie Pélican with Agathe Mélinand in 1989. He has staged plays at several major theatres, such as the Théâtre de Chaillot (for example, *Un coeur sous une soutane – Tentative de commémoration* as part of the 'Années Rimbaud' programme in 1991); the Théâtre Gérard Philipe Saint-Denis; Le Cargo de Grenoble and the Théâtre Paris-Villette (Alan Bennett's *Talking Heads* in 1994). Recent productions include Philippe Adrien's *La Baye* at the Cargo and Théâtre Gérard Philipe (1996), as well as Strindberg's *Dance of death* (1997) and *En caravane*, an Elizabeth von Arnim adaptation, both at the Cargo (the latter transferring to the Théâtre Paris-Villette in autumn 1997).

Jean–Claude Penchenat
b. 1937

Penchenat began his career as an actor and founder member of the Théâtre du Soleil, playing in productions including *1789* and *L'Age d'or*. In 1975 he left to form his own company, the Théâtre du Campagnol, which became a CDN in Corbeil-Essonne from 1983 to 1996, mixing collective creations with text-based productions. The best known of these was *Le Bal* in 1981, subsequently made into a film by Ettore Scola. In 1996 the Théâtre du Campagnol was forced out of its venue by political pressure from the local authority and became an independent touring CDN.

Olivier Perrier

b. 1940

Perrier is an actor, director and the director of Les Fédérés, Montluçon – now the CDN for the Auvergne region – which he originally helped found with Wenzel and Hourdin. In the 1960s his acting career took him to the Théâtre Populaire de Lorraine, the Théâtre Populaire Romand, and to work for directors including Brook and Gatti. He has written and directed many plays since the 1970s, a good number involving animals, such as *Les Mémoires d'un bonhomme* in 1976 at the Théâtre National de Strasbourg; *L'Engeance* at Villeurbanne in 1982 and *La Sentence des pourceaux* for the Avignon Festival in 1987. He has also worked on projects at the Strasbourg theatre school and in community theatre.

Dominique Pitoiset

b. 1959

Currently director of the Théâtre National de Dijon, Pitoiset began his career as assistant to Jean-Pierre Vincent, Manfred Karge and Matthias Langhoff, after training at the Ecole Nationale des Beaux-Arts and the Strasbourg national theatre school. In 1983, he set up the En Attendant company, which became the Dijon-based Compagnie Pitoiset in 1988. During the 1980s he directed at a number of theatres nationally, including the CDN in Burgundy; in the 1990s his work included prize-winning productions of Goethe's *Faust* at Brest, and *Oblomov* by Gontcharov at the Théâtre Vidy-Lausanne and the Théâtre MC93 Bobigny. He also directed the opera *The Marriage of Figaro* at the Lausanne Opéra and, at the 1996 Avignon Festival, Kafka's *The Trial*, which toured France during 1996 and 1997.

Roger Planchon

b. 1931

A major director, actor and playwright, Planchon is one of the leading figures in the directors' theatre of the post-war period. His career began at the time of decentralisation in the 1950s (see p.174) and he made his name from his re-interpretations of Brecht, Molière, Marivaux and Shakespeare. He has attracted huge audiences to his theatre in Villeurbanne, near Lyon, which was given Centre Dramatique National status in 1963 and the title Théâtre National Populaire ten years later. He has staged Vinaver and Pinter there, as well as many of his own works, including *Fragile forêt*, *Le Vieil Hiver* (1991) and *Le Radeau de la Méduse*, which he took on to the Théâtre de la Colline in Paris in 1997. He has also worked in film, as an actor and director of works such as the 1992 *Louis, enfant roi*. He set up the European Cinematographic Centre in the Rhône-Alpes in 1990. (See pp.45–7 and 173–6.)

Olivier Py
b. 1965
One of the new generation of playwright-directors (as well as a stage, television and cinema actor), Olivier Py has enjoyed remarkable success, staging his own and other's works. Notable productions so far have mainly been of his own plays. They include *Les Aventures de Paco Goliard* at the Théâtre de la Bastille in 1992, his twenty-four-hour-long, five-play cycle *La Servante* at the 1995 Avignon Festival and *Apologétiques* at the 1996 Avignon Festival. In 1997 his play *Le Visage d'Orphée* was performed at the Cour d'honneur at the Avignon Festival.

Claude Régy
b. 1923
Régy, who began his career in 1952, has collaborated with several contemporary playwrights, including Marguerite Duras in the 1960s and Nathalie Sarraute in the 1970s, as well as introducing German authors such as Peter Handke to the French repertoire. Since 1981 Régy has taught at the Paris Conservatoire, while continuing to work as an independent director. During the 1990s he has also been responsible for introducing a number of Gregory Motton plays to France, including *Falls* in 1992 and *The Terrible Voice of Satan* in 1994. He has directed opera too, including the dramatic oratorio *Jeanne d'Arc au bûcher* starring Isabelle Huppert at the Opéra-Bastille in 1992.

Jacques Rosner

b. 1936

Rosner is noted for a varied repertoire including Heinrich Böll, Thomas Bernhard and Eugene O'Neill, as well as the classics. He has actively encouraged many young companies and Rosner often co-directs with young directors. Rosner began his career with Planchon as an actor and assistant director at the inauguration of the Théâtre de la Cité at Villeurbanne (1957–62). Between 1962 and 1970 he staged productions at the Comédie-Française and the TNP, as well as the Théâtre de la Cité, where he directed Armand Gatti's *La Vie imaginaire de l'éboueur Auguste G.* In 1971 he became director of the Théâtre du Lambrequin, CDN du Nord, then in 1974 took over from Villégier at the Paris Conservatoire. He also ran the Jeune Théâtre National (National Youth Theatre) between 1975 and 1980, and continued to direct at major Parisian theatres (national and private). He became director of the Grenier de Toulouse in 1985; this became the CDN, Le Sorano–Théâtre National de Toulouse Midi-Pyrénées in 1987. He remained there until his retirement in 1997. Recent productions include Thomas Bernhard's *Simplement compliqué*, also staged at the 1996 Avignon Festival, and Shakespeare's *Julius Caesar* in 1997.

Jérôme Savary

b. 1942

A director, actor and author, Savary is most famous for his foundation of the Grand Magic Circus company in 1965, with its anarchic, provocative approach, designed to bring culture to the people by ridiculing the existing cultural establishment. Since 1988 Savary has been noted for his large-scale theatrical spectacles as director at the Théâtre National de Chaillot. Recent productions include *Le Bourgeois Gentilhomme* in spring 1997 and *Nina Stromboli* in summer 1996, a Grand Magic Circus revival.

Christian Schiaretti

b. 1955

Schiaretti worked for the Festival d'Automne from 1975 to 1980, before assisting directors such as Jean-Christian Grinevald and Daniel Romand. In 1983 he staged his first solo production, *Ariakos* by Philippe Minyana, at the Quai de la Gare in Paris. He has subsequently directed at many top regional and Parisian theatres, including the Théâtre de la Tempête (Harald Mueller's *Epave*, 1989); the CDN, Angers (*Léon la France, hardi voyage vers l'ouest africain* adapted by the director from letters by Léon Mercier, 1989) and the CDN at Reims (Johannes von Saaz's *Le Laboureur de Bohème* in 1990 and Euripides' *Medea* in 1991). Most recently, Schiaretti has staged Alain Badiou's *Les Citrouilles* at the Théâtre des Quartiers d'Ivry in 1997. His own plays are *La Nuit du Taureau* (1982), *La Terrasse* (1984), *Le Serment d'Aldebert* (1985) and *Léon la France, hardi voyage vers l'ouest africain* (1989).

Stuart Seide
b. 1946, USA

Seide is an avant-garde director from New York, who has staged various productions at the request of the French at prestigious venues including the Comédie-Française and the Théâtre des Quartiers d'Ivry. These have included *Les Précieuses ridicules* (1970) and three Feydeau plays (at the behest of Vincent in 1984) at the Comédie-Française; John Ford's *'Tis a Pity She's a Whore* (1975) and *Mourning becomes Electra* (1980), at Ivry, and Caldéron's *Life is a Dream* (1978) at the Cartoucherie. In 1994 he directed Beckett's *Dramaticules* and mounted an all-night version of Shakespeare's *Henry VI* at Avignon. He is currently director of the Centre Dramatique Poitou-Charentes.

Bernard Sobel
b. 1936

Director of the CDN in Gennevilliers, Sobel began his career by founding the Théâtre Gérard Philipe in Saint-Denis in 1961, before basing himself in Gennevilliers with the amateur theatre troupe which became the Ensemble Théâtral de Gennevilliers (ETG). His first entirely professional staging was in 1970: Brecht's *Man for Man*; to date his repertoire includes German authors from Brecht to Heiner Müller. Notable productions have included *Marie Stuart* by Schiller in 1983, in collaboration with the Comédie-Française, and *Entre chien et loup* by

Christoph Hein (1984), as well as classics such as *Tartuffe* (1990) and *King Lear* (1993), with Maria Casarès in the title role. In spring 1997 he directed *Zarkat, Soleil couchant* by Isaac Babel, whose *Marie* he had staged in 1975 and again in 1992.

François Tanguy
b. 1958
Tanguy is based at the Théâtre du Radeau in Le Mans, where he works on co-productions with other theatres and festivals including the national theatres of Brittany and Dijon, the CDN at Gennevilliers and the Festival d'Automne, all of which were involved in his latest production, *Bataille du Tagliamento*, part of the 1996 Festival d'Automne. During the last ten years he has been involved with numerous tours by the Théâtre du Radeau throughout Europe.

Laurent Terzieff
b. 1935
Terzieff is best known for his direction of many international avant-garde works and discoveries of new plays. He began his acting and directing career in the 1950s, and has also interpreted many powerful roles for directors such as Barrault, Serreau, Planchon and Brook, his acting style being noted for its physicality and characterisation skills. A notable recent production of his was T. S. Eliot's *Murder in the Cathedral* in 1995, which Terzieff not only directed but in which he also performed the role of Thomas à Becket.

Charles Tordjman
b. 1947, Morocco
Tordjman has been head of the CDN of Nancy-Lorraine since 1992, where he promotes young authors and regional companies, and organises theatre in unusual locations in the town and country, as well as running the Passages Festival in Nancy (see p.204). Tordjman began directing in 1972 at the Théâtre Populaire de Lorraine in Thionville, becoming co-director with Jacques Kraemer two years later. It was Kraemer who staged his first play, *C'était*, in 1978. Since then, Tordjman has directed, among others, Durif's *Tonkin-Alger* (1990); Duras's

L'Amante anglaise (1986 and 1993); Valletti's *Saint Elvis* (1990) and an adaptation of the Robert Bober novel *Quoi de neuf sur la guerre?* at the Théâtre de la Tempête in 1997.

Eric Vigner
b. 1960
Vigner has been director of the Centre Dramatique de Bretagne à Lorient since 1995, where his productions have included *L'Illusion Comique* in 1996, which toured most of the big stages in France, and *Brancusi contre Etats-Unis*, created for the Avignon Festival the same year. Vigner was trained at the Rennes conservatoire, then at ENSATT and the Paris Conservatoire, directing his first play in 1988. He founded the Compagnie Suzanne M., which began staging plays in 1991 with Roland Dubillard's *La Maison d'os* and continues to train young actors, having frequently taken part in workshops at the Paris Conservatoire and at the invitation of Peter Brook in 1993.

Jean-Marie Villégier
b. 1937
Director of the Théâtre National de Strasbourg between 1991 and 1993, Villégier came late to the theatre, having begun a career as a philosophy teacher. He specialises in the seventeenth century and has directed at numerous important theatres over the last twenty years, including the Opéra Comique and the Comédie-Française. He is particularly well known for his productions of Corneille, and has made the promotion of France's theatrical history during the seventeenth century his main goal through a prolific output at home and abroad. Still active in the late 1990s, he directed Corneille's *L'Illusion comique* at the Théâtre de l'Athénée, Paris, in 1997. His work at the national theatre school (attached to the theatre in Strasbourg) has helped raise its profile, so that it is considered the equal of the Paris Conservatoire.

Jean-Pierre Vincent
b. 1942
Vincent became director of the Théâtre des Amandiers-Nanterre in 1990. Recent productions there include his spring

1997 theatrical study *Karl Marx Théâtre Inédit*, based around texts from Shakespeare, Marx, Chekhov, Heiner Müller and Jacques Derrida. In autumn 1996 he also directed Nerval's *Léo Burckart* at the Comédie-Française. He began his theatre career in the 1960s, co-directing with Chéreau at Sartrouville, where he became noted for his promotion of visual theatre by authors including Bernard Chartreux and Michel Deutsch. Vincent was director of the Théâtre National de Strasbourg between 1975 and 1983, when he took over the running of the Comédie-Française, introducing new authors into the repertoire. He left in 1986 to direct independently and teach at the Paris Conservatoire, before moving to Nanterre four years later.

Antoine Vitez
b. 1930; d. 1990
One of the most influential theatre directors of recent years, Vitez is famed for experimentation with staging non-dramatic text, as well as his communist beliefs and faith in *'un théâtre élitaire pour tous'* (an élitist theatre for all) (see pp.37–40). His career began in 1966 at the Maison de la Culture in Caen, although he subsequently became well known for his productions at the Quartiers d'Ivry theatre in the communist Parisian suburb of Ivry-sur-Seine in the 1970s, where he staged classics as well as contemporary works by Vinaver, Kalisky and Pommeret, and adaptations including his famous version of Aragon's novel *Les Cloches de Bâle*, entitled *Catherine*. In 1981 he became director of the Théâtre National de Chaillot, where he worked with stage designer Kokkos on celebrated productions including *Hamlet* (1982) and Claudel's *Le Soulier de satin* in 1987. The following year he became general administrator of the Comédie-Française, where his last production was Brecht's *Life of Galileo* in 1990. He also taught at Jacques Lecoq's school (1966–70) and the Paris Conservatoire (1968–81), and translated and produced many Greek and Russian plays throughout his career; thus the international centre for translation, the Maison Antoine Vitez, is named in his honour.

Jacques Weber

b. 1949

An actor as well as a director, Weber has been in charge of the Théâtre de Nice (CDN) since 1986. A graduate of the Paris Conservatoire, he went on to direct the Théâtre du Huitième in Lyon between 1979 and 1985, before moving to Nice. His repertoire of productions has included Molière, Sartre and Diderot, and he has also played many classic roles himself, from Petruchio in *Taming of the Shrew* to Figaro, Don Juan and Tartuffe.

Jean-Paul Wenzel

b. 1947

After the national theatre school in Strasbourg, Wenzel started his career acting for directors including Peter Brook and co-founded the company Théâtre du Quotidien in 1975. He has written many plays, including *Loin d'Hagondange* (1975) and *La Fin des Monstres* (1994) (see playwrights for more details, p.253). As well as being a fervent supporter of decentralisation, Wenzel has collaborated on new writing projects with Théâtre Ouvert and has been director of the CDN at Montluçon, Les Fédérés, since 1976. He also directs the Rencontres d'été d'Hérisson Festival and is in charge of teaching at the Ecole National de Bretagne in Rennes. Recent productions at Les Fédérés include Brecht's *Drums in the Night* (1988), *The Chopalovitch Touring Theatre* by Lioubomir Simovitch (1990–2) and his own *Fin des Monstres* (1994).

Robert Wilson

b. 1941, USA

The avant-garde American director Robert Wilson came to fame in France following his *Deafman Glance* at the Nancy Festival in 1971. Drawing on his background as a painter and architect, Wilson directs using images rather than narrative as his main vocabulary, illustrated in productions such as his twenty-four-hour-long *Overture* (1972) and *Einstein on the Beach* (1976). In the 1980s his stagings included Heiner Müller's *Hamlet-Machine* and *Alcestis*, a Euripides adaptation, as well as many operas throughout Europe. More recently his work has included a one-man show called *Hamlet, a Monologue* in 1995, an adaptation of a text by Marguerite Duras entitled *La Maladie de la mort* in 1996 and *Time Rocker* in English and German at the Odéon in 1997. His production of *La Maladie de la mort* was invited to the London French theatre Season in 1997.

Claude Yersin
b. 1940, Switzerland

After training with Lecoq and Valde in the 1960s, Yersin became actor, then assistant director at the Comédie de St Etienne between 1962 and 1967. During the 1970s and early 1980s he directed productions for numerous theatres and events around France, including the Comédie de Caen, the Théâtre National de Chaillot and Théâtre Ouvert at the Avignon Festival (Besnehard's *Les Mères grises* in 1978). He became director of the Théâtre Nouveau d'Angers in 1986, and has staged productions by contemporary dramatists, particularly Daniel Besnehard and Jean-Pierre Sarrazac. These include first productions of Besnehard's *Mala Strana* in 1988, *L'Ourse blanche* in 1990 and *L'Enfant d'Obock* in 1994, Sarrazac's *Harriet* in 1993 and *Teltow Kanal* by Daoudi in 1995. He has also translated many plays from German and English, by authors including Bond, Achternbusch and Kroetz.

FURTHER READING

Abirached, R., *L'Etat et le prince*, Paris: Plon, 1992.

Abirached, R. (ed.), *La Décentralisation théâtrale* (4 vols), Arles: Actes Sud, 1991–5.

AFAA (Association Française d'Action Artistique), *Guide des 129 metteurs en scène, Théâtre/Public*, Hors série No.7, 1993.

Aslan, O., *Roger Blin*, Cambridge: University Press, 1988.

Bablet, D., and Jacquot, J. (eds), *Le Lieu théâtral dans la société moderne*, Paris: C.N.R.S., 1968.

Baecque, A., *Avignon, le royaume du théâtre*, Paris: Gallimard, 1996.

——— *Les Maisons de la culture*, Paris: Seghers, 1967.

Bradby, D., *Modern French Drama 1940–1990*, Cambridge: University Press, 1991 (revised edition).

——— *The Theater of Michel Vinaver*, Michigan: University Press, 1993.

Bradby, D., and Williams, D., *Directors' Theatre*, London: Macmillan, 1988.

Busson, A., *Le Théâtre en France. Contexte socio-économique et choix esthétiques*, Paris: La Documentation Française, 1986.

Cardona, J., and Lacroix, C., *Statistiques de la culture*, Paris: La Documentation Française, 1996.

Champagne, L., *French Theatre Experiment since 1968*, Michigan: University Press, 1984.

Chollet, J., and Freydefont, M., *Les Lieux scèniques en France 1980–1995*, Paris: Editions AS, 1996.

Cohn, R., *Just Play: Beckett's Theater*, Princeton: University Press, 1980.

——— *From Desire to Godot: Pocket Theater of Post-war Paris*, Berkeley and Los Angeles: University of California Press, 1987.

Copeau, J., *Le Théâtre populaire*, Paris: P.U.F. ('Bibliothèque du Peuple'), 1941.

Corvin, M., *Dictionnaire Encyclopédique du Théâtre*, Paris: Bordas, 1995 (revised edition).

———— *Le Théâtre de Boulevard*, Paris: P.U.F.('Que Sais-je?'), 1989.

Couty, D., and Rey, A. (eds), *Le Théâtre*, Paris: Bordas, 1980.

Dasté, J., *Voyage d'un comédien*, Paris: Stock, 1977.

Delgado, M., and Heritage, P., *In Contact with the Gods? Directors Talk Theatre*, Manchester: University Press, 1996.

Dort, B., *Théâtre public*, Paris: Seuil, 1967.

———— *Théâtre réel*, Paris: Seuil, 1971.

———— *Le Théâtre en jeu*, Paris: Seuil, 1979.

———— *La Représentation émancipée*, Arles: Actes Sud, 1988.

———— *Le Spectateur en dialogue*, Paris: P.O.L., 1995.

Faivre d'Arcier, B. (ed.), *Guide-Annuaire du spectacle vivant 96–97*, Paris: Centre National du Théâtre, 1996.

Fumaroli, M., *L'Etat culturel*, Paris: Fallois, 1991.

Godard, C., *Le Théâtre depuis 1968*, Paris: Lattès, 1980.

Jomaron, J. (ed.), *Le Théâtre en France* (2 vols), Paris: Armand Colin, 1989.

Kiernander, A., *Ariane Mnouchkine and the Théâtre du Soleil*, Cambridge: University Press, 1993.

Knowles, D., *Armand Gatti in the Theatre: Wild Duck Against the Wind*, London: Athlone, 1989.

Knowlson, J., *Damned to Fame: The Life of Samuel Beckett*, London: Bloomsbury, 1996.

Lallias, J-C. (ed.) et al., *Koltès, Combats avec la scène*, Paris: Centre National de Documentation Pédagogique, 1996.

Lang, J., *L'Etat et le Théâtre*, Paris: Librairie Générale de Droit et de Jurisprudence, 1968.

Lassalle, J., *Pauses*, Arles: Actes Sud, 1991.

Latour, G., and Claval, F.(eds), *Les Théâtres de Paris*, Paris: Ville de Paris, 1991.

Laurent, J., *La République et les beaux-arts*, Paris: Julliard, 1955.

Lecoq, J. (ed.), *Le Théâtre du geste*, Paris: Bordas, 1987.

Miller, J., *Theater and Revolution in France since 1968*, Lexington: Fench Forum, 1977.

————— (ed.) *Plays by French and Francophone Women: A Critical Anthology*, Michigan: University Press, 1994.

Miquel, J-P., *Le Théâtre des acteurs*, Paris: Flammarion, 1996.

Roubine, J-J., *L'Art du comédien*, Paris: P.U.F. ('Que sais-je?'), 1985.

Rudlin, J., *Jacques Copeau*, Cambridge: University Press, 1986.

Sarrazac, J-P., *L'Avenir du drame*, Lausanne: L'Aire, 1981.

Sarrazac, J-P. (ed.), *Les Pouvoirs du théâtre: Essais pour Bernard Dort*, Paris: Editions Théâtrales, 1994.

Schumacher, C. (ed.), *40 Years of mise en scène*, Dundee: Lochee, 1986.

————— *Artaud on Theatre*, London: Methuen, 1989.

Surgers, A., *La Comédie-Française. Un Théâtre au-dessus de tout soupçon*, Paris: Hachette, 1982.

Temkine, R., *Mettre en scène au présent* (2 vols), Lausanne: La Cité/L'Age d'Homme, 1977, 1980.

————— *Le Théâtre en l'Etat*, Paris: Théâtrales, 1992.

Thibaudat, J-P., *Le Théâtre Français*, Paris: Ministère des Affaires Etrangères, 1994.

Ubersfeld, A., *Antoine Vitez, metteur en scène et poète*, Paris: Editions des Quatre Vents, 1994.

Vilar, J., *De la tradition théâtrale*, Paris: L'Arche, 1955.

————— *Le Théâtre, service public*, Paris: Gallimard, 1975.

Vinaver, M., *Le Compte rendu d'Avignon*, Arles: Actes Sud, 1987.

————— *Ecrits sur le théâtre*, Lausanne: L'Aire, 1982.

Vinaver, M. (ed.), *Ecritures dramatiques*, Arles: Actes Sud, 1993.

Vitez, A., *Ecrits sur le Théâtre* (3 vols), Paris: P.O.L., 1994–6.

Whitton, D., *Stage Directors in Modern France*, Manchester: University Press, 1987.

Williams, D. (ed.), *Peter Brook: A Theatrical Casebook*, London: Methuen, 1997 (revised edition).

Yaari, N., *Contemporary French Theatre 1960–1992*, Paris: AFAA and Entr'Actes, 1995.

INDEX

(of proper names and titles for pages 1–195)